The Perfect Story

Reece E. Peace

1

Dedication

I will like to dedicate this book to my angel, my daughter, VISION PEACE, who knew no sin. She went straight to Heaven before she came into this world. My precious seed to God. Baby girl, I name the company after you…

Peace Vision Global.

CONTENTS

Chapter 1

The Divine Intervention

"I want to find me a man who's rich!" Athaliah cried, "I want to find me a man who's tall and settled, a guy who's handsome. I don't want these clowns! I want a guy who's amazing."

There in New York, a group of beautiful and aesthetically pleasing ladies talked about things that they had wanted from life, things that most of them had always looked forward to. Amongst them was Athaliah, a girl much lively, too pleasing, and too beautiful. Hers were the eyes that would sway people toward her, the eyes that would show of a spirit so very divine of a girl so magnificent. She was a girl who had gone to college, receiving her degree in Management. Somehow, talking in the group, the center of discussion, would always transition from a number of topics to conversations about guys. They had wanted it all, all the good things that a guy would have to offer; they had wanted it all. Athaliah had wished all that for herself, but perhaps more than anything else, she had wanted a man who feared God. I was that; though not too tall and not settled as of yet, I was a man of God.

See, fate is a strange, strange thing. We are left with things to know, things yet to figure out, things yet to adore, and things yet to explore. We are introduced to this world with no knowledge at all and something that is promised to be free will. We have the authority, the power to do things, make decisions, and have what we want from life. Yet, at the same time, fate plays its part. There are things that fate plans for us rather carefully and with much contemplating. But the things that it had planned, the things that fate keeps in store for us, are, at times, the very things that hurt us, the things that make us break down to pieces and into shreds. We see things that we had never expected to see, and we see things that we might have never really wanted to see. And at the end of the day, we know it to be uncertainty that adds thrill to our lives, that adds exhilaration to it. But we are led to think.

We are led to ponder over questions that great minds in history have pondered over, the questions that have never really found the answers to. So, oftentimes, I was compelled by my mind to wonder about some things, things that all of us have pondered over at some point in our lives. "Do I pilot my life? Am I actually in charge of it?" We think to ourselves, "do I decide the path it takes, my life, the way it eventually comes to its inevitable conclusion, the very end? Or is it all written? Is it all fated? Do I have anything in my hands, or am I all but a puppet, walking to my death the way I had forever and always been destined to?"

It troubles us… to see that what we know is but a drop in the oceans. But if we stop for a moment, if we learn how to breathe in nature's blossom and truly feel the smiles of children, we will find that happiness is in pursuit of us. It happens when we see around us. It happens when we believe that if God got us, then we are going to be all right, that we are going to be just fine. It happens when we put our trust in the Lord who is in the heavens above, eagerly waiting for us to join him. It happens when we see that this world around us is entwined into our hearts. And when we see, when we actually look, when we feel to the core of our souls that this life is sacred, that it is beautiful, that we are all a part of the amusingly massive tapestry of creation, then we will finally live. Only then will we ever truly be home.

It was a fine Sunday, a rather sunny day there in New York. Perhaps it was like that throughout the rest of the country. I know it was a delightfully sunny day here in California – that I had known for a fact. Back in New York, Athaliah stood there with her friends at the Sunday church service, thinking about how it was that her life was about to turn. She wanted her life to change: perhaps the same environment had felt somewhat old, much too familiar to stick around in. So, she had been thinking about a change, a change in scenery, or maybe a change in the scenery. And with the end of the church service, she walked up to her car.

As she wrung the key, pulling the door open, she saw a car. It was a charming Mercedes, looking all delicate and absolutely magnificent in its glossy black color. It drifted and revved, throttling and pulling up a few feet away from her Nissan. A tall, handsome guy stepped out from the left side, adjusting what seemed to be his already perfectly-gelled hair. "Oh!" she sighed, "I want that. I want me a man like that!"

I was chiming and singing along to the hip-hop music in my car; there was a hard, solid vibe. The sun was eager to climb up to its zenith, rising from behind the Californian seas that ran beside me. I was driving back home from my early morning Sunday church service that ended a little early. As mentioned, I was a man of God, a man of God who happened to have an undying, irrevocable ambition for hip-hop music. I was bumping my head, not finding enough room in my nice, beloved jeep to relocate into some fine dance moves. So, the fingers would move into a beating rhythm against the steering wheel, my shoulders dancing and my left thigh jarring. It was the most I could do at that instant.

I had been on the road when I finally developed a sudden hunger – I had to get some food. And so, I drove a little further, pulling up at a restaurant near my home. I had been to that place before, and it was not all bad. But this time, perhaps fate had something fun planned for me. As I went in, I ordered my typical breakfast, bacon with eggs. Excited to have my breakfast and be on my way, I waited for the food. When it finally came, I dug in, saying my sincere thanks to the God above me. Little did I know what I would find in there.

As I moved forward with eating, I saw what seemed to be a hair. "What's going on in here?!" I tried to keep my calm as I called the waitress. "There's a hair in this!" I tried to gulp the food particles that were there in my mouth already. "I'm so very sorry, Sir; let me just change this really quick. My sincere apologies!" She ran to the kitchen, coming back with the passage of a few minutes.

"What?!" I yelled this time. "What is going on with you people?" She came running again this time, and I showed her what it was that was in there; it was a fly! There was a dead fly… in my eggs and bacon. I walked out though she insisted she wanted to get me new eggs and bacon this time. I was not feeling like eating that anymore. I was disgusted. So, still rather hungry, I decided to drive all the way across the town. It was lunchtime already, and I hadn't had the best breakfast.

So, I drove up to the steakhouse that was on the other side of town. I went in, sitting all alone, all by myself and my steak. To my good luck, I did not really find a hair or a fly in there this time. I was somewhat happy; there was a smile on my face. Again, saying my thanks to the Lord above me, I dug in. Sooner, I saw three older white women sneaking looks at me as they talked among themselves; I was unsure about what they wanted.

Sooner, I saw them coming up to me. "What's your name, dear Sir? Can we ask?" I looked at them, still not sure what they had wanted from me. "Sure, sure," I swallowed my food and said, "Peace. My name is Reece Peace, almost like the chocolate peanut butter candy." We all laughed! They looked at me and asked, "Sir, can we pray for you?" It felt good being asked that. "Yes, please, please!" I cried, "Do that! Pray for me!"

Soon as they said the verses that they had to say, the supplications that they had to say, they told me that I was in for a surprise. They told me that I was going to see everything that I had ever wanted to see in my life. They said to me, "Sir, you are going to go all around the world. You are going to be famous. You are going to have your name as one that people would know. You are going to see everything it is that you have always ever wanted to see."

Well, as they prayed in their heavenly language, I could sense something different swaying within me, something much spiritual happening inside me. I felt as though it was a miracle happening to me, for me, within and without me. It was the feeling that left me at peace, knowing that whatever it was that was yet to happen was going to be just right. The other two ladies had come into one accord with the first one, and they added, "You are going to be traveling around the world. You are going to be famous. You are going to have your name known to people. But… you are also going to help a lot of people!"

And I was happy hearing that; I was sure that all of my hardened efforts were not going to go to waste. Oh, little had I known that I actually was in for a surprise! Little did I also know that it was not precisely going to be the same surprise that I was expecting and hoping for. Oh, how little had I known!

Living in my fantasy world for a few seconds, I kind of dazed out and faded away into my happy place. I flickered my eyes open to see that the ladies had gone away and out of sight; it was as if they had somehow vanished into thin air!

See, I thought something to myself just then. A thought raced the back of my mind. It said to me, "Perhaps that's why I had that hair and that fly in my meal. Perhaps that happened to me so I could come here to get prophesized and prayed on by these women! Anyhow, God really has a great sense of humor!" With that, I had a smile on my face, one that made me sure that it was all going to turn out just fine.

That week passed by without really feeling like anything. I was happy. There were not any real problems that prevailed in my life. I spent my days as a devoted man of God, confessing and asking for forgiveness because, like any man, I had sinned. I had been with girls, but I had known that God was still there for me. I had sinned, and I had been saved. But this time around, I was actually trying. I was actually trying to do right by my Lord, my beloved creator. I was truly working on myself, trying to keep myself away from any sins and prejudices, far away from all the things that would make Him angry at me.

So, the week passed. And as Sunday arrived in New York, Athaliah went to her Sunday church service. She was sitting there with her group of friends when the pastor started to talk about some unexpected topic. He started talking about something that would change Athaliah's life, something that was about to influence the upcoming decisions that she was about to make about her life. The pastor was talking about leaving, and he talked about Abraham. He told the people who sat there along with Athaliah about how Abraham moved to the south, leaving everything for a new life, a better one. And it hit Athaliah suddenly. A sudden feeling of realization swept in, making her run parallel with what it was that she had kept all along in her subconscious mind. She did not want to live in New York anymore!

The place that popped there in her head was Atlanta, Georgia. Sure, she was fascinated by and attracted to the nice cars that the guys would have there in New York, but she had wanted to start life all over again, and she had wanted to start life anew. She had wanted to do what Abraham had done all those years ago. She wanted to start a new life, hoping for the best of what was written by fate for her. And so, Athaliah researched Atlanta, and she was convinced that she wanted to move to the new state all by herself.

She went home to talk about it to her family. Her sister, Vicki, told her that Atlanta was actually a really good place. When she walked up to her mother to talk about it, her mother told her, "No, you are not going anywhere!" She was still young, and she had not been on her own ever before. But Athaliah went into a rebuttal, telling her mother how she had to go to Atlanta. Her mother seemed rather confused, hinting at the fact that she was not going to let her move all the way from home so very easily.

In the meantime, there I was, driving to Los Angeles, California. I had a music-related errand to do, and I was just driving. I had the usual playlist on, and I was again trying to be able to dance in my car while driving. I had been in California for way too long, and I also needed a change in my environment. I had wanted a change. In California, I had heard people talking about Atlanta, Georgia, and it had gotten to the point where I wondered what it was that was so very good, so intriguing about that place. So, I took my right hand off of the steering wheel to turn off the music. I had done that so that I could talk to God. I had needed to speak to Him about the things that had prevailed over my mind, the thoughts that I had been thinking.

"Yeah, so," I whispered in my heart, "what's all this about Atlanta? Everyone's been talking about Atlanta, Georgia. Right? They've all been talking about that place like it's some sort of a beautiful place. I don't know much about it; I haven't researched about it yet. But I know that it's good if they are all talking about it. So, what I want from you, my dear God, is to show me a sign. Show me a sign if you want me to move to Atlanta, Georgia. Show me a sign if that's what you have written for me, and I will move there, all the way to Atlanta, Georgia."

While I had been waiting for my sign to show up, the highway started to get a little busy. There were too many trucks and cars on the road. I took an exit onto the backstreets – a means to avoid all that traffic. I had taken some turns along the streets yet managed not to look at the names of the streets; I was just trying to run parallel with the highway. But the first time I actually took a look at the name of the street, I saw it to be labeled as Atlanta Street.

"Oh!" I exclaimed, "Alright, God. Alright." I was surprised, rather fascinated. "But, just to be on the safe side, this may just be a coincidence. So, God, show me one more sign, you know? Just show me one more sign. One more sign, and I will move to Atlanta, Georgia! God, show me one more sign, and the next big decision about my life will be Atlanta, Georgia." I was excited to see what it was that was written for me.

I was now moving on the side streets, seeing that the highway had started to move again. I turned, and I drove up to the highway again. As I turned, what I saw was beyond my imagination. There was a red car in front of me, and I never really read the number plates on the cars driving in front of me. This time, I did, in fact, take a look at the number plates. There was Georgia's peach license plate on that car. It was a sign!

"Okay, then," I said, "it looks like I'm moving to Atlanta, Georgia." Thinking that, I moved forward, overtaking that car. I took a look inside the car as I was driving by it, and I came across two white people. They were enjoying themselves. They were clapping and laughing and smiling and dancing. They seemed happy. "Well," I said to myself, "if people are that happy in Georgia, then I'm definitely going to Georgia!"

Those were the events that led me to the finalization of my decision to move to Atlanta. But there, in New York, Athaliah still struggled to convince her mother to agree with what she had wanted. There were quite a few arguments. But right when her mother asked her about whom she was going to stay with, the thought of a friend of hers dashed into her head. She had made a friend on a cruise ship, and she had known that she lived in Atlanta. So, she ran to pick her phone up, and she started dialing.

"I want to move to Atlanta," she cried, "tell me about it, will you?" The girl on the other side of the phone replied, "yeah, well, you should come!" She had offered Athaliah her place to live if that was the problem that was standing in her way of moving to Atlanta. She had gotten encouragement to move to Atlanta, and it was happening. Her heart had wanted her to move to the new place, and with each passing second, the desire was only increasing. The plan that seemed somewhat unrealistic was now coming to life.

So, she sat with her sister and talked about all that was about to come. "I'm still a virgin, and I have been with no man ever in my life before," Athaliah said, "I want to find me a man who will take good care of me." "Yeah, girl," her sister said, "go get yourself a good Jamaican man." Athaliah said in a rebuttal, "Oh, no. I want me a tall, handsome, rich American man." Vicki had given her 800 dollars to start with. That was all that she had, and she had given all of it to her so that she could have a nice trip to the new place. She had told Athaliah that if she needed more, she would just send it to her account. Athaliah's eyes shone with the fact that she was going to start life all over from the very scratch.

And there I was, in California, with my stuff packed. I was sure that I was going to move to Atlanta quite soon. But before that happened, I had made a decision to make myself right by God. I had decided that I did not want to be with girls anymore. Because of the fact that I was about to move to Atlanta by fate, I was sure that I did not want to sin anymore. I had been getting money from all those who had owed it to me, and I was giving away my furniture. But in the meanwhile, I had been getting calls from girls as well.

There was this one lady who called me. She called me, and she said to me, "Let's go out." I told her that I did not want to do that, and when she asked me why, I said to her that I was getting right with God. I told her how I was moving to Atlanta, and I hung up soon after. The day passed, and she called me again. I clicked my tongue, and I picked up the phone. "Who are you?" the woman asked. I was rather curious, much unsure about what was going on. "Who are you?" she asked again. "You know who I am," I replied, asking, "what's going on?"

"You didn't want to go out with me," she replied. "You brought this upon yourself. You did not want to go out with me, so I went to a friend's house. She's a witch, and I told her to put a curse on you. I told her your name was Reece Peace, and when they started with the curse, the house started to shake. Right then, the friend, who's a witch, said to me that they could not touch you: your blood was "too thick." The daughter, then, tried to put the curse on you, but she could not do it either. Her hand started to bleed, and the house was shaking again and again. So, who are you? Why can we not put a curse on you?"

"I'm just a cool dude. I'm just a cool guy," I said, hanging up. "She's crazy," I whispered to myself, knowing that if she had heard me, she would have tried to put another curse on me. I had not wanted that.

I had moved to the mountains with a friend of mine, knowing that I had to keep myself safe from all that these women had wanted from and with me. I did not want to do that: I was making myself right by my God. Just when I had gathered my stuff and gotten to the mountains, I got a call from another woman. "Do you want to go out tonight?" she asked me. I told her that I did not want to do that. I told her how I was in the mountains, and I told her how I had wanted to do right by God, how I had wanted to stay away from any sins. I had told her about my decision to move to Atlanta, and I told her about how fate itself had played the most important part.

A little while later, a lady friend called me. It happened again. I told her how I did not want to go out. She asked me, "Why are you moving to Atlanta?"

"To get my life together," I replied. I told her everything that I had said to the last two of them. Let's have some sex before you go then," she suggested. I told her how I had not wanted that. "Well, okay," she replied, "let's just get married then if you want to stay away from sinning." I was stunned to hear that, not knowing what to reply to her. "No," I said, "I don't want to marry you! I'm not marrying you." I hung up.

See, growing up, I was a man who liked the thrill of getting into trouble. I had done all the things that a child growing up is advised not to do. I was from the streets, and due to that, I had grown a special attraction toward the drugs that revolved around the streets, right along with alcohol and women. But when it was time for me to see things the right way, I started to see them the right way. I became a man who was shown the way of God.

Anyway, by this time, all my finances were in place. Everything was thought about, and all that I required was prepared and primed. So, my friend had wanted a pastor to pray for me so that I would have a safe and prosperous journey to the place that awaited me. After praying for me, the pastor said to me, "Make sure you find a brook, the main brook."

"What's a brook?" I asked.

He replied, "When you get to Atlanta, Georgia, make sure that you find your church home so that you can find your establishment."

Just when I had prepared to be on my journey, Athaliah was staying with her mother in New York, spending the weekend with her. She prepared there, while I prepared here. And just when the time came, she left from New York, while I left from California. Our roads were different, and our desires stood much distant from one another's, yet our destinations were the same. Fate had a thriller written for the two of us, and there were quite a few things that we had yet to see, yet to go through. I was sure that life was going to get better: I had put my trust in my God. I was convinced that I could be the one I had always wanted to be, and I was willing to work for it. So, with high hopes and heightened expectations, we got on our very own journeys, not knowing about one another, not recognizing one another' mere existence. Yet, there was very little that I had known. There was very little that the two of us had known.

Chapter 2

The Departure

The wind pushed on my car to no avail. I was going forwards, and nothing but a blessed tragedy could have changed that. The tires made their monotonous hiss over the clean, deserted highway, and the air that managed to make its way through the filters was meadow-sweet. All around, through these tinted windows, were fields. Inside this tin box destined for the horizon, the world outside continued like some choreographed dance, but without the soul's purpose and God's will, it would not have. What reason under the sun was there that I could not stop and walk barefoot in the grass and feel the keen rays of the spring? Was there none that could hold up a brave hand and say stop?

And thinking the thoughts that resided within my head, the thoughts that made me sure to get going, I was the passenger as well as the driver in that jeep of mine.

So, with the radio to fill my ears with the latest popular tunes, starlets, the hip-hop songs, I endured that long, long journey through many states. And so, I knew that if I were to close my eyes, I could feel the gentle rise and fall of the road beneath me. I could not imagine what it was that was in store for me, what fate had planned for me, but it was not as bad as things could be. That ride, that car, that meeting of mine with nature – they had found a use for me, and somewhere, at the end of this road, I knew the answer to what that could be.

I left on Friday, September 10th of the year 1999. I had filled up the tank of my car and got on the highway. But first things first. What I did was pray. I prayed to the Lord above me to bless my journey and to make sure that I did not go astray from his path or from mine. I made sure that I prayed. I had actually wanted to put the music as the first thing that I did when I got into the car, but then, I thought to myself, "What the hell am I doing? Pray first, man. Remember your God!"

But when I put my music on, I knew that there was no stopping me. The roads were straight, for I was about to be driving through many states of the country. *Don't Stop What You're Doing* was the song that prevailed amidst all others, for I had always had a soft spot for it. Yet through it, through all of it, the music dared not stop. It was about to be a very long drive, and so I had kept with me a bottle of water to drink from. And I had known that there would be no stops.

I had known that the journey would keep going until I had reached my destination—Atlanta, Georgia.

But you know, nature has a weird way of showing you who it is that is actually in charge. "Oh, God, no, no, no, no, no!" I cried. See, just when I thought that I would go non-stop to the state of the country that awaited me rather eagerly, I found myself in need of going to a restroom. I had wanted to save money, so I had decided not to book myself any schmancy hotel rooms. But what can a man do when he needs to go to the restroom? He stops the car. But what does he do when he cannot find a restroom anywhere around? He panics.

And just like that, I was taken back to the time I

was driving from Las Vegas to California, back home after a rough couple of days. I had to use the restroom, but the moment I pulled up the car in front of the restaurant, it was already too late. I looked down to find out that I had used the restroom on myself. So, what did I do? I did what any person would do. I walked to the restroom, dropped my pants and my underwear, and I left them there... hanging high and dry. So, the people around me wondered. They were left wondering. "He went to the restroom wearing pants; why is he coming back without them?" I had heard their whispers. But no, I had not wanted to do the same this time. So, perhaps to my good luck, I found a nice, cozy restroom to go to in Arizona. It was, in fact, a moment of great relief, a significant sigh. Right there, in the hotel's parking lot, I parked my car, and I took a little nap, just enough to let me drive ahead freshly.

Soon after getting a little nap somewhere in Arizona, I entered New Mexico. And yes, it was just like they show it in the movies – hues of brown and yellow throughout. I was too alone on that long road, on that deserted road that ran along the desert. The vegetations were a little too scant, and there was very little greenery to be looking at. So, rather bored, I kept driving, and driving, and driving.

Sooner, the vegetation increased a little – not a lot, but just a little. I was in Texas. And I kept driving, knowing that my destination was not too far anymore. I had pulled over at a sandwich place to get myself some fries and a sandwich somewhere in Dallas, Texas, and I had not known how to get back on the highway. I asked a guy about it, and he directed me. But when I actually tried to follow the directions that he had given me, I got more lost. But then, my eyes stopped at this wooden area. I drove up to that place, hoping that the blessed people who lived there would guide me. But to my surprise, I pulled over to see something rather unusual. The sun had fallen, giving way to the magnificent stars that shimmered above. There were just some people with white sheets over their heads, gathered around a wooden fire. I simply turned around and speeded off.

In all honesty, it has always been a treat, driving

there in the calmness of the night and the stillness of the desert under the light of the stars, with no bright city lights to dim them. It was therapeutic. And just when I was getting to the point where I would get frustrated by the boredom that prevailed, I saw something magnificent. It was something that put an end to the tears that managed to roll down my eyes.

From my windshield, I saw bright, bright stars in front of me that fell ahead, far behind the hills. I was petrified to think that there might be a fire because of that, but the closer I tried to get to where it had gone, the further it seemed to be getting from me. But, on the good side, there was no fire, after all. There were no tears in my eyes anymore. My hopes had just gotten higher with the sight of that. The sun came up to tell me that it was Sunday, and I had to attend the church service. I had wanted to talk to a pastor. So, I got off the highway just as I saw a church, but it was closed.

So, I sat there by the church's stairs, and I started to cry. Tears had managed to roll down my cheeks as I pondered over the decision that I had made to move to

Atlanta, Georgia. And all my mind could tell me was how I should not be going to Atlanta. So, for guidance, perhaps, I called my friend Charlie. I had known him from California, and when he heard the sound of my voice, he told me to come back home, back to California. Since I had left my job, I told him, but he, in turn, told me that I could stay with him. So, I made up my mind. I made up my mind to turn around and go back to California. I went to get gas for the car, and while I was there, a lady asked me if I was doing well.

My eyes were all red, and my face screamed that there was something wrong that was going on with me. So, I told her. I told her about how I had set out to go to Atlanta and how I had managed to make up my mind to turn back toward California. "No!" she yelled at me. "No, you are going to Atlanta!" "Huh?" I asked. "Do not go to California! Go to Atlanta!" So, once again, I was convinced to go to Atlanta, Georgia, after all. So, as a courtesy, I called Charlie back to let him know I was going to Atlanta after all. And I filled the car's tank up, got some chips and drinks, put the car on cruise control, and kept it moving. I was getting out of Texas, and for that, I was very happy.

There were a few stops; I would pull over and straighten my back for a bit before hitting the road again. And once I got out of Texas, I found out something weird about the people who lived in the south. As I went to a hamburger stand, the accents had changed a little too much, so much so that I could barely understand most of the things they were saying. And one more thing that I found rather weird was that they were used to putting sugar in their tea. So, confused, I called my mom to ask her about it. She assured me that it was the way it was in the south.

As I almost reached my journey's end, I drove through Mississippi. I decided to find a Brook when I got to Alabama. I wanted to attend the church service, for I could go no longer without it. To my good luck, perhaps, this time, I did not find the church doors to be closed.

The pastor was teaching about moving to different places. He talked about the life of Abraham, how the devoted man of God moved from his home to a place he had not known, a place where he thought he could see and live the better days of his life. The pastor was teaching about walking by faith and how a person should let it be the driving force of their life.

After the church service ended, I looked through the phonebook to find a friend of mine, Kango, who lived in Alabama. I had anticipated making it to Atlanta by Sunday, the 12th, but I had not been able to achieve that. So, I decided to rest a little there in Alabama. Somehow, I ended up telling some guys that I was making music and was going to Atlanta to pursue my life, my career, and my dreams. He told me about the boxer Green Field, advising me to take my music there.

Well, it was not long before I was back on the road again. I was punching it, playing my music, enjoying the most I plausibly could. And on Monday night, the 13th, I finally made it to Atlanta. I saw the sign that said "Atlanta, Georgia," and I sighed. I looked at the buildings that seemed much new to me, and I knew that this was … the start of a new chapter in my life. I had not known how it was going to be, but I had known that I was going to persist through it, come what may.

Little had I known that a beautiful, beautiful girl was also arriving from New York that very day. Little had I known what fate had planned for me, for her, and for us.

Athaliah was driving, playing gospel music, and praying to God. Her car was going really fast; then it slowed down. She kept driving even when she saw cars. But then, she saw a highway patrol person with a switch caught up, being called with a speed trap machine. She saw the officer with the speed trap machine, and she hit the acceleration paddle even harder. And after she passed the officer, her car started moving faster. "Oh, my god, look how I just got out of a ticket!" She sighed to herself. She had not really known that her car had been moving fast.

Anyway, she had to go through New Jersey, DC, Virginia, North Carolina, and South Carolina to get to Atlanta, Georgia. Her journey was a little shorter than mine, but we got there the very same day, not really knowing what it was that would make us meet one another, how things were about to unfold shortly right after.

Yet I held on to the better of life. And she held to the better of life.

Chapter 3

The Arrival

How did I get here?

Fate? Destiny?

Was it written in the stars? Was it all just a coincidence?

Everything that had been... did it lead me here?

Or was it God?

Was this His plan all along?

As I sat there in my car, a million thoughts raced across my head. I just rested my head against the murky window. Well, it was the sight of the stars that had always managed to make me dream. It was the stars that shimmered above me that had always made me wonder about all the questions to which I had not been able to find the answers. There were many things that I asked myself, many things that I needed the answers to. But my faith in my Lord in the heavens was what had kept me going all along, all the way I had been. Yet, as a curious guy, I wondered.

See, someone will sigh, bat their eyelashes theatrically at you, and say, "It was fate." Fate is paradoxical and contradictory; either you will be taught that you must make your own decisions, or you will be told, "It was fate." Who, in the end, makes the decisions for us? Are we to believe that our lives are being guided by a semi-controllable force?

You might claim that you found yourself in the same church with a man from California by chance, or perhaps you found yourself trying to be killed by the woman you had loved. But, at the same time, you could equally argue that your inner drive pushed you there.

"Which is it, to be precise?" I asked myself.

"It is both," the voice inside me whispered back almost instantaneously. "It is both!"

It is the two – combined, at once, at the same time. See, fate is the sum total of all the choices you have ever made. It is essentially true everything you have been told about is selecting your fate. It is determined by your decisions. It is determined by the choices you opt for and the choices you leave behind. These decisions might range from anything as basic as turning right instead of left at a stop sign to something as significant as quitting your job. The difference is that each one takes you to a new realm, one filled with hundreds of different options, people, and experiences that you would never have had if you had chosen differently. Your fate is determined by your collective decisions and the history of all of your decisions, each of which is impacted by the previous one. It is a foreshadowing butterfly effect that affects not just your future, but everyone else's as well.

Our greatest fear is fate. The unknown is the future, and everything unknown has the potential to be good or harmful, to lift you or lower you. True, only God knows your destiny. Is your fate, however, cast in concrete, written in the stars, unchanged, unhinged? It is, without a doubt, a fascinating issue to explore. At the end of the day, we are not God's toys, and we have complete freedom to live our lives. He is aware of what is best for us and demonstrates it to us in signs and the voice that resonates within us. In the end, we make our own decisions.

In the meanwhile, Athaliah arrived at Tina's house. She was there, having food, dancing to music, and having the best time of her life. It was all that she had ever wanted to do, and now that she was finally able to do it, she felt quite satisfied, much gratified. She had come there straight from the roads of New York to take a shower, and her friend showed her around the place. It was all too beautiful, a place anyone would want to call home. Sooner, the conversation was taken to the remembrance of God. Tina had told her about the church that she attended there, in that part of the country. They were going to have a Bible study on Wednesday that was about to arrive shortly.

Athaliah was not used to going to big churches with a large number of people and wealthy pastors. Tina had told her about the Rolls-Royce and private jet that the pastor had owned and all the things about him. She was not really into that, for the church was the one place where she had gone to find herself, not to be taken over by her worldly desires.

Anyway, she agreed to go. And so, they prepared to go to the church on Wednesday that was to come quite sooner.

And there I was, somewhere in Atlanta, Georgia, trying to get out of my car and into a hotel room to get a decent shower. I had gotten there by 1:30 AM, and I had found myself in desperate need of a hotel room. I always have been a simple man, always wanting the simplest of things, perhaps. Well, I did want a million dollars, too, but that, too, is simple, isn't it?

I tried to check into the hotel room, but the receptionist told me that I would have to pay for two days since I was very much close to the check-out time. So, she moved the check-in time to 11 AM, and I just had to spend around 10 hours in my car. That did not seem like much since I had been in the car for three or four days.

Just then, a lady came over to me, asking me if I wanted to have sex with her. I, a devoted man of God, turned her down, knowing it to be something that my God would not like very much.

The woman, named Head Nurse, and I had a conversation, and I ended up telling her about how I was there because God had shown me signs, how I had wanted a record deal. "Can I introduce you to Lord Jesus Christ?" I asked her, "Have you been born again?" She looked confused, and she asked, "What? What's that? What's being "born again?" I was born years ago from my mother's pussy!"

She was too straightforward with her street vocabulary. So, I told her all there was to know about being saved, and I made her a Christian, a devoted woman of God. "You turn to your Lord Jesus Christ," I assured her, "and He will take you. You have been too far from Him for too long. When you go back to Him, He will not push you away; He will embrace you. And your life will be better. Everything that you have wanted will come to you, and you will find yourself thanking

Him for all that you have been through. You will know, then, the real reason for your life, the very purpose of it."

Whether or not she followed God from that day forth had to be a matter between God and her. But I told her to try to go to church and that I will keep her in prayer. She said to me, "Wow! I feel good. I feel really, really good. I feel like I'm new somehow!" Anyway, she asked for 5 dollars, and I gave her the money, and she went on her way. I spent the night in my car, which reeked of old clothes, dirt, and a long journey. Yet, I was proud that I had done this. "Wow! I did it! I made it to Atlanta!"

I checked into the hotel room the next morning, and there, I was finally able to take a shower. I shaved, and when I came out of the restroom, I felt somewhat like a clean machine. Then, I hit the streets, looking for a place to quench my hunger at. I came across this place named "The Egg House," and I knew then that there, I would have my breakfast for that day.

As I came out, I saw this big man who stood there. He was a local, I guessed. So, I walked up to this guy, and I talked to him, asking where Green Field lived. I said to him, "I heard about his big, hit record company, and I'm a rapper. And I want to take my music over there because I know that they'll all like it here in Atlanta. I'm from the West Coast. And I just moved out here, man, and I am basically by myself. I think that my music will bring good things to the record company and to me. I want to try to find this record deal. I believe he will really like my music. So, please tell me which way to go."

He was impressed. The guy assured me of the big mansion that Green Field lived in, saying, "When you see this big-ass house, you'll know that it is where he lives." He had promised me that there was a lot more to come my way. He told me the directions, and he cried to me as I walked to my car, "You be on your way, mister, and you better find that big motherfuckin' house! You better go and get yourself that deal!"

And I followed that man's directions, what he had told me, and I pulled up before this massive and beautiful mansion. And when my eyes stopped at it, I was sure to know that it was where Boxer Green Field lived. I was awe-struck, for it was the place of my dreams, the place I had aspired to own. I walked up to the house, and that is where the security stopped me.

There was this person who was cutting the lawn, and he was just looking at me having conversations with the security. I had been telling them how I had come from California, how Green Field had to listen to my music. They kept telling me no. And that was when the lawn guy jumped in, asking me to give the music cd to him, and he will get it to Green Field and all the right people. I left the house excited because Boxer Green Field was going to hear my music!

Driving down the street, I saw this huge, orange church. I stopped to see if they had a homeless shelter since I had found myself in need of that. It was a big church. I knew that they had a place for people to sleep at. Moving from California, I did not really have any properties at the place. I went to the office area, and they gave me some information about programs and offered me a shower. I talked with the people whom I had found myself to be amidst, and I prayed with them. I told them that I was there because of the fact that I was pursuing God and music.

When I got to see the attendant, I told her that I had moved from California. I told her that I had gotten there after a four-day journey in my car. I asked them about the homeless shelter, and they told me that there was none. I was then passed on to the counselor. I told her the same that I had moved there from California. She asked me about my occupation, and I told her that I was pursuing the field of music and I told her that I was a rapper. She then told me that they had a record label there by the name of Point Records.

They called up some people, and I went to talk to people who worked in the studio at the church. There was this A&R person I was talking to when I got there. And while I was talking to her, the back door opened quite suddenly.

She asked me to go and see who it could be, but when I went to see who it was, I could not find anyone. There was no one there, so I closed the door. I told her I was from California. I told her how God had wanted me to move here and how I thought it was destiny to be here. Just then, the door opened again.

She, yet again, asked me to check if there was anyone there. There was no one: I closed the door again. As I resumed the conversation where I had left it off, it happened again. The door popped open once again. She got up, and she said to me, "The Holy Spirit is present amongst us!" I chuckled, but I had believed her when she had said that.

I had let her hear my music, and we talked. At the end of the conversation, she told me that she liked the music. She was telling me about the record label, and she told me about who it was that was running it. "We are looking for talented, young artists," she told me, "especially those who are willing to pursue a career in it. First Lady Benjamin herself is looking for people; do you know who she is?" I told her that I had been hearing that name for the first time ever. "Well," she said, "she's the wife of the man after whom this church is named. Reverend Lite Benjamin of Planet Dome Church."

At that time, during the whole conversation that I had had with her, she kept looking at me because the door popped open three times while I was there. The lady who was praying offered me to come to service that Wednesday, and in reply, I had told her that I did not really like big churches. She told me that they had prayer before bible study on Wednesday. When she said that, my eyes brightened up because I liked praying. And she talked to me about the record label some more. At the end of the conversation, she told me that she had heard my music and she liked it. She assured me that she was going to let the Reverend Lite Benjamin hear it, as well as the First Lady Benjamin. She assured me that she was going to get back to me, and so I gave her my pager number, knowing that I would keep waiting for her message.

The next day, I finally decided to attend the prayer service after all. So, I went to service that night also, after the prayer.

The reverend preached on faith, talking to the people about how Abraham had left his country and changed his name. I could not stop thinking. My mind just could not stop saying to me, "He's talking about me! He's talking about me!" I did see a lady who was sitting at the front, and I could not help but wonder whether or not it was his wife, the First Lady. When I knew for sure that it was her, I said to myself, "That's the First Lady Benjamin! She's the one who's got the record label!" I had wanted to walk up to her and ask her about the music, my music.

Little had I known that there was someone else present in that church, too, that same night that I had found myself there.

See, it was Wednesday night, and Athaliah was there too. Yet, as fate would have it or as God had intended it to happen, I did not see her. My eyes did not cross hers for the first time that night. Oh, little had I known what it was that was about to come my way! Little had I known that my world was about to be knocked upside down, quite literally!

So, as I went back to my car to sleep another night in it, trying to save money, Athaliah was staying with Tina in Lawrenceville, Georgia… just about 30 miles from me. I was still staying in my car because I did not want to spend money on motel rooms. I was in extreme survival mode!

Just that night, I met a girl, Tee-Tee, who was staying in the motel. She came across my car, asking if I had wanted sex. I told her that I most certainly did not want to have sex with her. She was, too, a prostitute. I talked to her about Jesus. I enlightened her about how Jesus had always loved her, how He still loved her, and how He always will love her. I told her how He had in His hands the power to fix her life. She told me, "After this hooker job, I'm going to find Jesus." I told her, "You can have him now by being born again. Do you want to confess Jesus as your Lord?" She said, "Yes," and I gave her the repentance prayer. She had said it and confessed it. She was born again. Tee-Tee said to me, "I feel good." It was that Friday when she invited her friend to come over to listen to me. Tee-Tee told Lucy, "This is my friend Peace, and he's a preacher!"

"That dude ain't no preacher!" her friend, Lucy,

cried as she saw me for the first time ever. "That dude ain't no preacher! He's a gangster! He ain't no preacher!"

"Girl, come here," said Tee-Tee, "at least listen to what the man has to say! Peace, tell Lucy what you just told me. Tell her all of that!"

Lucy groaned as she faltered toward me. And I ended up talking to Lucy about God. I told her all that I had told Tee- Tee before her. I said to her, "God desires for His children to be joyful, and He wants them to be happy. He has gifted us with so many blessings. He cares about you and wants you to interact with Him via prayer. Jesus has said, Your Father in heaven will give you good things only if you ask Him."

And by the end of the conversation, they said to me, "We are bad women! We take guys to motel rooms, and we have sex with them. And after we are done, we give them drugs and put them to sleep. And when they are asleep, we take their wallets and go away. How would Jesus still love us?"

"Jesus still loves you," I said. "You could be a

sinner, or you could be a saint. Jesus would still love you if you sinned being a saint or if you did the right thing being a sinner! Be born again, ladies! Be introduced to Jesus, and He will make your lives better!"

"What's being "born again?" What does that mean?" Lucy asked, confused, bewildered. And so, I edified her all there was that she had needed to know, what all they had missed out on for all this time. And I ended up getting her friend Lucy born again. So, she cried to me in happiness, "I feel really good! I feel like I am a new person! I feel very good! I think I want to get rid of this hooker job and do something moral!"

For the next day, I took a shower in Tee-Tee's room and gave her rides to the store. I still could not risk staying in her room, though, so I still slept in the car for the night.

It was the next night that Tee-Tee had told me that if I wanted to have sex, she would give it to me for free. I got in my car and left. I was lying in the car, talking to God about how I wanted to shower, comb my hair, freshen up a little, and rest my back. I had wanted to wear a suit for church. I wanted to look good when I went into the house of the Lord on my first Sunday. I had wanted to dress up appropriately, all for Him.

So, later that night, around 11:55 PM, There so happened to be a girls' basketball team that was staying at the hotel. But they were leaving. The last girl that came out shut the door, but the door popped back open. I was very certain that I had heard God's voice in my head, saying to me, "Go! Take your shower. Freshen up. Rest a little. You have a long way to go, still!" So, I went into the room quickly before anyone saw me. I took a shower, laid down, prayed, and went to sleep. When the sun dawned for the next time, it looked as though the first miracle that I saw was the first one that I had noticed.

See, miracles happen each day. They happen every single day. Yet, they remain unseen to us, unknown, really. I knew that; I had known that. But this was the first in a very long time that He had wanted me to see, or so I thought.

As I stayed in the motel room, Athaliah was staying in the big house that her friend had to herself. She would get in her car and drive to church whenever she felt like going there. She was regularly and religiously going to church and praying for all that she had wanted, all that she had ever dreamed of, never having any problems.

Tee-Tee knew a guy who had an apartment and was looking for a roommate. He also had a window cleaning business. Tee-Tee told him about me. I went to pay him a visit, and he let me stay with him. His name was Sherman, and he had given me a room with a king-sized bed to sleep in. It was good to finally fall asleep in a normal, usual bed and not the back seat of my car with my legs rolled up to my chest. From there, I joined him in cleaning windows and ministering to folks as I worked for him. He said to me, "Cool, you will pray for people when they pass you by." He was not putting in enough money for me, and I felt like I was working a little too much for a little too less of an amount to go by. So, I thanked him for the roof over my head, but I really needed spending money as well.

I looked for another job, and I found a job as a

waiter at Slice Kitchen's, which was great since I could eat there and make good tips. Sherman was surprised when I told him I was a rapper; he informed me about "The Nest" Club. In Atlanta, it was my first time rapping on stage there. I did that every Tuesday night, and I seemed to grow on the crowds and the audience there. I would rap an inspirational song. The crowd would join in my chorus line. After my rap song, I would say, "If anyone likes prayer, please meet me outside in the parking lot. Come join me!" I had people from the club come outside, and I prayed for them and then got them born again. The owner of the club liked what I was doing. So, he kept telling me to come and rap there. He said, "I don't care about the Gospel, but your Gospel rap is good. I like it!"

Sherman had a place that he was renting out for $400 per month. He had told me that. I moved out of his place and moved into my new townhouse. It already had furniture in it, and the power and the electricity were on at all times. One day, coming home from work, I was driving to my complex and saw four lads playing basketball who began to start running as soon as they saw me. So, I decided to drive around the complex to see why the boys were running and where they were running to. It was quite unnatural, and I was confused and curious. They there were trembling, hiding behind the bushes, looking at me with fear in their eyes. But without answers, I let them be.

A little while later, I remember hearing a teaching of a preacher who talked about how devils flee from the anointed, it hit me. "That's why those boys were shivering!" I speculated to myself. Those boys had demons in them and had seen Jesus in me. I looked up at the skies, and I asked my God, "Okay, God, what's really going on? Who Am I?"

As I went to see the place that I had to myself, I was relieved. "Oh, my God!" I cried in exhilaration, "I got my own place now! I can stretch my legs now! I don't have to sleep in my car anymore!" I was excited. That was when life in Atlanta, Georgia, began for me.

My routine was very much on track and defined. I went to church every Wednesday. I would go there again on the night of Friday. And then, I would attend the Sunday service, and always before each service started, I would join the prayer service. I started going to the new members' classes, ones where they taught about church standards. I was still going to rap shows every Tuesday. And at the same time, I was an employee at Slice Kitchen's. It was not much, but I had known it to be my road to the greatness that I had yet to see.

One workday, the pastor's wife – First Lady Benjamin, who runs the record label – came into Slice Kitchen's. See, I had always been praying to meet her. She had a seat in my section, but I wasn't on the clock yet. She had started eating inside. I gathered the courage that it took to walk up to her, and I opened my mouth, saying, "Hello, First Lady Benjamin, my name is Peace. I'm a rapper, and I've wanted to meet you for a very long time!" I thought to myself, jumping and dancing with exhilaration in my thoughts, "My prayers are working!" I asked her, "Can I kindly give you my music and resume?"

First Lady Benjamin said, "Okay, show me what

you got!" she replied. And so, I ran to my car without even thinking anything else. My heart was beating much too fast, and I brought her my CD and resume. "I rap Gospel Rap," I said to her, adding, "I attend your church Planet Dome Church. I have been faithful in coming to the prayer services and growing in the Lord."

First Lady Benjamin was looking over my CD and resume, smiling while eating. She had finished her breakfast and left the restaurant. But before she left the restaurant, she said, "Have a blessed day, Brother Peace." I replied to her with a wide smile on my face, "You have a blessed day to yourself, too, First Lady Benjamin."

I whispered to myself, "Am I dreaming!" I had to pinch myself. She knew my name, my rap name, Brother Peace. This was a great day, and all it had done to me was bring happiness.

In the intervening time, Athaliah was going to a Temp Agency. She had gotten a job working for an insurance company. She, too, was happy and going to the church she loved rather dearly.

While I was still working at Slice Kitchen's, weeks passed. This time Rev. Lite Benjamin and his son had come into Slice Kitchen's. I introduced myself to him, and he asked me, much confused, "Your name is… Peace…?" He was looking at my name tag. I told him, "Yes, it's my last name. My first name is Reece, and my last name is Peace." He said, "Wow, your name is powerful." He made a joke which went somewhat like, "Your name is like chocolate peanut butter candy."

I laughed and said, "People call me that all the time!" So, I let them eat as I help my other guess. I saw they were finished. And when he was about to pay for his meal, I told the pastor that I would pay for his meal. I liked a prophet's reward; I knew about treating well a man of God like him. I walked him out the door, and he patted me on the back. It was a feeling too good to be replaced, and I was happy. It was the first time in a very long time that I had felt as though my life was actually heading somewhere, as though those three ladies' prophecies were actually nothing but the truths in themselves.

I was still praying early morning, making my positive confessions, going to church, and working faithfully. On one of my workdays, I was serving a family. I was talking their orders, and when I got to the older gentleman, about to take his order, all the guests and I heard a loud pop, and the older man who was ordering almost jumped up out of his seat.

"What was that?" he asked. His wife and family asked, "Are you okay?" He said, "I'm okay. I feel better. It was somehow like an electric shock ran through me."

Everything calmed down, and I was taking his order. While I was taking his order, The Holy Spirit whispered to me, "The anointed of God inside of you healed him."

Now I was trying to hold my peace. After I took their order, I went to the back, talking to God. I said while looking up at the skies, "God, I don't deserve this! What are you doing to me? How are you using me to help people?" He did not talk back to me. He did not reply to me this time, and there was no sign that I got to see. I was still trying to hear something, see something out of the usual, expecting a response from him, but there was nothing.

So, I got back inside the restaurant that I happened to work at, and I was just working. A little later, there came a man. He had walked in with a security uniform on. He had asked me whether or not we had soup chicken noodle soup. I told him that we, in fact, did have chicken noodle soup. He ordered it, and he was telling me that someone was not feeling too well. I went around the back to go prepare the soup. While I was preparing it, I was praying over the soup, packing some lemons and some hot sauce in the bag to go.

I brought the security guy the soup, and I said to him, "I prayed over the soup. Also, make sure that you squeeze the lemons and put hot sauce in it. They are going to be healed." He sighed, "Wow! Thank you, sir. The world really needs good people like you; I hope you know that. Do you know whom I am taking this soup for?" I told him that I did not know. He said, "It is going to Mother Benjamin, Rev Lite Benjamin's mother." I was perplexed, puzzled, and stunned. He said, "I'm the security there at Planet Dome Church." I sighed, mouthing, "Oh, my God!"

He asked me, looking at my name tag, "What's your name?" The security guard asked me, "Your name is Peace?" I told him that it was, indeed, my last name. He told me, "I'm going to go tell Mother Benjamin that Peace prayed over her soup! And I hope that through your prayer, God brings her health and wellness, that she gets better very soon."

I was still attending church faithfully and prayer services before church. Sometimes, I would have the favor of sitting in the front area of the church. There would be times when I would see First Lady Benjamin, and whenever I would see her, she would look at me, smiling. I would pray to myself, "She's going to sign me. Please, God, make her sign me." I would be thinking about how God had planned all of this. I had always been in amusement of how God had brought me to the face of the Glory, how he had made everything happen.

My job at Slice Kitchen's was never boring. It was always an adventure in there, one or the other. There was a time when a group of men walked in and were about to have breakfast. Before I took their order, I saw one of the gentlemen whom I remembered to be a preacher back in California. He was surrounded by his bodyguards and entourage. I said to him, "Sir, I remember you from California. You're a prophet." He asked me, "Why do you say that?" I said to him, "I went to one of your services in Ontario, California. You were prophesying over people." I thought to myself, "You are a joke. You are not real."

His entourage was looking at me crazily, with frowns on their faces and their eyebrows shifting downward in anger, "Watch yourself, boy." I continued, "So, you started prophesizing over my friend who was with me. You were saying that he was dead one time, and God rose him up." I said, "I'm getting out of here, man. This man is a clown!"

His bodyguards had stood up, looking at me like they were about to remove my head from my body with not much power. The pastor told them to sit down. I said, "No." My friend stopped me and said that you were right.

He told me that he died for an hour, and God brought him back to life. I said, "What?!" So, I asked my friend, "This guy is not lying?"

I said to the pastor, "I was hiding in the back because we had just got drunk and had women at the house. And I didn't want you to say that to me in front of the church. I started hiding behind people so that you won't see me." All of a sudden, the pastor started laughing quite hard. He kept laughing and laughing and laughing. His bodyguards and entourage were also laughing. The pastor said to me, "Young man, you made my day!" I had not had a laugh like that for a long time, and it felt amazing. He told me, "God loves you." The pastor saw my name Peace on my name tag and prayed for me. After they ate and had their meeting, he gave me a big tip. I said to him with a smile running wide across my face, "Thank you, sir." The pastor said, "Thank you, Peace. You really made my day!"

It was a Sunday morning, and I was up; I was praying and doing my positive confessions before church. I heard the Lord's voice, as clear as day, and He said to me, "You are signing a multi-million-dollar contract deal." I jumped off the floor and started running around my place. I was so much in delight and gratification that I had heard God's voice. He just told me about the thing that I had been dreaming of. I went to church, and before I could even walk through the church doors, a lady named sister Bern stopped me at the door. She said, "Hey, Peace."

"Hello, sister Bern," I replied.

"Don't tell nobody I told you this," she said to me,

"but I found out that First Lady Benjamin is signing you." "What?" awestruck, I couldn't believe it.

"A multi-million-dollar contract deal. She really loves your music. They were playing your music in the studio all day yesterday at Point Records."

"Wow!" I cried. "God told me this morning that I was about to sign a multi-million-dollar contract deal, but He never told me with whom. So… now that you're telling me this, I feel it must be with First Lady

Benjamin."

We are all God's creations. We, as humans, are all created by the one who sits in the heavens up above. This notion is largely evident in the scriptures. First and foremost, we have the freedom to live our lives as we like and to carry out the behaviors that our bodies and minds desire. We don't know if we'll succeed or fail in life. We are expected to do and be our best; we should not blame fate for our poor decisions or thank fate for our excellent ones. Second, we all take various roads and arrive at different places in life. We have complete flexibility to pick a course based on our beliefs: the good path or the negative road.

Choosing a route typically entails deciding whom you want to be and, as a result, your own fate. The pathways are marked; however, you may decide whatever location you wish to visit. Nobody knows what we are meant for! It is critical to trust that our good fortune will come to us. Choosing the appropriate conduit is critical for our road to success in life. Furthermore, there is no question that there is a fate. The term "destiny" refers to the fact that you will be given two options and will be punished or rewarded depending on which one you choose. So, sooner or later, one thing becomes clear: the options are written down.

And so, giving in to the God who created me with much love, I asked for love in this world – not to replace him, but to make it feel a little less lonely… perhaps.

Chapter 4

"You Are Beautiful!"

It was a Saturday morning, and I was going to the new member's class. I saw this beautiful lady by the altar; she was getting her paperwork done. She was unlike any other woman whom I had come across.

I whispered to myself, "Wow! She's beautiful. I've got to meet her!" So, the teacher was teaching and telling us about the church, but all I could do was stare at her. When she smiled, her face looked like one of an angel's. With her red lipstick on over her dark colored-skin, she looked pretty.

I am a guy from the West Coast, and I happened to have this gangster aura around me. Even though I was not scared to meet her, I was scared of what she might say to me.

I went into the restroom to go talk to God. I said,

"God, she is beautiful! How can I approach her? I can't use my street lines. I cannot say to her, "You got me all tired: you've been running through my mind." I cannot say to her, "heaven must miss you: you fell from heaven like an angel, you beautiful woman.""

So, I simply decided to write my number on a piece of paper, and I said, "Holy Spirit, help me once I walk outside this restroom! Lord, behold!" She was outside, right in front of me, and all I said to her was: "You are beautiful! Can I give you my number so we can talk a bit?" Athaliah took it, and then we went our separate ways. I noticed she was pretty tall, a little too taller than I was. But I didn't worry about that. I had dated taller women before. I guess... I can say that I like long legs.

I had many females liking me from the church and outside the church. They used to call me cute; they talked about my eyes, the way I talk, and everything else they liked about me. But I was just seeking God. There was a lady, named Wanida, who liked me a lot. She didn't go to my church, but she liked going out to dinner.

She liked cooking for me, but my heart was on Athaliah. I had wanted to know her more. She was the only one on my mind as if she had bought herself a place there.

Sooner, Athaliah gave me a call. On my voicemail, pager rap music came on. She just hung up. I guess she didn't like rap music and the loud sounds. I knew it was the music.

Now every Wednesday, Friday, and Sunday, I would see her at church, and I would just give her flowers, teddy bears, and cards. Every time I would see her, I would have something for her. I just kept giving her gifts, because I really liked her. She would look at me with a little smile and thank me. But at the same time, she would not let me walk with her into the church. She was kind of running away from me. And I had caught on to that. I did not want her to run from me. I wanted her to run to me.

I told her, "Yes, I'm a rapper, and I will be signing a multimillion-dollar contract with First Lady Benjamin." She didn't believe me when I said that, but she said something about some guy whose music she liked. I told her that it was me. But she didn't believe me. I was still coming on to her as other ladies kept coming on to me. They knew that I was signing with First Lady Benjamin. Yet, I had found myself wanting her.

It was one Wednesday evening at the church that another Pastor preached about how Abraham told one of his servants to find his son, Isaac, a wife, but not from the land they were in. He had told them to go to his hometown, where his fathers and family lived. He told them that there were good women who lived there in that land, wholesome women, holy women. So, the servant of Abraham went to the land that Abraham told him to go to. The servant really wants to please Abraham, so he prays to God. He said, "God, help me, please, my master Abraham and the first woman who comes and draws water for my Camel and me will be Isaac's wife."

I was so amazed at this story in the bible. I said to myself, "I'm going to do just that. I'm going to fall in love with the first woman who says to me, "You're a man of God." She will be my wife."

There were so many women who liked me: I was

about to sign a multimillion deal, but I just wanted to get the right wife. I wanted to be married again. I believe I learn a lot about what to do and what not to do from my past marriage and relationships.

Wanida had come by my home that Saturday, and I asked her, "Do you believe I'm a man of God?" She didn't say anything. She just looked me in the eyes. I asked her again, and she just looked at me with this strange stare, barely moving her lips. So, I just changed the subject. She wanted to have lunch; I said, "Cool. Let's go." I came home early to get myself ready for church the next Sunday. I had a plan to have Athaliah go out with me for dinner after church. I wanted to take photos of my home with me in front of it and send them to my mother to show how good I was doing. I would ask Athaliah to take the photos for me and then let us go have dinner. I thought she would say, "Yes, I'm kinda hungry after church." And I thought I would reply to her, "Anywhere you want to go, my queen!" I thought that to myself. I did not know how it would actually go.

After church, I saw her, and I went up to her. I

asked her, "Can you take photos of my home with me in front of it so I can send them to my mother?" She had this frown on her face and said, "No. But I'm sure you'll find someone. You're a man of God!" I said to her, "Will you like to go to dinner?" She said no to that too. She walked away, and I was left heartbroken. Even being a grown man, I had a little teardrop in my eye. I said to God, "I like her a lot! You have been doing so many miracles in my life; can I get another one?"

I went home, but I saw Wanida's car parked in my driveway. Before I could get out of my car, she looked at me and said, "You are a man of God, Peace!" I said, "Thank you," but my heart was tripping. Then I asked her if she could take some photos of me in front of my house so I could send them to my mother. She said, "Yes, sure, anything for you."

She took the photos. She noticed something was going on with me. I said, "It's all good! I just want to chill alone tonight." I decided to take a long bath with my candles and talk with God. But before I could even open my mouth to speak, I heard the Holy Spirit say,

"The first woman who said to me, "you are a man of God," is your wife." I jumped out of the bathtub, butt-naked, and ran around the house, still dripping, saying, "I heard you, God! Oh, my God! She's my wife! Athaliah is my wife! That's why Wanida couldn't speak the first time I asked her. Wow! God had shut her mouth not to speak! Okay, God, this is some weird stuff that is going on!"

Then I started thinking to myself, "I'm a man of God! Wow! The Holy Spirit just told me that I'm a man of God!" I threw some clothes on without even drying myself off. I got into my car and went to a phone booth to call Athaliah. I had to tell her what God had said to me. She answered the phone, and I was just telling her what God had said to me, how she was about to be my wife. She said to me, "No, I'm not!" I told her how I asked God that the first woman to say I am a man of God was going to be my wife. I said to her, "... and you said it first when you decided not to take photos of my house with me in it." Athaliah said, "I just said that to make you feel good, so you can find someone to take photos of your home." I told her about the other woman who couldn't speak and then later said it the second time. She hung up the phone right in my face. But I was happy with joy because I heard God speak to me so clearly about Athaliah being my wife. He had told me that I was a man of God.

The next morning, I woke up feeling good because I knew who I was now. I went to work that morning. I was in the back, fixing food for guests, and a few teenagers from a college arrived. One of my coworkers was acting crazy and wanted to punch me. I said, "Homeboy, you're tripping. I'm from the West Coast, and you don't want none of me. I've knocked out many guys bigger than me, and I would have no trouble knocking you out." I just started praying and holding my peace, speaking the word quietly in my mouth, saying, "No weapon that is formed against me shall prosper."

In my mind, I knew I was a man of God. My coworker who wanted to hit me ran out of Slice Kitchen's. Then I started to hear the college students being very loud. So, I went into the lobby area to see what was going on. Then I saw this strange man sitting in my area. I felt annoyed by him. He was a white, brown, dark man with long hair; I couldn't tell his race. He was looking right at me. I didn't like him, so I ran to the back. I said, "That is the devil. Oh, my God! That is the devil!" I started praying, and I was not scared of him. I felt this boldness that came upon me. I went up to him and said, "What's up?" I already knew who he was, and I was not scared of him.

I asked him, "Do you want to order something? He said, "I'm looking at the menu." Just then, he put his head down. While I was talking to him, I could notice his nails were long and pointed. So, when I tried to get a closer look at his nails, he put his hand under the table. Now the college students were still making loud noises, cussing, and just being very bad people. And that was my table too. So, I went over to them and told them to stop it. You need to Quiet down or leave. Now I went back to the stranger man that I knew was the devil in the flesh. I went back to him, looked him in his eyes with no fear, and asked him, "Are you going to order something?" He said, "I'm not hungry now." He got up and left, and I watched him. He got into a white car and drove off. I said to myself, "I just talked with the devil! God, this is some weird stuff that you are doing to me! Why are you letting me see all this stuff?"

Now, my coworker had come back to apologize, starting hugging me, saying, "I'm sorry. I'm sorry." I said, "Bro, it's cool. I forgive you." Then two people – a lady and a man – had this glow on their faces, two beautiful smiles when they walked in. They sat at the same seat that strange man who I know who was the devil in the flesh had seated at. Now everything got calm, and the college students calmed down also. So, I'm looking at the man and lady who came in. They were putting their cheeks together, like some kind of cheek kiss. Everyone was looking, even the college students. But the couple kept on doing it. So, I walked over to them, asking for their order. They said that they weren't hungry. They just kept on kissing each other with their cheeks as I was looking at them. I convinced myself that they were angels. That's why everything got calm, and when the devil was here, everything became crazy. All of a sudden, they got up and left. I said, "Okay, God, this has been a weird day at work!"

Now when I got home, there was a lady named Esther on my porch. She was yelling, saying, "This is my house." I told her, "No, ma'am. I'm renting this house from Sherman." When I said his name, she knew that he had lied to me. She told me that it was not his house in the first place. She had been out of the country, and he was only supposed to watch it for her. But he was out there, trying to make money off of it. I came back early. She smiled and said, "Young man, just live in it and pay me, not him." She kept looking at me up and down, saying to me, "You are kind of cute." Sooner, she left to go deal with Sherman. An hour later, Sherman came by and told me to give him the rent money. I told him, "No, you lied to me about this place, saying it was yours. I'm only paying Esther. You should leave." He said he would turn off the power because it was in his name. I said, "Go ahead. I'll turn it back on. I'm not scared of you." So, he ran off in his car. Less than 2 hours later, the power went out. There were no lights, no hot water. I went to the store and purchased candles. That night, I ran bathwater and put all the candles around the tub. Somehow, the candles heated up the water. I just sat in the water, talking to God. My plan was to get up and turn the power back on. It had been such a long day!

I did get the power back on in my name. Days and weeks passed by, and we finally graduated from the new members' class. I did see Athaliah. I asked her if she wanted to go out and have lunch. And just like the last time, she said no. I didn't worry because I knew what God had told me. He had told me that she was going to be my wife.

The next morning, I got a page from Athaliah. I called her, and she told me how God had told her to stop running from me. She had told God, "Okay, I'll go on one date, and that's it!" So, she said she would have dinner with me. I was so happy. I washed my car and got a fresh haircut. I got some new clothes. It was a Sunday, and we went after our church meeting. She left her car, and I had brought flowers and candy for her.

I opened the door for her, she got in, and we drove to the restaurant.

We ordered food, and we talked and ate. Athaliah was having a good time. She was smiling from cheek to cheek. She was saying, "You're kind of cute." She was starting to tell me how she drove from New York by herself. I then told her I drove from California by myself. We look at each other. I asked her about when she left, and she told me that she left on September the 13th early in the morning and arrived in Atlanta later that night. I cried, "Oh, my God! I left on September the 10th and arrived on September the 13th. We looked each eye to eye, and we both were amazed. She told me more about her college and everything about the life she had left behind. I had to tell her some of my stuff because I liked her. I felt the need to come out straight. But she had started asking me questions. Have I been married? I told her yes. But I didn't tell her two times. I told her I had a child in California. She asked me if I had been in jail. I told her yes. She was as looking at me funny. She thought that this was her first and last date with me. She was saying to me, "First Lady Benjamin will not sign you with all that past drama." We talked a little more. The food was good. We left the restaurant, and I took her to her car; we went our separate ways.

That week, First Lady Benjamin was having a book signing for her new book. I purchased one, and Athaliah purchased one because she loved reading books; she told me that since we had been cool friends. But I want her to be my girlfriend. I couldn't make it to the book signing because I had to do a rap show. I asked her if she could take my book and have it signed for me by her. I told her to make sure she said, "Brother Peace." She went to First Lady Benjamin's book signing, and I heard it was packed at the church. So, when it was Athaliah's time to get her book signed, she did. Then she asked First Lady Benjamin to sign her friend's book. She asked her about the person's name. She said, "Brother Peace." First Lady Benjamin, with brightness in her eyes, said, "Yes! I know him! He's a good rapper. His music is really good!" Athaliah couldn't believe it. She whispered to herself, "Wow! She really does know him!

She likes his music!"

That night, Athaliah called me. And I called her back. She told me everything about how First Lady Benjamin knew me and how she liked my music. Athaliah said to me, "We can meet up so I can bring your book, or I could just bring it by the church on Sunday." I said, "Cool." She asked me, "Will you like to have dinner after church?" I said, "Yes." I was surprised. After church, we went out to dinner again. We had a great time. I had to come real with some more of my pass. I told her about my second wife, who was a famous rapper's cousin, and the only reason I married her was that I thought her cousin would sign me. But also, because she always wanted to have sex, and we weren't married. I had to marry her so I wouldn't mess up God's plan on my music deal. But later, I told her that I had divorced her. But after I divorced her, she purchased two guns, looking for me to kill me.

Athaliah just looked at me with her eyes wide open and said, "That's your pass. So, you have been married two times? Wow! Why did you divorce your first wife?" I started to tell her, "We were dating and living together, but I wanted to change my ways back then. I went to church and got saved. She came with me and got saved. But the pastor at that church didn't like people living together and having sex without being married. So, we joined the church, and he married us a week later. I was just trying to do the right thing. We were married for two years. She started fighting so much; she was extremely jealous. She didn't like girls around me. She was very protective when it came to me. Later, I came home from rapping a late show. She hit me with an iron rod in my eye. But for some reason, it didn't hurt. Long story short, I divorced her ass. Now by me divorcing her, she got her gangster cousin, who killed people, to kill me."

I continued to tell Athaliah, "One day, I was at a local pancake house. She and her cousin came inside. She said, "There he is. Go get him and kill him!" They looked at me and spoke, "We are not doing anything to him. We are about to order some pancakes and eat." I looked at her and said, "No, you didn't bring them all the way here to kill me." They said to me, "Man, you're cool. Come join us and eat." So, I sat down and ate with them."

I added, "I divorced my first ex-wife because she was crazy and liked to fight. Now, she was looking at me, sad and dumbfounded because I was eating with her gangster cousins who she had sent to have me killed. But she had like gangster guys anyway. I was not so deep in the gangster life world because I loved my music. I learned that you can't really make music in jail or in the grave." Now I was telling Athaliah about my second ex-wife.

"And my second ex-wife really liked drug dealers. She was 5 years older than me. She had two children, and we were married for 2 years." I was telling more detail to Athaliah about my second wife. I said to her, "I had a millionaire who was going to bless me with $500,000 dollars for my record company I was getting started. And then, I had a member from the rock group who wanted to help my career in music. That's why I had to marry her. I couldn't keep having sex without being married. I was messing up with God and maybe didn't get my deals with the two people who wanted to help me."

I continued to tell Athaliah about me, "But when I married my second wife, the millionaire who was from Iran was being sued. He had a lot going on, and people were coming after him to bring him down. He called me and told me all of it, why he could not do it. But he told me to keep going after my dreams. I was upset. Then one of the members of the rock group found out that I got married and didn't want to work with me. I was so confused. I married just so I would not fornicate with more women in sin. I married to do right by God. So, while two years of marriage with my second wife, stuff was rough with her. Her children were being mean to me, and she was acting up. One night I was praying to God, and I asked him, "God, what happened to my deal with the two gentlemen who wanted to help me?" God spoke to me and said, "You married the wrong woman. I didn't care about the fornication. I had taken care of that already on the cross. I just didn't want you to marry her. I tried so many times to stop you, but you wanted her so bad. You married her because you didn't want to fornicate with her. I saw your heart, how you will say no and run. But I couldn't stop your strong will on the earth. So, I had to stop the two gentlemen from helping you. You were out of my will with that wife." I said, "Oh, my God! God spoke to me about what was going on. God, show me how she started cheating with drug dealers because I didn't get the deal." The reason I didn't get the deal was her. So, I divorced her, but she didn't want a divorce. So, after I divorced her, my friends were telling me to watch out. She purchased two guns to have me killed. But God had hidden me from her."

By me telling her all this, I wanted her to like me for me and not my past. I was a changed man now. But Athaliah, with her eyes big, would say, "Wow! That's your past!" She was kind of liking me now because I was about to be a rich man. Athaliah would tell me how she liked tall men. She was a pretty and tall woman, about 5'10" but really didn't care now. She just wanted the man of God for her. She just wanted the will of God for her. So, I explained to her about the time when God told me that she was going to be my wife. I said, "It is the will of God, after all – a woman of God for me. Now I can get the multimillion-dollar contract deal because I will be right on His will on marring you."

I'm in the right state and the right church. So, everything looks perfect. We just kept talking.

I was also telling Athaliah how I confessed Psalms 91 each day. She said, "You really are a man of God to survive those two women trying to kill you. Wow! You can't be touched." But she still kept her shoulders up, not telling me that she liked me. But I noticed that she liked me. She also heard from God to stop running from me. Now Athaliah was looking at me really crazily, and she said, "That's your past! Look at you now... you're about to sign a multimillion-dollar contract deal with First Lady Benjamin!"

One Saturday in a new Discipleship class, Reverend Lite Benjamin was teaching, and he was saying, "I remember seeing you at Slice Kitchen's. You have that strange name... Reece Peace. Everyone laughed. Then he said that your name is great; your last name Peace means prosperity, wholeness, complete, nothing missing, nothing broken. You are a blessed man! The whole class started to clap." I was shocked. After class, people were coming up to me, shaking my hand. There were women looking at me because I just got spoken over in a good way by Reverend Benjamin.

That Saturday, Athaliah didn't come, so I called her and told her what had happened. She said she already knew; her friends had told her, "That guy named Peace, who likes you, Reverend Benjamin spoke over him." Athaliah was really starting to like me. She asked me, "Don't you want to go out after church? Let's go out to dinner after church."

So, I got home that Saturday, and I heard a knock on the door. It was Esther. She came to ask me how I was doing. I told her that I was doing just fine and that I was great. Then she came close up on me, trying to kiss me. I moved back. Then she grabbed my pants, trying to take them off. I pushed her hands down, yelling, "What you doing?"

She said, "Give me some sex!"

I said no.

She said, "Give me some or get out of my house!"

I said, "Okay, I will get out."

She said to me, "You have one week to be out. You have to be out by January 7."

I said, "One step up, three steps back!"

But I wasn't worried because I was a man of God and had the most beautiful woman who liked me. I didn't tell Athaliah because I didn't want her to know my issues. And I couldn't stay with her because she living with Tina. On the second day, Esther decided to put me out early. I asked her, "Why are you doing this? I have a week to leave!"

She said, "Get out now!"

So, I packed my stuff and went to the parking lot at the same motel I started at. I slept in my car, and I said, "God, what's up?!"

I get a page from Wanida. I called her back. She

asked me, "How are you doing?" I ended up telling her about the situation I had found myself in.

She told me to come over to her place, telling me that I could stay there until I had found myself a place to live at. So, I stayed that night at her house, followed by another night. I couldn't call Athaliah because I didn't want her to know what was going on with me. One night, Wanida put on the tight red dress and started saying, "We are going to get married, and you are going to be my husband." I said, "No, I'm not!"

She said, "Yeah, you are!"

So, I grabbed my clothes and ran out of her house. She started crying and telling me to come back. I just left, got back in the car, went to that motel's parking lot, and fell asleep, trusting that God would soon find a roof for my head, a bed to comfort my back, and a pillow to comfort my neck.

Chapter 5

The First Kiss

Things were not really going quite well for me, and I was having a hard time seeing any good side to life. The only good that I had was God accompanying me and being there for me no matter where I was. Well, that was enough for me. That was more than enough for me. But in my head, there was something more than I had wanted. There was something more than I had been looking for, and so, I turned to God, asking for all that I had wanted, pleading for it, begging for it, knowing that only He was the one who could grant me all of it.

I got myself a hotel room and stayed there for a couple of days. I had explained to Athaliah about Esther, who I was renting from, and also about how I had to stay with Wanida for a while to figure out what my next step was going to be. Athaliah wasn't mad. She assured me, saying, "You will be alright. God is with you."

Thomas, a friend of mine, asked me to come and volunteer at an elementary school in the cafeteria. I said, "Okay, cool," thinking how working with children would make me forget about all the trouble that I was going through.

When we got to the school to start helping, Thomas told the children at the elementary school that I was a famous rapper. The kids' interest in me had awoken. Thomas was a cool guy. He and I both had come to cherish the friendship that we had. He thought that I was a good rapper and that one day, I was going to sign a big record deal. Perhaps for that reason, he always kept telling everyone that I was a famous rapper. So, when the children asked me to rap, I could really not say no.

I started flowing, showing my skills. The children were dancing and clapping their hands to my flows. Singing and rapping for them, seeing all the smiles on their faces and the excitement that they had held in their hearts, I was sure to forget and let go of my problems for a while. It did not look like everything around me was falling apart, crumbling to the ground. It felt like I was truly and completely happy. It was something that made me sure that there was much more to come from my career as a rapper. It made me sure to know that giving up was never really an option. It never could be. More importantly, it made me sure that there was a lot more to life than I had seen or believed to be. I was happy.

Soon as I got done with that, they wanted autographs. So, I had a couple of photos taken with the kids, and I signed some autographs for some. The bell started to clang, telling the kids that it was time to come back to class from lunch, but they would not want to leave until they had gotten an autograph. I told the kids to go back to class, but their reaction was quite a rebuttal.

They started snatching the photos out of my hands. They jeered at me, "We don't need an autograph. Just give us the photo!" As much as I was able to, I started passing the picture on to the kids who tried to come at me. Even then, those who had not gotten the pictures were coming toward me, jumping at me, and trying their best to take off my shirt. "Give me your shirt and your hat." I scoffed, "No! You've got to go to class now, children."

Seeing all the chaos that had begun, all the teachers and the principal paced toward the scene of the frenzy. "What's going on?!" the teachers asked, while the others blew whistles. The lunchtime bell was still ringing, and it had gotten to the point that my eardrums had begun to hurt. The children were still all around me like a cluster of bees, and I was feeling a bit too suffocated.

But with the calmness of that storm, one of the teachers saw me and asked, "Who are you?"

There was a little boy who cried, "He's a famous rapper!" Thomas and I had started running against the children who were still chasing after us. In the meanwhile, we were crying, "Stop it, kids! Stop it!" The teachers were now chasing after the school kids as well. Just then, my buddy and I managed to jump over the fences. It was not easy, but since there was a will to get out of the messy and tumultuous situation, we had found a way. We sat on our knees, panting as though we had run a marathon.

"What the hell just happened?" he chuckled in confusion. I replied, "Man, I don't know! You're the one who told the kids that I was a famous rapper!" We faltered up to our car, got inside, and drove off, not being able to control our laughter.

Perhaps due to all the kids who jumped me or perhaps due to the hysterical laughter that followed after, I felt quite a few cramps in my stomach. At any rate, it was then that I heard something. It was a familiar voice, and it came to me in my head at the most unexpected of moments. "Get ready for that," God said to me.

I asked in an instant riposte, a reflex of sorts, "What God?!" I had not realized that a little of my voice, the one that was supposed to stay inside, had found its way out a little bit. Thomas asked in confusion, "What you say, Peace?" I knew that it would never be an easy conversation to have, not one that I would be able to explain to him very easily, so I opted for an awkward silence instead.

There was a guy, Jazz, who used to come to The

Nest and watch me perform. This one night after performing, he came up to me and went into a subtle admiration, "Great performance, sir!" I said, "Thank you." Jazz was a great singer as well. Seeing him there perform quite a few times, and very well, I was sure to let him know that. Well, one talk led to another, and I ended up telling him about my living situation, saying to him, "The lady kicked me out of her townhouse that I was renting from her because I wouldn't give her sex as a payment!" Jazz said, "Oh, man, I have a big house. I have many rooms in my house. You can come and stay with me. I'll charge you little to nothing! You're like a brother to me, and that's what brothers do, right? They take care of each other." I asked in amusement and disbelief, "Seriously?" Jazz said, "Yes. My wife and I… we… are planning on going to Vegas in a few days, so you can move in before we go."

I moved in just a little later. I had much of the house to myself, and I had someplace to rest. I was sure to thank my God above me for showing me that there were, in fact, better times to come. I had enjoyed being there, and I was grateful for Jazz to have led me into his home. I knew that to be very big of him, a gesture that not many were willing to do.

It was not long when Jazz and his wife came back from Vegas. And as soon as they came in, they cried, "Man, you can stay here all you want! You do not have to pay us any rent money either! We just won $40,000 dollars in Vegas! We know that it was God's gift to us because we let you move in here."

I was amused. There was a sense of exhilaration that I felt, one that I had not really felt in a long while. I had a place to live. Though it was not permanent, I knew that I would not have to go out looking for a place. I had time to concentrate on all the other things that were going on in my life, all the problems that were coming back and forth to trouble me.

In the basement of his house, Jazz had a nice and massive studio. We would go downstairs and make music. I was rapping, and he was singing. We were making some nice songs in the studio, and doing that with him was quite fun. It came to me as some sort of break from the problems, a break that I had much desperately needed.

Jazz asked me once, "Did God say that you were signing with First Lady Benjamin and Point Records?"

I had previously told him about the conversations that I would have with God. I replied, "No. God just spoke to me and said that I was signing a multimillion-dollar contract deal. The next day, a lady named Sister Bern walked up to me and said that First Lady Benjamin and Point Records were going to sign me a multimillion-dollar contract deal. She was telling me how they were jamming to my music in the studio."

Jazz replied to me, hearing all that and having a smile on his face that told me that he really did believe in me, "Man, Peace, you can sign with anyone! God is with you! God raps through you! Sign with one of those big companies."

I replied to him, "I like my church, and I'm just trying to do everything through and for my church." Jazz replied to that, "God's will, right?"

I nodded in agreement, telling him that he was right and also telling him that I had appreciated all that he had done for me so far. "Yes," I replied, "God's will."

At that very instant in time, we were working on music, creating something new. So, I asked him to help me make a song for Athaliah. I said to him, "Let's go for a nice old-school slow beat. I'll rap, and you sing on it." When we were done with it, when I finally got to hear what he had spent so much of our time on, it sounded nice. It was something that I thought she would really like.

The next Sunday, after church, I gave Athaliah the CD. On it was the song that Jazz and I had made for her. Athaliah could not wait to hear it, and so we ambled up to her car. We sat together, and she put it in the CD player. No more than thirty seconds into the song, she cried in exhilaration, shying away from her face in happiness, "I love it! Wow, Peace! You have talent! I didn't know you could make romantic love songs with a rap!"

Well, it was her, and I was happy to do that for

her; I had known it to be something that would make her happy, and well, it did. It made her happy. Seeing that smile on her face, all the efforts that I had put in were suddenly worth it. I knew that I had not wasted my time doing that. She was happy, and that was all that had mattered to me.

We said our goodbyes, and she left, screeching her car away, but I could hear her still playing the song. I was happy.

That same night, at Tina's house, Athaliah was playing my song in her room. Tina heard the music and spurted into her room. She told Athaliah to turn it off, telling her that it was worldly music and she had not liked it. Athaliah explained, "It's a gospel rapper I'm listening to, Tina. Tina replied, "It doesn't sound like gospel music." Athaliah replied to her, "Gospel rap is not Jesus' music, you know? It's the devil's music!"

Athaliah was infuriated, screaming within in fury that was much more than any she had ever seen, "I'm out of here! No one tells me what to do!" That morning, Athaliah went out and found her an apartment and moved her stuff out right away.

I was still going to church, making the same positive confessions each day. In each of my heartful confessions, I would talk about how I wanted the beautiful woman to be my wife. The rest of the confession would be about how I believed in God for my signing with First Lady Benjamin a multimillion- dollar contract deal.

One Saturday morning at prayer service, I was praying, and I heard God say to me, "Go tell that lady in the blue by the door that she's going to have a baby." I replied, "Alright, that's easy because she's a female, nice lady, and she is married to a nice guy." The couple was familiar since I had been seeing them at the church for quite a while now. I walked over to her while the husband was next to her, and I said to her, "You are going to have a baby." With that, I walked away.

Sooner came Thursday, and with that came Athaliah's call. She had called me, telling me about her new apartment, and asked me to come over for dinner. She said, "I'd really like to cook for you."

I was out of words, surprised, and I never really could explain that feeling since I had wanted that for way too long. I tried, however, to keep my cool, and I replied to her, "Cool." If I had to put it simply, I would say that I was feeling like a king who was happily and calmly sitting on his destined throne.

"She really does like me!" I whispered to myself, knowing it was something incredible. The feeling was unmatched. Just then, I went out and bought her a promise ring with a green birthstone on it. I also got her a plaque that said, "My Promise To You."

I could not wait for the much-awaited Friday night. So, that Friday morning, I got up earlier, got myself a nice haircut, and got my car washed. I picked up some flowers and my favorite candy to present to her the moment she opened the door; I knew she would really like it; it was sweet.

With all the gifts that I had to give to her, I sat in my car, carefully placing them in the car. I drove up to her house and made it there safely. Trying not to be nervous, I knocked on the door. When Athaliah opened the door, I was left in awe.

Never had I seen someone looking so very beautiful, and never had I ever seen someone taking my breath away so very often. The apartment smelled good, as though a meal was carefully and wholeheartedly cooked inside. I went into a hug, giving her the flowers and the candy. Dinner was already cooked; she had made me a plate of baked chicken with rice, vegetables, and salad. It was quite thoughtful of her, and it felt like it was the best date I had ever had. We ate, we talked, we laughed, and we had a really amazing time overall. We talked about the birds that flew too beautifully, the bees that hummed, the trees that stood too proudly, and the flowers that grew to bloom.

Just then, I lit a candle, turning off all the lights. There was a beam of light that found its way into the living room from the streetlight far away. As I got on my knees, opening up the fancy box of the ring that I had got for her, the scene set felt somewhat like it had come straight out of a movie. It was just us in that room, under what seemed like a spotlight created carefully just for the two of us. And I asked her, "Will you be my lady, Athaliah? Will you be my girlfriend?"

"Yes! Yes! Yes!" she cried, jumping and giving me a hug that I had never gotten before in my life. It was the type of hug that told me that I was going to be alright, that life itself was going to turn out just fine. Then I turned the lights back on, giving her the plaque that said, "My Promise To You." It felt like a dream that I was living too factually, one that I never wanted to wake up from. Yet, I pinched myself, and to see that it was not a dream, I was happy.

Athaliah, just a little after that, started telling me some of her secrets. She thought about it as though she was carefully thinking about letting her walls down for the first time ever.

"I'm a virgin," she said to me, taking a deep breath, sighing as though a hefty weight had been lifted off of her chest.

"Really? Wow!" I exclaimed, adding, "I knew a guy in California. He used to be a pimp who would have women on the streets as hookers. Now, he's a preacher.

He prophesied over me one time that I was going to marry a virgin. I didn't believe him because of his past, which revolved all around pimping women. But he had prophesied over me, and if I married you, I guess he would be proven right."

Athaliah replied, "I almost had sex one time with the boyfriend I had in New York. But just then, I heard God's voice, and God said to me, "Athaliah, if you do this, you are going to be behind three years of your life." So, I push him off of me." If it isn't quite clear as of yet, let me tell you: I was impressed with the woman. Athaliah was amazing.

Athaliah started telling me more about herself, things that she had not really talked about with others. She said, "When I was little, I would read a romantic book about tall men. They would come and be a prince to a woman like me and make love to me. My parents kept me in the house. I couldn't even go out the front gate because they were very protective of me. My friends had to come to play with me in the front yard that was surrounded by a gate. I had been this good girl forever."

I had known her to be a woman who had been through a lot, and through all of it, she had endured; she had persisted. It was something that drew me into her, something that made me sure that I was going to love her for a long time.

Athaliah also confessed how she wanted a man who had many women, a man who knew what he was doing with her when he was doing it with her. My eyes, just then, spread wide open, and I said to her, "I have some more stuff to tell you."

"Okay," she replied, confused, wondering what I was about to tell her.

"Well, I've had many women in my life," I told her. "It's not just been the two of my ex-wives. I used to have sex with my babysitters when I was 7 years of age. When I was 13 years of age, I had a 21-year-old girlfriend. She and I would get drunk all that time and have sex. I believe that happened because I was having sex at a very young age. I was known as a "Male Hoe." I used to call myself The Erotic Lover."

Athaliah's eyes got bigger and bigger; perhaps

these were the things that she was never expecting me to say, given I was a man of God. "What?" she exclaimed.

I said to her, "My family used to call me by my nickname Puta. It's a bad word in Spanish that translated to "Bitch," so basically, I was a male bitch, a male hoe back then."

Athaliah said, "Well, you have a nice name, Reece Peace. It's like how Reverend Lite Benjamin says, "Chocolate peanut butter!"" We laughed. "Peace," she sighed, "Wow! With a name like that, why did you go through so much?"

Then I explained to her that my last name was changed. I said to her, "My first name has always been Reece, but my last name used to be Barnes. My rap name, however, was Brother Peace. So, I rap by this name. There were times I would rap, and the people would pay me by checks. So, the check would be to "Reece," "Brother Peace," or "Reece Peace." Then I would have to tell them to change it. So, I had to go through that for a while. When I got tired of it, one of my buddies told me about how he had his last name changed.

He told me to change my last name to Peace." I paused for a while, not sure if she was already getting bored of me.

"And…" she asked, wanting to know more and more about me, "What did you do?"

"So," I added, "I asked him whether I could do that. He told me that I could, that it was easy. I told him my name would be funny, Reece Peace. But then I thought that it would be cool. So later, I started the process with the court system. There was no one named Reece Peace. So when it was time for me to go to court, the judge declared that my name could be changed. I was in line with many people who were getting their names changed. Now the Marshall walked toward all of us and asked everyone if we had all the paperwork. Everyone, including myself, said no, but the Marshall said that no one could come in without the paperwork. Everyone was upset after waiting in line for hours. When I started to walk away, the Marshall told me to stop, telling me that I could go inside the courtroom. Everyone exclaimed in anger, "Why does he get to go to the courtroom?""

Athaliah chucked just then, humming, "Oh, special treatment… I see."

"Yeah," I agreed, continuing, "Well, while they were all out there fussing with the Marshall, he told them that they could not come in if they did not have the paperwork. He walked into the courtroom and shut the door on all those people. I asked him just then, "Is everything okay? Why am I in here by myself?" I thought that maybe I had done something wrong, and they were going to arrest me for some kind of crime that they found out about me. I was almost about to run up out of there. The Marshall told me to have a seat, and I did just that. I saw the judge come to her seat, and it was a lady judge. The Marshall told the judge that I did not have my paperwork. The lady judge said, "His name gets changed right away." She stamped over some papers quite loudly, and it was the sweet sound of accomplishment. The Marshall gave it to me and said, "Congratulations, Mr. Reece Peace." I said, "Cool. Thank you, your honor." I went out of the room. Everyone was gone, and I asked myself, "what just happened in there?""""

Athaliah said to me, holding my hand in hers, "It was God who changed your name for the end times." I had agreed with her. I guessed that God had something for me to do. Just as God had changed Abram to Abraham, Jacob to Israel, Simon to Peter, and Saul to Paul in the Bible. They all had a purpose for God.

Athaliah sighed, "Wow! You really are a man of God!"

She reached out to hug me, and I hugged her right back. Only this time, though, there was something else. There was something more. Only this time, our lips had come closer together, and they entwined. It was my first kiss with her. It was her first kiss with me. It was our first kiss.

I could not hold myself there, not being able to resist further leaning in. The beautiful eye contact was broken as we both leaned in for a kiss. Yet another one still felt like it was the first one that we had ever had – still glorious.

Her heart pounded, uncertain of the direction, fighting to let go of the parts that struggled to convince her to stop. She raised her impassively hanging arm and placed her hand on my chest, persisting me into pulling her closer. She had never wanted a man more. Nothing in her past could compare to the desire she was experimenting with now. She sensed my feelings as genuine; she was weak with acceptance.

My hand swiftly shifted from her waist to her long slim neck; my lips placed an inch away from her lips. It was between the irresistible first kisses that I saw her face and fell in love. I knew that I wanted her there with me through my rough days and sleepless nights. There was a longing in her voice – a longing that wanted to know no restraints.

Our kiss was impassioned and demanding. Her mind was dizzy as my tongue searched out the tip of hers. There was no power that could hold them back, not yet.

Athaliah was overcome; she could not cease to think. My hands moved gradually, unhurriedly up her back and down again. Our kisses became hungrier and longer. She had no resistance when my hands moved up to her beautiful breasts. She was no longer hugging me but massaging my chest, upward to my collar, carefully caressing my throat and the back of my neck with her fingertips that glided over my jaw and into my rough, dark hair. We were breathing hard into moans that grew louder and louder with each passing second.

Aggressive and fast, much like a Corvette, she moved onto me, and downward I went, on the floor. The way she was, it did not turn her off. A sweet giggle escaped her mouth, and she jumped onto me yet again. I gripped her by her waist and got on top of her.

My mouth left hers, searching first the curve of her throat, then down to her breasts. Without looking away and without taking my lips away from hers, I unbuttoned her shirt. The hungry burning augmented as I put my lips on her bulging bra. I sequentially undid the hooks on the back of her bra with my teeth. I pulled the straps of the bra away from her shivering shoulders, spitting it to the side.

I had pulled her bra off, and my eyes met hers as

her breasts spilled from the lace. "Oh, my God!" I moaned, looking at the breasts that left me wondering about all the beautiful things in the world. A slight moan escaped her when, aggressively, I cupped both her breasts, one in each hand. Her eyes were closed as my tongue wet first one nipple and then the other. Her back arched against my chest as she felt my mouth open; a gentle suckling began. A deep, ecstatic moan escaped her when the hauling sensation rippled through her.

We were quite past being strangers, yet her own desires prevented her from resisting our passion. At that point, she knew what made her feel alive. She knew who made her feel alive. It was me.

Her touch was unambiguous; it was exquisite. Her hands slid gently down my body, hot, gentle, and claiming. I sensed that she was more than moved by genuine and lasting emotions, just as I was.

Still dressed, to some extent, at least, I ecstatically rubbed my cock on her vagina. Her moans emerged into screams, encouraging me to go on without even thinking about stopping. It was hot, and all the things that were happening made it even hotter. Trails of sweat dripped from our bodies and onto the coffee-colored carpet in a rain-like pattern.

But it was wrong. I could not do that. My brain kept reminding me that. That was when I came to my senses, pulling myself away. She lay on the carpet, almost undressed, and I stood over her, calling out her name.

She was just smiling, as though a daydream that she did not want to wake up from. It was, in fact, just as much of a dream to me. She was with me. But I knew that it was God who was telling me to not do it. I knew that it was God speaking to me, telling me to stop. And so, I stopped.

"Athaliah?" I whispered. She didn't listen.

"Athaliah?" I spoke, a little louder than before. She was gradually coming back to her senses.

"Yeah?" she asked.

"We just sinned," I replied. "I apologize to you." Getting on my knees, tears rolled down my eyes as I said,

"Sorry, God. Please forgive me, for I have sinned."

Athaliah buttoned her shirt, hugged me from the back, and said, "I'm not mad at you."

I said, "We can't do that again." Athaliah nodded in agreement. So, we cleaned up, and I helped her wash the dishes. I said my goodbyes and left with my head facing downward in shame and mere guilt. It had felt good, but the cost was too much. I had made my God angry, or so I thought.

While driving, I was still crying out to God with tears in my eyes, saying, "Lord, I'm sorry. I'm sorry. Please forgive me!"

I got home, walking up to the door. I had the keys in my hand, but I could not open the door. The clouds rumbled and growled, and it started to rain. I was still locked outside, with nothing to cover myself with.

I knocked on the door, but no one answered. I knew that they were home; I could see the car and the lights on in the bedroom. So, I walked up to the backyard and started to yell Jazz's name. The rain started to grow more and more intense with each passing minute, and I could not do anything about it. I ran back to my car, dripping, and said to myself, "God is punishing me for what I did with Athaliah." I closed my eyes, and I started praying. I started to plead to God to take the lust spirit out of me, and with that, I fell asleep in the back of my car, slowly and then all at once.

My eyes flickered in the morning due to the harsh and warm beams of the sun that escaped through the windows of my car. I woke up, sitting up and rubbing my eyes, and I found in front of me a rainbow that appeared too lively from the car's windshield. I heard God's voice. He said to me, "I have a covenant with you."

I had understood about the covenant rainbow. I went into a deep sigh, knowing that He was not mad at me anymore. I felt relieved. I said to myself, "That's why God made me sleep in my car! He did that so that I could see the rainbow this morning!"

My clothes were still damp, and I desperately needed a change of clothing. I walked out of the car and onto the porch of the house. I put the keys into the knob, but before I could turn it, Jazz opened the door. "Where were you?" he asked.

"I've been here, man," I replied. "I called out your name all night, but you didn't open up. So, I fell asleep in the car."

"I'm sorry, man," he replied almost instantaneously. "I didn't hear you."

"It's okay," I replied. "No worries."

Time passed by, and Athaliah and I were dating. It was going quite well, and we were having too much fun. It was one Sunday after church that we were walking out of the church, and a lady walked up to me and said something. It was the lady about whom God told me that she was going to have a baby. She walked up to the two of us, and she spoke to me, "Peace, you're a prophet."

"Why do you say that?" I asked.

"I just found out that I'm pregnant," she replied with

a joyful sense of exhilaration on her face.

"Congratulations!" I cried. I could see that Athaliah was too impressed.

"No," she replied. "You don't understand! I couldn't have children! So, when you came up to me and said that I was going to have a baby, my husband was mad at you. He wanted to hit you for saying that because we had been trying for years."

I said to her, "I didn't know that. I just told you what God told me."

With a wide smile on her face, Athaliah put her hand on my shoulder. The lady thanked me, telling me that she was happy that I obeyed God. I replied, "All glory is of God."

So, Athaliah and I arrived at the restaurant. We were about to walk through the door when another lady ran up to me and said, "Peace, you remember me?" I told her that I didn't.

She reminded me. "I'm the lady who you got born again. My friend, Tee-Tee, introduced me to you, telling me that you were a preacher. My name's Lucy, and when she told me that you were a preacher, I could not believe it. I told her that you were a gangster. Also, I told you that we were the ones who would have guys get high, have sex with them, and then steal their wallets. But you got me born again that night. Ever since that night, good things started to happen to me. I got my husband back. I got my children back. I'm in church now, and I go there regularly."

Hearing all that, Athaliah and I could not help but praise God. Lucy thanked me, and I told her what I had told the lady before, "All glory is of God."

A little while passed, and Athaliah and I were eating. We were sitting in the restaurant when she said to me out of nowhere, "Peace, you really are a man of God!"

I was happy, and I portrayed that with a smile. She said to me, "I have been blessed with a man of God! God has blessed me. I love you, Peace." A teardrop rolled down her eye and onto her cheek, one that told me how happy she was to be with me. I took a tissue, scrubbing the tear away.

The following Sunday morning at church, there was a guy who walked up to the two of us. He said, "You guys are dating, right? Just go to the courthouse and let the judge marry you two. God put you two together. If you get married, you can have sex, have kids, and live well."

Athaliah and I were looking at each other, thinking that the idea kind of sounded good. she and I talked about it a little more, putting some more thought into it, and said, "We'll pray about it." We were planning on going back to the church that evening. They had a service that evening, talking about finances and elaborating on the ways to live without debts. Athaliah and I wanted to go to that to learn more about being debt-free. That evening when we got there, Athaliah whispered in my ear, "Let's go and get married tomorrow."

I looked at her and asked, too confused and too happy, "Are you serious?" She told me that she was, in all honesty, serious. The smile on my face extended from one ear to the other. I was so very happy, and putting it all into words could never really do justice to that happiness. I was truly happy.

See, I had been good. I had abstained from sins, and I had been celibate for more than three years now. Athaliah was still a virgin. So, the church service started. Athaliah and I were seated all the way in the back of the church, holding hands because we were about to get married. So basically, she was my wife now. We both had a joyful look on our faces, and I could not wait to spend the rest of my life with her.

Reverend Lite Benjamin came in and started tutoring about financing, expounding over the ways to be free of debt and the ways to perfectly manage your money. In the middle of his teaching, he got really loud and said, "Stop going to the courthouse to get married by a judge! Don't do that! You should not do that!"

My fiancé and I looked at each other and were confused, mouthing, "How did he know that?!" We were caught in awe and amusement, trying to figure out what had just happened. I said to her, "God told him to say that."

Athaliah replied to me, "I guess we have to trust God, don't we?"

In my mind, there were quite a few thoughts that raced around. But one of those thoughts had managed to prevail.

I guess I'm not having sex tomorrow.

In Athaliah's mind, there were quite a few thoughts that raced around. But one of those thoughts had managed to prevail.

I'm still going to be a virgin tomorrow, just like Mary, the mother of Jesus.

There was one time that I went to bible study without Athaliah. The usher had seated me in the front row, and Reverend Lite Benjamin was teaching. He started to pray in tongues. Then he stopped by me and said, "Yes, your name is Peace." He started to prophesize over me, saying what the Lord told him to say to me. He also knew and said that I had been confused about what it was that was going on in my life.

Then, Reverend Benjamin said, "This night,

there will be no more confusion. If you want guidance, listen to your name; study your name. God will cause you to be the example of what God called you. So begin to rejoice and know that nothing is missing, that nothing is broken. Prosperity, wholeness, and completion shall be yours."

I was amazed and exhilarated. "Oh, my God! Reverend Benjamin just said what the Lord told him to tell me. He told me that in front of all these people!" I whispered to myself, a grin all over my face. I was happy. People were clapping and cheering for me. After the church service ended, I purchased the tape and drove to Athaliah's house. I knocked on the door, and she let me in. I could not wait to tell her what had happened. I told her to listen to the tape, how Reverend Benjamin just prophesized over me. She heard the tape on her tape box, and she, too, was joyful. She hugged me so tight that I felt like my ribs would crash into each other and break. She cried, "We are going to be rich and blessed!"

With the passage of a little while, I had gotten Athaliah an engagement ring. I had it custom-made with a cross made with diamonds. On top of that, I rented a white limousine. I was still working at the restaurant at Slice Kitchen's, but I was making good tips for doing all of this for her. I wanted her to be treated like a queen, and I wanted her to know her worth. I wanted her to know that she was my queen and I was her king.

I played a little trick on her and told her that my car was in the shop. I told her that a friend was going to let me use his car, so we could go out for dinner. I was at her apartment, and she was looking out of the window, asking me, "Is your friend still coming?" I said to her, "He should be here in a little while."

Still looking out of the window, she could not help but notice the white Limousine standing outside too proudly, a royalty. She said, "That's a nice white Limo outside." It was then that I took her outside and walked her to the car. The driver hopped out and greeted me, "Welcome, Mr. Peace."

I helloed him right back, introducing him to the woman I had loved. She got into the schmancy car, and she could not believe it. The driver drove us around the city while we gulped down apple cider in those pretty wine glasses. She could not help but smile, and that was enough for me. I knew that I was going to do everything it took to make her smile for as long as I could. I wanted her to be happy.

We got to the restaurant, enjoyed our food, and had a great time with one another. Then after we had eaten, I got on my knee and asked her the question that she had wanted to hear, the question I had wanted to ask.

"Athaliah, my love, will you marry me?"

"Yes! Yes! Yes! I'll marry you, Peace! I'll marry you!" she exclaimed, too happy.

People were clapping, on their feet, rooting for us. We had gotten engaged, and it was official this time. It was now time to meet her family. Thanksgiving of that year arrived very soon, and I was excited to see New York for the first time ever. But it was not just that. I was excited to meet her family. We had taken a road trip to New York, the city that apparently never slept; I had heard so many stories about the place. I wanted to see what the hype was all about.

We were driving, and driving, and driving, taking turns to switch from the driver seat to the passenger seat. It was fun to see all the states we had to pass to get to New York. One time, we were a little hungry, so we stopped at a fast-food restaurant's drive-thru to get some food.

The lady took our order at the speaker area; we drove up to the payment counter and picked up food at the window. We got our bags of food, but Athaliah was missing her sauce. Athaliah told the lady that she had forgotten her sauce. The drive-thru lady told her that they were out of sauce at that time. All of a sudden, Athaliah started to yell, "You don't have no sauce?!"

She opened the door to try to go through the window and fight the lady. I had to pull her back. I said, "No, Athaliah. It's okay. Let's go. Let's go. It's only the sauce, and she said that they didn't have any. It's not that big of a deal!"

Athaliah replied, "They don't know who they're messing with!" I looked at Athaliah with my big eyes and started talking to myself, "Lord, what was that?" It was almost like I saw another person in her, a demon, a monster, someone that I never expected to see.

Perhaps that was my cue to not go through with her. Perhaps it was God's way of telling me to run away from her.

Run, nigga! Run!

At any rate, we finally made it to the fancy state – New York. We were visiting her family, especially her mother. Her mother was tall, smooth-skinned, and a very beautiful woman. She had loved me at first sight. Athaliah said to her mom, "This is my fiancé, Peace. We are getting married soon!" It was at that time that I could feel my heart racing against my chest, almost like it would break through my ribcage as though it was nothing but caramel strands.

We finally went to New York City on the day that followed. We shopped, and we ate the famous NYC pizza that I had grown up hearing about; it was amazing! We went to the top of the Empire State building, looking at the Twin Towers. We could see the Statue of Liberty, and the sight was just too romantic. I was glad that I was experiencing that with her for the first time.

Athaliah was showing me everything, all the places where she had created memories that lasted in her mind and heart. It was getting late, and we had to go back to get some rest. We had stopped by her father's house before we went back to her mom's house. She introduced me to him, and I instantly knew him to be a very nice man.

He was married to a nice lady, Athaliah's stepmother. The guy could talk a lot, just like me. He was short in height, just like me. I was sort of surprised because Athaliah was tall. I had noticed her mother was way taller than him. I had liked that because Athaliah was some taller than me, maybe an inch or two. Her mom, however, was way taller than her father.

Now we really had to get back; it was late, and Thanksgiving was just a day ahead. We woke up, and we went to her sister's house for Thanksgiving. The dinner party was at Vicki's place, and when we got there, Athaliah was so happy to introduce me to her family for the first time officially. She was holding my hand, telling everyone I was her fiancé and that we were getting married soon. She kept introducing me to everyone by my last name, Peace.

She had a big family – her brothers, sisters, nephews, and nieces. And it felt too good being there. Later, I found out that there were some issues going on, a small argument with two ladies and Vicki. Vicki didn't play; she was really bossy, and she told the two ladies that they needed to leave. I was just looking, too confused and awkward to say anything.

Athaliah whispered to me just then, "My sister, she can be annoying, I know."

She then introduced me to Vicki. She said to her, "Sis, this is my fiancé, Peace. We're getting married soon."

Vicki didn't smile. She simply said, "Hello, Peace. It's nice to meet you." With that, she chose to walk away. I understood that, however. She had a lot going on with the food preparation, hosting the party, and the argument.

A short while later, Vicki called Athaliah to the kitchen. Vicki was telling her sister that I was different. She said to her, "He looks like a gangster or some kind of pimp."

Athaliah said, "No, Vicki. He is a really nice guy."

Vicki asked, "Where's he from? What college did he go to? What kind of job does he have?" Vicki was asking all these questions to Athaliah.

Athaliah replied to her, "Sis, Peace is from California.

He didn't go to college. He went to acting school."

Vicki scoffed, "Acting school?"

Athaliah replied, "Yes. He is going to sign a multimillion-dollar contract deal to make music with First Lady Benjamin. Peace and I are going to be rich. God had blessed me with the right man."

Vicki asked her, "Why do you not want a Jamaican man?"

Athaliah replied, "I already told you. I don't want no Jamaican man! I wanted an American man… and I got that. I found him. And I am going to marry him."

Vicki replied, "He's not tall. I thought you liked tall men."

Athaliah replied to her, "Sis, I just want the will of God for my life. I just want a man of God, the husband that God has for me."

Vicki said, "Okay, if you're happy, then I'm happy for you."

With that, the time for dinner had gotten there. We were just eating, talking about different things. I could tell that her family had started to like me already, and it felt good. They kept asking me if the food was any good, telling me to try all the dishes. It was my first time eating Jamaican food. So, I made sure I prayed twice because I didn't even realize what some of the dishes were; they were all very new to me.

I was telling jokes, and I had her family laughing to the point where their stomachs turned. They were then talking to Athaliah, asking her, "Where did you find this nice guy?"

Athaliah, smiling, said, "Peace and I met at a church."

They were happy. The conversation passed, and before I knew it, they were telling me about Athaliah. They were telling me about how she was the first daughter of her parents, who was born in America. I thought to myself, "Wow! That's cool."

They said to me, "No, listen, Peace. When we tell you that she was the first daughter of our parents born in America, we mean that she made it possible for us to move here from Jamaica."

I said, "Cool," looking at Athaliah.

All the siblings were teaming up against Athaliah in a funny way, making everyone laugh by making fun of her as much as they possibly could. After all, that's what siblings do, don't they?

They started telling me about how when they moved into the house, Athaliah saw them and didn't like her sisters and brothers from Jamaica. She told them to go back. "Get out of my house," she said. "Y'all are black monkeys! Leave! Go back to Jamaica!"

Athaliah was only nine years old but was very selfish and mean. I was looking at her with my eyes wide open, and, in my mind, I was asking God, "Okay, are you sure this is my wife? I'm seeing and hearing too many red flags."

Perhaps that was my cue to not go through with her. Perhaps it was God's way of telling me to run away from her.

Run, nigga! Run!

Athaliah told me to not listen to them, telling me that they were jealous of her because she was in the house first and was born in the States. Apart from that, Athaliah had younger brothers who were also born in America.

All in all, the time I spent in New York was quite fun. I had fun with all the people there, and it was the time that I kept close in my memory for quite some time.

We had come back home, and life was getting even better for us. I got myself a better job, working as a tow-truck driver at Double-X Tow Truck Company. I was making nice money, and hence, was also able to get my own apartment. I had moved out of Jazz's house, but I made sure that I thanked him for letting me live there. He was a good man, and I was lucky to have him in my life. That convinced me that I wanted to keep him around, and so we remained friends.

It was one time that my car had broken down and was very expensive to fix. I had my rent and bills to pay. But I did not have enough money for my rent due to my car getting fixed. Really, I just needed 40 dollars to make up the difference to pay my rent. So, "No worries," I thought to myself. I asked my soon-to-be wife for $40 dollars.

I had always treated her right, and I had always bought her the best of things. I had helped her pay for the furniture that she had in her apartment. I even purchased her groceries for her. I just said to myself, "I'll just ask her when she gets off of work. I'll stop by her house to check on her as well." So, I went by her house.

She opened the door, and we hugged each other like we usually did. I asked her how she was doing, and she told me that she was doing just fine. She asked me how I was doing, and I told her that I was doing just fine. She said to me, "You got your car fixed, I see."

I replied to her, "Yes, it was expensive. And it got me behind on my rent payment."

"M-hmm…" she mumbled.

I asked her, "Can I borrow 40 dollars till my payday? I'll pay you back as soon as I have my check."

Athaliah looked at me and rolled her eyes. She said, "No."

I couldn't believe it. I couldn't believe it after all the stuff I had done for her. I kept my Peace, and I said to her, "It's okay. I know that God will provide for me." With that, I left. I drove back to my apartment and just could not understand why my soon-to-be wife wouldn't let me borrow 40 dollars. Before I got to my apartment, I came across a man who had a flag in his hand that he waved in his hands, telling me to stop. So, I stopped.

He asked me, "Can you help me with my flat tire?" I was sure to help him, knowing that I was never the one to turn down a cry for help. So, I helped him fix his tire. He thanked me quite a few times and handed me two brand-new 20-dollar bills. It was 40 dollars! It was exactly what I needed to pay my rent!

As soon as he was about to leave, I shouted in happiness, "Thank you, Jesus!" I told him, "Sir, you won't believe this. I needed 40 dollars to finish paying my rent, and you just gave it to me. Thank you so much, Sir! Thank you!"

The man was happy, and perhaps for that reason, he gave me another 20-dollar bill to buy some lunch. That had made it 60 dollars, and it was more than enough. I said again, "Thank you, sir."

He said to me right before leaving, "The world needs more people like you, brother." That was something that made my day, something that made me more than happy. It was something that added some exhilaration to what had been a rather rough day.

I left and started praising God in my car. I said to myself, "God just provided for me! God is my provider! He is my ram in the bush. I can't wait to tell Athaliah what happened."

So, I called her and started telling her God gave me the money through a man. She just sighed, "Wow!"

I thanked her for not giving me the money, but I was sure to let her know that my tone was sarcastic. But a part of me actually thanked her. At the end of the day, if she had given me that money, I would have never seen this miracle; I would not have seen how God was there for me through all of it and more. I said to her, "God is real! God is Good to me! God is good to us!"

With that, I just hung the phone up in her face. I wanted her to know that God was with me even when she was not. I felt a feeling of confidence racing through my blood, each ounce of which was telling me that if I had no one, even when I had no one, I had God.

Chapter 6
Debt-Free Wedding

With God's divine will, we had determined a date for our much-awaited wedding. I could not wait; our hopes soared. Athaliah was bursting with joy, and she could barely contain her happiness; she did not want to contain it. She was happy to be marrying me, and her mood was lightened. In the meanwhile, my spirits were brightened, and hope bloomed inside me. Happiness glowed inside me, and I felt a sudden flare of joy the moment our date was set. I could barely conceal my delight, and we were flabbergasted with joy. It felt much like sunshine flooded my soul; happiness had found a way into my life yet again, and it finally felt as though things were falling back on track, as though every piece of the puzzle was finding its very rightful place.

I was still pursuing my rap career, and I had high hopes. I knew that God had things planned for me, things that would make it all the better for me. I believed in Him, and I knew that he was going to be there for me… always. Still driving a tow truck for Double-X Towing, I felt like I was making Him happy. To be perfectly honest with you, it felt liberating. It felt awesome, and I believed that I was making a positive impact on the world. I felt as though I was making a difference. I got to help people on a regular basis, and I knew that I was making them happy. I was there for them when they found themselves in need.

I was there to fix their cars for them, and if I could not do just that, I would tow them to where they needed to go. In doing so, I believed as though God had sent me to them like I was sent to them to pray for them.

I remember it was one of these times that I came across a lady who needed my help. She was driving an extravagantly expensive car. I had taken a good look at it, wondering all the ways that I could help her. I, however, could not help her, and therefore, she had to be towed to one of the shops nearby. I could not help but wonder about the two big guys on her side, almost like they were her bouncers. I asked her, "Are you alright?"

She did not think all that much before bawling out, "No! I'm exhausted from this job!" I could not help but wonder what she did for a living – the car and the bodyguards gave me the impression that it was something significant. So, I asked her, "What kind of a job do you have? Are you a movie star? A model? Or a businesswoman, perhaps?" I chuckled and then scoffed, hinting at how wrong I was. "I'm just a call girl," she replied, "I have sex with businessmen, celebrities, sportspersons, and all the wealthy men who need it!"

I instantly replied to her, "Lady, Jesus loves you!" She was caught off-guard, perhaps, or I had said something that she never really saw coming her way. A teardrop rolled down her eyes, and she came to me and embraced me in a hug. She did not let go of me, and she cried, "No one has ever told me that they love me!" Still being hugged, I was not certain of what I could do. So, I replied, "Lady, Jesus loves you... I don't."

She chuckled a bit, instantly blinking her eyes back and forth and scrubbing away her tear with that trembling palm of hers, and she told me, "My parents are pastors at a church in the city." I was happy, but I did not really know what to do with that information. So, perhaps sensing that from my face, she asked me, "Can I hang out with you?" I replied to her, "I'm working."

By then, I had gotten to know that the guys she was with were her bouncers, in fact. They asked her, "Are you coming with us or going with him?" I told her, "I can take your car to the shop." She just thought, and she decided to go with them, and I said to her, "Jesus loves you. But you should certainly start going back to your parent's church again. It's going to be very good for you." She replied, "I will do just that, thank you." She hugged me again with tears of joy streaming down her face that was now relieved. I knew that she had felt better, and I was happy that I was of help.

In the meanwhile, Athaliah was still working her insurance job. She and I heard about how Reverend Lite Benjamin had a new book coming out quite soon. We got to know that he was having a book signing at the local bookstore. We were so excited to go and support him since he was our pastor. I knew that I had to be there; I owed it to him because how he had always told me that my name was a powerful name. And so, holding happiness and excitement in our hearts, we went for the book signing.

Athaliah got her book signed, and I was right behind her. Reverend Lite Benjamin was signing my book when he started talking to me. He wrote something on the inside of the book, and he wanted me to have a look at what it was that he had written. I replied, "Okay, alright, I'll do that very soon. Thank you so very much, sir." Athaliah was looking, standing right behind me. When I walked back to her, she asked me, "What did Reverend Benjamin say to you?" I replied to her, "He told me to look at what he wrote for me in the book." When we got outside, I looked at what he had written. It said, "Your name is power, and God will manifest what your name means in all of peace and prosperity."

I was overfilled with joy and ecstasy. Athaliah was too happy as well. We had a little chat about it. I just wondered how we had gone with happiness in our hearts and came back with the same happiness, just intensified too significantly.

We were taking premarital classes; the classes were preparing us for all the things that we needed to ensure and take care of before we got married and while we were married. They were quite good, and I enjoyed attending them with her. The one and the only thing I did not like was our marriage counselor. He was a tall man, and on him was a darker shade of skin. Everything about him was handsome, everything that Athaliah wanted in a man.

A part of me was a bit insecure about her, but then, I would be reminded by another part of me that would say, "She's going to be your wife!" So, I pushed the bad and jealous thoughts away, not worrying. She was, after all, about to be my wife.

The man's name was Minister Butler, but I called him Reverend Lamb Chops. The first time he counseled us was when he unbuttoned his shirt, chopping his lips at my fiancé. So, every time we had a marriage class, I would always remember to say to her, "Here we go again with Reverend Lamb Chops!"

On one occasion, he asked us, "Are you saving yourselves for marriage? Are you holding back on having sex?" We told him that we, in all honesty, were doing just that. Somehow and for some reason, I said to him, "Athaliah is still a virgin." Just when the words came out of my mouth, I regretted them. I knew that I should not have said that to him... not then, not ever. Anyway, just as I said that to him, I thought he was going to rape my fiancé in the middle of the classroom. It was the eyes that lit up, and he really started to unbutton his shirt some more, showing off the hairs on his chest. I could not wait for these classes to be done and dusted with.

It was not long before we finally finished our classes, and that was when we had to pick three different ministers who we would like to make the two of us official. We picked Reverend Lite Benjamin as the first choice, of course. As the second, we chose the First Lady Benjamin since I believed that she was the one who was going to sign me my multimillion contract deal, the one that I deserved. For our third choice, we chose the minister who had preached the message about how Abraham had told his servant to find his son a wife – Pastor Jack Miller. I liked the way he preached when Reverend Benjamin was not preaching.

Time flew by, and we were just a few weeks away from our wedding day. Most of the things were done and prepared.

Athaliah had her magnanimous wedding dress, and I had my handsome Tuxedo. She had chosen the bridesmaids, and I had chosen the groomsmen for the wedding. Everything was set for the day of the wedding, the hall for the reception, the people who would cook the food, the cake, the people who were going to be there, the decoration, and everything else. The wedding party was going to be amazing, and I knew that it was going to be a day to remember. She and I had arranged everything, and we had worked for everything too hard. Just like that, there was only a week remaining on our wedding day. I was so excited, as though I felt a stab of hope in my heart, and satisfaction settled in my very soul.

And I knew that it was the same for her. Whenever I would look at her, I would see how a feeling of happiness would wash over her face, and her soul would take flight toward the skies above. It felt as though she was living in the heavens above; she had a smile on her face that she woke up with and went to sleep with.

Looking at her impeccable face, I knew that everything was going to be flawless. After all, God had already told me that Athaliah was going to be my wife. So, for that reason and more, I had left everything to God.

I had gotten booked for a show in Atlanta, and it was a big show with one of the very famous radio DJs in Atlanta. I felt an inkling of joy to be called to do this show. Now, my buddy, Mr. Singer, was performing that night as well. Mr. Singer was also one of the groomsmen for my wedding. He was also about to help me do a special song on my wedding day for the bride.

On the day of the show, I was welcomed at a packed place – a full house. The famous DJ was there, along with many performers and celebrities. I was so ready to get on that stage and rap; it was going to be immense and laudable; I was sure of that.

The radio DJ was a very tall dude, around 6'4. He walked up to my table, and he let me know that I would be performing first to get the crowd hyped and dancing. I said, "Cool."

The DJ had already heard about me from other people; they were sure to sing praises with me. They had put in a good word for me, and they knew that I was worthy of the honor. They had told him that I was a good rapper.

A little while passed, and Mr. Singer, Athaliah, and I were sitting together. When the DJ left my table, letting me know that I was about to perform very soon, Mr. Singer said, "Man, if I was that tall, I could do a lot of things!"

Athaliah started to smile, agreeing with the friend of mine sitting with us, "Yes, I know!" She said that to him, and she started to look at him up and down as he walked away. I knew what she was thinking, and I knew that he was exactly her type; I was not. I did not feel that good about it, but I chose to let it go. I had a show to perform, and I had to leave an impression that was going to last. I had to keep my mind at peace. She was still staring at him up and down, and it was like she just could not keep her eyes off of him. She was drooling all over the thought of him, and there was nothing that I could do about it. So, I said to myself, "Peace, be still. We are getting married in one more week. Don't worry. Just try and concentrate on the show. That is what's important right now!"

And with that, the show started.

The show started, and the DJ introduced me to the people. They welcomed me with screams that reached the clouds above me, and I was too fascinated. The music started, and I found myself on the stage. The feeling of being there with all those people was unmatched, and I knew that I was not going to leave them unsatisfied.

And so, I opened my mouth, and words started to flow right out into perfect rhythms – a collaboration that every person there had needed. I was rocking the house.

I did no more than two songs, and throughout them, the people were dancing, shouting, and feeling my performance. In the crowd, my eyes only looked for one. While singing, I tried and found the love of my life, sitting at the back. One look at her, and my adrenaline shot up beyond the skies. There was a smile on her face, one that made me sure that she wanted to keep me around for a long time. And I knew that in her lay the confidence that I had always been looking for, the confidence that was the key to all my success.

Just when I finished, the DJ got on stage and yelled out, "Peace! You rocked the house, my man! We just had a party here, and y'all know that!" The crowd could not stop screaming in happiness and excitement, and I was happy. I was proud of myself.

As I walked back to my seat, people were all around me. Athaliah had her eyes set on me. She knew that she was proud of me. As I got there, she stood up for me. She waited, and when I reached her, she gave me a kiss. It felt exuberant, one that made me sure to perform like this a lot more. She cried, "Baby, that was good! You did a great job, honey!" I smiled, "Thank you, babe. All glory is to God!"

In my heart, I said to myself, "Yeah, she knows who her husband is! She knows who the man is!" After the show was over, people were swarming up at me, asking if they could book me for their respective shows. I agreed to all of them, knowing how big of a step that would be for my rapping career. Athaliah loved it, seeing her future husband getting booked for more and more shows. She loved how the people had fallen in love with my performance. And so, in her head, she just awaited the Saturday to come, the day she would get to spend the rest of her life with me.

And before we knew it, that blessed Saturday finally came. It was our wedding day: 27th July 2002. At the time, I knew it to be the best day of my life, closely followed by the day I met the love of my life.

All of Athaliah's family was in town from New York – her sisters, her brothers, her nieces, and her nephews – and they all waited to see her get married. I was just as impatient, if not more. I was waiting just as much. I wanted to see her walk down the aisle and get married to me. I could not wait!

Her mom and dad were there. Her stepmom, however, chose not to come; she was not too comfortable with Athaliah's family being around. None of my family from California showed up, but they sent money, wishing the two of us well. I had some people I knew, and there was Athaliah's whole family attending the ceremony.

Athaliah was already at the church with her make-up artist, her bridesmaids, and her family. I was leaving the apartment for the chapel. I was driving like I was the happiest man in the whole wide world. It is a feeling of pleasantness. I felt this surge of energy within me, and everything suddenly felt much lighter. I felt as though I was gliding on a thin layer of air, never ready to come down. It was this bliss, this harmony that was experienced within. It was a feeling that I never managed to forget. After all, I was about to marry the most beautiful woman in the world.

As I screeched to a halt, I saw their cars already

in the parking lot. I met my buddy, Mr. Singer, in the dressing room. See, we had a special song planned to sing during the wedding ceremony. We had planned this song for a very long time, going over it over and over again. I was going to surprise the love of my life. I was going to rap for her while my friend, Mr. Singer, followed me with his singing. We had named the song "Athaliah, This Is Your Wedding Day." We were ready.

A bit nervous, I could hear the guests in the chapel talking. It was about that time that my best man and the pastor came in and asked me, "You ready, Mr. Peace?" I replied instantly, knowing that I was growing more and more impatient with each passing second, "Yessir. I'm more ready than I ever could be." A plot twist, though. Can you guess who the pastor was, the person who was going to marry us? No, it wasn't Reverend Lite Benjamin, First Lady Benjamin, or Pastor Jack Miller. Yes… I couldn't believe it either… it was Reverend Lamb Chops!

When I found out that devastating news, I said to myself, "I'm not going to even get upset! The music is playing, and we are walking towards the altar. The people are smiling at me, and, most important of all, I'm getting married to the woman of my dreams!"

With that thought spinning round and round in my head, I walked out carefully with my best man and Reverend Lamb Chops. I stood there at the altar, trembling at the emotions that swayed right in to overwhelm me. We were looking at Athaliah's mother being escorted down. Then came in the wedding party – the maid of honor, her sister Vicki, all the bridesmaids and groomsmen walked down the aisle and up to the alter. With that, the music changed to a slower tone for a few minutes, eventually coming to a halt. The door was shut, and the people were quiet.

I was getting a little hot, a bit too nervous, but most importantly, I was excited to be married to the woman I had fallen in love with, the woman that God had made for me. A beautiful song started playing, and the doors opened up again. The ring bearer walked toward me, up the aisle, and stood on the side. Then came the girls who were bearing flowers and bouquets in their hands. The music stopped, and the door was shut again.

Sooner, the music started playing again, and the doors opened up. With that, my heart stopped. I was looking at an angel. I want you to trust me when I say that there are no words to describe the feeling you get when you see the love of your life walking toward you to get married to you.

Her father held her hand and gently squeezed it. He told her, "Everything is going to be okay," since he knew that her biggest fear was to freeze and not move or fall over. His reassurance gave her enough confidence that she managed to lift what felt like a brick, move forward, and before she knew it, she was walking down the aisle toward me. Everybody staring could have been a glare of misfortune for her, but she could not even notice all the people who were standing and staring at her. All she noticed was her future husband, me, waiting for her at the end of the altar.

Her tunnel vision was only letting her see her husband. That one look at her, and I knew that she felt an amazing feeling to see me standing there and looking back at her. I knew that she felt like we were the only two in the entire church. I then realized how much love and emotion was in the air of the church at that moment; there was some crying, clapping, and smiling – all in all, people could not help but congratulate us.

Dressed in white, her wedding dress was one that made me fall in love with her all over again. Her face was shining like a star, one that gave light to all the other stars there were in the whole universe. Minister Butler asked her father, "Do you give your daughter for marriage?" Her dad replied with tears in his eyes and a smile on his face, "Yes, I give my daughter for marriage."

"Oh, it's on now," I whispered to myself.

I just looked at her as she stood there in front of me. The white dress was nothing but royalty in itself – a little bit of cleavage showed, and I could not wait to take her home. I knew I would be all over her. As I stood there, her hands in mine, her eyes with mine, I knew something else as well. I knew that these were my best friend's hands, the hands that would cradle my children, the hands that would always care for me, the hands that would still reach for mine when I was grey and old.

I would see Reverend Lamb Chops, looking and licking his chops at the woman who was about to be my wife. I looked at him right in his eyes, and I let him know that I was seeing him. In my mind, I said, "Okay, Minister Butler, let's do this right, or I will change your name back to Reverend Lamb Chops." I was just talking to myself in my mind.

The ceremony started. We did our vows, confessing our undying love for one another. We lit the candle as one. Minister Butler asked me the question that I had wanted to be asked. After me, he asked her.

Mr. Reece Peace, do you take Ms. Athaliah Soft to be your lawfully wedded wife?

Of course, I do!

Ms. Athaliah Soft, do you take Mr. Reece Peace to be your lawfully wedded husband?

Yes, I do!

I slid the beautiful ring on her finger that was

shivering, and she slid the ring onto my finger that was trembling just as much.

I now pronounce you two husband and wife. You may kiss the bride.

And, oh, boy, did we kiss at the altar for a long time! Her lips on mine, and my tongue with hers, I forgot that there was anyone around us. It just felt as though it was the two of us, mingling, dancing, singing, and doing all the beautiful things in a world that welcomed no one other than the two of us. I did not care about what the people had to say because, in that kiss, I felt the feeling of the first kiss you ever had. In that kiss, there were fireworks and rainbows and sunshine and unicorns and all the happiest of things. In that kiss, there were just the two of us – her and me. In that kiss, we were both happy – husband and wife.

Minister Butler had to stop us; everyone was laughing.

The music started to play, and it was the song that I wanted to do for her. Mr. Singer rushed to the stage, singing the song that he and I had prepared for the love of my life. He sang, opening the song, and Athaliah was awe-struck, wondering if the lyrics had truly read "Athaliah, This Is Your Wedding Day." She could not believe that there was a song named after her that was being sung on her wedding day. To augment and add to her incredulity and surprise, I started along with my verses of rap – real, cool, and smooth.

I had lost myself while I rapped there, on my wedding day, at the church, right after being married to the woman I had loved too dearly, the woman who I thought God had made specifically and carefully for me. As I put on the stage one of the best performances of my life, I was sure to remind myself of the club where I had previously performed at. It was a rather slow, romantic, and beautiful song, and it felt good to see that Athaliah was smiling.

All the while, I could not stop looking at her. My eyes were set on her beloved face, the one that I had adored more than anything in the whole wide world. As she looked at the crowds, I sang; I kept looking at her, reading every emotion that was racing across her mind, every feeling that she was feeling, every thought that she thought, and every happiness that made her day even better. And I could not stop thinking how beautiful my life had just gotten, out of a sudden, out of the blue. And I was happy. I was happy to have married her, and I was happy that I was about to spend the rest of my days with her. I was excited to spend the remaining nights of my life in her arms. It was what I had wanted from my life, and I was sure to thank the God above me for blessing me with the biggest of blessings. I was happy.

Just as I finished the song, she looked right back at me. With a smile on her face that I had never seen before, she looked at me and blew me a kiss. That was the kiss that knocked me out, my heart almost skipping a few beats. It was certainly the song she had loved most in her life; I saw tears in her eyes that she scrubbed off rather quickly, thinking about the expensive mascara that she had on. It was a song that made her sure that she had married the right one, a song that made her sure that I was actually and truly the one she had always been waiting for. Though not precisely her type, she was sure that I was the man for her, and she was happy.

As I ended the song, I caught a few glances with her, and it felt like time had stopped for me. It felt like the world around me had stopped moving for a while, and I looked at the satisfied crowd. I looked, and each of them looked at us right back. Some of them had tears streaming down their eyes and onto their cheeks. The others just stood, too surprised to see the absolute and perfect love first-hand, the love they thought had vanished and faded off from the face of the earth a long while ago. In the two of us, they saw the love that they wished to have. And they just applauded and admired, celebrating and adoring the two of us – the perfect couple.

Minister Butler then said, "Everyone... I introduce to you... Mr. Reece Peace and Mrs. Athaliah Peace... Mr. and Mrs. Peace!"

The music started to play, and we started walking out of the chapel toward the schmancy Limousine parked right outside. I opened the door for her, and my wife got in first. I got in next, wanting to sit with her, my wife.

But Vicki, her sister, just raced and jumped in front of me, trying to sit in my seat, which was right next to my wife's. I said to her, "Vicki, that's my seat. Get up."

Vicki got up and moved to the wedding party seats in the Limousine. She was looking at me with mean looks, rolling her eyes at me while she moved to the wedding party seat. The look on her face was one that made me realize that she could actually kill me, one that made me realize she did not approve of us. Other than that, the wedding reception was faultless; the food was delicious, and everyone ate to the maximum capacity that their stomachs allowed them to. The music was wholesome, and everyone danced to the maximum capacity that their legs allowed them to. We all had a great time.

During the reception, Vicki pulled Athaliah to the side. Vicki asked her, "Where is your husband's family? I'd like to meet them."

Athaliah said to her, "His family didn't come, but they sent their love, wishes, and money." She added, "But that doesn't matter. We are his new family!"

Vicki looked at Athaliah with an uncanny look, one that made my wife think some wicked thoughts. "But what about his father and mother?" asked a rather curious Vicki.

"His mother couldn't make it, but I talked with her yesterday over the phone. She was congratulating us!" Athaliah explained to her, adding, "…and his father passed away when he was 12."

Vicki asked her sister, "What about his sisters or brothers?"

Athaliah told her, "He has one sister that couldn't come. He had an older brother, but he passed away before his dad passed away, when Peace was 12 years old."

Vicki said, taunting her, "Okay… his father and brother are dead…."

"Yes," said Athaliah.

"What about uncles, aunties, or cousins?" asked Vicki, adding, "Are they dead as well?" Athaliah just nodded her head sideways, catching her sister's bad tone.

Vicki continued, "That's a cursed family that you've just gotten yourself into. There's still time; it's not too late. You need to file a divorce now!"

Athaliah said to Vicki, "No, we have been redeemed from the curse of the law. Peace is alright. He is blessed."

Vicki asked, ignoring the fact that Athaliah mentioned me being blessed. "How did they die?"

My wife said, explaining, "Well, his older brother had Epilepsy in the bathtub, and he drowned. Peace was at the park, playing baseball. That was when his sister came and picked him up from the park. She said to him, "Our brother is dead." He left the park crying. After no more than six months, his father passed away as well, and it was due to cancer in the liver or something. Peace told me how he was pitching a baseball game at that time, and they were winning. He had to get the last strike-out. Just then, his sister came to the park and told the coach that her brother had to leave the game, telling him that their father had just died. The coach stopped the game, went to the pitcher mold, and told Peace that he needed to leave because of his father's sudden death. Peace didn't leave the game. He stayed, pitched the game, and they won. While he was pitching, he had tears rolling down his eyes. He was 12 years old, but he was strong enough to finish the game. He has always been a strong man in the Lord!"

She looked at Vicki, who still had a look of disapproval on her face. Noticing that, trying to convince her some way or the other, she added, "And now that we are married, God is about to bless us with this major record deal from First Lady Benjamin."

Vicki said, still judgmental and condemning, "Okay, sister. I'm praying that you have the right husband."

Athaliah replied, "Yes, I do." Vicki was talking to Athaliah with an evil grin on her face, one that hinted at the felony she had held in her heart, the prejudice, the chauvinism.

"Well, sister," said Athaliah, "You should have married Minister Butler. You know, he's tall, dark, and handsome. More importantly, he may have all his family together."

Athaliah looked over at her sister's face, smiled, and replied, "I trust God. Peace is my husband. He's my man of God. God is blessing us with this major record deal."

Vicki replied, "Okay, sister. I'm praying that you have the right husband."

Athaliah said, "Yes, I know that."

People were hugging us and putting money in our hands before they left. They were all happy for the two of us, and we were happier. Athaliah and I had to leave and rest up for our early morning flight. The flight was booked for the next day, and we were going to Florida to take a cruise for our honeymoon.

We made it to our apartments with all the gifts. We were putting them up so we could start packing our bags. But just then, we decided to open up cards and read our guest's cards. Every card we opened had money in it. We couldn't believe it when we saw money in each card that we received from the guests at our wedding. By the end of counting and gathering stacks, we had much more than the amount of money we paid for the wedding in the first place.

We both got up and praised the Lord, saying, "Thank you, Lord. We just had a Debt-Free Wedding! We got all the money back, the amount that we spent on the wedding."

Athaliah and I decided to lay down to go to sleep. It was our wedding night, and we were both very tired. As she lay beside me in that comfy bed, I could not hold myself back. I moved my face closer to hers, and I could see her lips wanting to feel the sensation of meeting with mine. I wanted to kiss her. And so, I slid my hand under her ear and to her neck, pulling her closer. My lips met hers, and my tongue fused with hers. I was kissing her, and she was kissing me right back.

Just then, she stopped. She looked into my eyes as deeply as she could. "Peace," she said, "Are we going to make love?" I thought about it. There was nothing more that I wanted to do at that moment, nothing that I would much rather do. I wanted to do that with her, and

I had desired that for the longest.

"No," I replied. "Let's wait until we are on the ship. Let's rock the boat!"

She giggled, and we were both laughing till our stomachs turned. With that, we went to sleep with her in my arms. We went to sleep, and I felt the peace that I had never felt before in my life. It was her presence that made my heart pound harder and harder with each passing second. It was her presence that made everything in my life better, more exhilarating, and much more beautiful. It was her that made it all worth it, and I went to sleep that night with a smile on my face, one that I never had before.

The following morning, we headed to the airport. We got on the plane in coach. That was when a guy came to our seats and asked us if we wanted to move to first-class. The gentleman had wanted to sit with the rest of his family in coach. We replied, "Yes." And so, just like that, we moved to the first- class. We jumped into the front seats. We said to one another, "Look at God favoring our honeymoon already!"

We made it to Florida. We took a bus to the cruise ship. It was so big and beautiful. We got on and gave them our tickets. We were so very happy, holding hands, walking around the ship. They had lunch for us. Later that evening, it was a honeymoon marriage dance for all the couples who had just got married. It was perfect.

All of us honeymooners were slow dancing. There was a couple dancing next to us. The man was a very tall guy with a very short woman; I believe she was his newly-wedded wife. But while I was slow dancing with Athaliah, she kept turning her head back, looking at this woman's husband. I asked Athaliah, "Why do you keep looking at them?"

Athaliah replied, "I was trying to see if he is a famous basketball player."

I replied, "I don't believe so. I don't think there is a famous basketball player on this ship with us."

In my head, I asked the Lord, "Are you very sure I have the right wife?"

Party was over, and we headed to our cabin on

the ship. We showered, and Athaliah put on this red lingerie. In her, she looked feisty, and I knew that if she looked like that for the rest of her life, I would always let her walk all over me. "Holy!" I whispered to myself. In that red lingerie, she looked like the woman I would never leave, one I would never be able to keep my hands off. I had just put on some red-hearted boxers. All I can say is that Athaliah was no longer a virgin when that night passed on.

We had much fun on our honeymoon for four days and four nights. I even won three day and three-night hotel getaway in Orlando, Florida, on the cruise ship contest. So, once our cruise was over, we went to Orlando, Florida, for three days and nights.

We just had so much more fun, making memories that would linger on for the rest of my life. The sex was always brilliant, and I would blow her mind each time. Those were the memories that I will never let go of. And with that, I knew.

I knew that God had given me the desires of my heart – my beautiful wife, Athaliah.

Chapter 7
Hell on Earth

The time that I spent with her seemed much like it flew right by us. It felt like the months that came right after our marriage were but memories, one that only left behind beautiful traces. And so, I realized how true it was when people say, "Time flies when you are truly happy."

I was that. I was truly happy.

The year 2003 arrived quite shortly, and we waited to see what it was about to bring along with itself. The newly- married couple, the one too deeply and madly in love, could not wait for the times to get better, for the happiness to ever end, for life to be more and more beautiful than it already was. But that was not really the thing that happened. Those happy circumstances were not really what stayed. Perhaps it was just the point where the happiness was going to end. Perhaps it was just the point where the chaos crept in and eventually prevailed. Perhaps that was the point that brought the demise of all happiness. I did not know. I waited to find out, hoping that it was all going to be good for me.

Married for around 9 months, we were both working our jobs and going to church, believing that the First Lady Benjamin would be signing a record deal with me really soon. And there was a reason I thought that. See, now that I was married to the right wife, the perfect woman, I thought that I should be receiving a call from her anytime soon. I was working according to the will of God. See, God had spoken to me, and He had told me that Athaliah was my wife, that she was the love of my life, the woman who was for me.

Each time that Athaliah and I would go to the church and the First Lady Benjamin would teach, Athaliah, my lovely wife, would always say, "There's your manager!" her eyes would shine with excitement for our future together, or so I thought. And so, I would just agree to what she had said, knowing that it was something that I was looking forward to just as much as she was, if not more.

It was one fine day that First Lady Benjamin had an event with the children at a Christian Book Store. I had gone there to support her and check it out since it was for the youth. I saw her working with the children, and it felt almost too wholesome. It felt as though the children were truly happy, and it felt no less than a sight for sore eyes. She also saw me, passing me a smile that made my heart flutter. Since artists had started signing with her on deals, I thought I should go on and ask her about the time that my record signing would come around. I knew that now that I was married to the right woman and had made God happy, I was in the right state and position to ask her about my signing. Deep down inside, I could feel. I could feel that my day was coming rather shortly. I knew that the much-awaited and too-desired day was just around the corner, that she would sign me soon enough. And so, I just decided to keep my cool and watch the event in peace without troubling her.

Just when that event was over, I decided to leave, not asking her about the deal. Why had I done that, you may ask. Well, I entrusted my fate with God. I knew that I was doing right by Him, and I knew that He would only ever give me what was good for me. I knew that if I did not get something or the other, it would be for my own betterment. I knew that He could see whatever it was that had happened before, and I knew that He could see what it was that would happen long after. Therefore, I just put my faith in Him, and I knew that the deal was coming to me very soon.

As I was leaving the parking lot of the Christian Book Store, I saw something out of the usual in my rear-view mirror.

I saw the First Lady Benjamin. She was just standing behind my car, writing down my license plate number. In my mind, I asked myself, not knowing the answer, "What's up with that? Why is she doing that?" I found out years later what that was all about.

That Monday, First Lady Benjamin researched me through my license plate number. She wanted to know more about me – perhaps all there was about me – before she signed me. By her being known worldwide, she knew people from high places who had in their hands the power to pull up my records. First Lady Benjamin came across some stuff on my record that she did not grow much to it. There was everything about me; arrest records, marriages, my given name, and everything else. What she did not know was that it was the life that I had left behind a long time ago. After all, I had traveled all the way to here to have a clean slate, did I not? She did not know that; after all, how could she?

She went back and told her husband, Reverend Lite Benjamin, all about me. "That guy, Brother Peace, you remember him?" she asked.

The Reverend replied, "How could I not?" His wife scoffed, "He is not a peaceful guy!"

"Why do you say that?" Reverend Lite Benjamin asked.

"Well, his real name is Reece Barnes. He has been in jail before. He has been married and divorced twice before. This is his third marriage. His credit is bad, and there happens to be no kind of education. He is a fake, and I do not want to sign him, that little bad boy!

He is probably related to Nicky Barnes, that big drug lord, and gangster. He needs to leave the church. I don't want to see him around."

Reverend Benjamin said, "What!? We almost invested in this dude a lot of money! I'm in agreement with you, honey. You can just use that money and go buy yourself a million- dollar car."

I never knew she was never going to sign me. I came to find this stuff out a few years later. So, amidst all this, I remained in the dark. I knew nothing about any of this, and therefore, I had no chance to redeem myself in front of them. I had no chance to tell them that I was actually a good guy, that I was right by God, and that all the bad things were those that I had left behind in my past. That is what it was… the past. Barnes was the name that I left behind with my past. God had changed my name to Peace for the future.

So, not knowing what had happened, I kept hoping to get a call from her a get to hear the golden and much-awaited words from her mouth. Weeks had passed by, and there was no call for a record deal from Point

Records. There was not a single call from them or anyone, not even one to tell me that they were not considering me anymore.

Fortunately enough, perhaps, I did not only have my music in Point Records' Studio. I was sending my music to many other record labels. In my heart, I was just holding on to God's word; He had told me that I was getting that deal in the December of 1999. He had told me that it was then when I would sign that multimillion-dollar contract deal, and it had been three years since that time had passed. I do remember that and heard it so clearly from God.

Athaliah and I were still together, going to prayer before church and during the church service. We did that quite routinely, each Wednesday, Friday, and Sunday that arrived, each Wednesday, Friday, and Sunday that we found ourselves to be alive. Everyone was still getting their record deals, but I was not catching my break; I was growing impatient. Regardless of the wait, the impatience, the desire, and the hope that was getting me nearly nowhere, I still had my faith in God, and I kept entrusting Him with everything that was going on in my head and my heart. I knew that He was going to come through for me, and that was more than enough for me. I kept remembering about the white ladies also, the ones who had once prophesized over me in that restaurant all that while ago. I remember Reverend Lite Benjamin when he spoke over my life, talking about my name.

Through all of it, I had no clue that First Lady Benjamin had decided to never sign me because of my history. I had no idea that Reverend Benjamin agreed with her. I respected the couple, and I knew that they would not disappoint me. Oh, little did I know that it was never going to happen, that miraculous deal, the very one that I had so desperately deserved.

It was one morning that Athaliah and I both left for our own work. But this time, when we got to the red light, Athaliah did not want to wait. So, she made a right turn, busting a U-turn, and got back on the highway. Too curious to go my own way, I did the very same. I took the U-turn, following her closely after in my car. After I did that, the police pulled me over. Athaliah was, by that time, already too far to see me getting pulled over by the police. The officer did not get out of his car yet; he was still checking my plates.

A few moments passed, and some more police cars showed up, to my surprise. I did not get out of my car; I just stayed in the driver's seat, trying to keep my calm, wondering what was happening, knowing that there was nothing wrong that I had done in a long, long time. Just then, the police car bull-horned me; they said over the speaker, "Get out of the car with your hands up!"

Each of the officers had their guns drawn, ready to shoot right at me if I made any sudden move whatsoever. Quite naturally and too curiously, I dared to ask, "What the hell I do?!"

They said yet again, "Get out of the car! Keep your hands up where we can see 'em!"

"Alright, alright! I heard you! I'm getting out! Alright!" I replied, frustrated. I got out of the car with my hands up. They pulled handcuffs and put them on me and said, "You are under arrest for this stolen car. You have the right to ask for an attorney. Anything you say can and will be used against you in the court of law."

"This is my car!" I replied.

"No, this car was stolen back in California," one of the officers rebutted.

"No," I replied instantly. "You policemen are tripping."

They did not have anything more to say. So, they put me in the police car and took me to jail. I was unsure of what was happening, asking myself questions that I did not know the answers to, the very questions that I had been asking them. "What's going on?"

I found out it was my second ex-wife who put a warrant out for my arrest. She said, "He stole my car." Even though the car was in my name, she had said that. I was trying to talk to an officer to look at the paperwork in my car, but they had already towed it to a repossessed lot.

When I got to the detention center, the police officer said to me, "You will see a judge on Monday." It was Friday, and I had to wait two more days in order to prove my innocence of a crime that I had nothing to do with whatsoever, a crime that was never even committed.

I finally got ahold of Athaliah. I told her where I was at and told her my second ex-wife put a warrant on my arrest for a stolen car. Athaliah came up to the jail to visit me that night. I told her that I was going to see a judge on Monday. "Go home and get some rest," I said to her, knowing that she was quite worried for me. Her face was flushed, and she was willing and ready to help in any way that she humanly could. I did not want her to worry. After all, I had never committed that crime. So, I told her, "Go home. I'm alright. I'm okay. I want you to go home and get some rest. I'll be back home on Monday." With that, she wished me luck and went away.

All that night, I was in the holding cell with all the criminals who had committed crimes of all sorts, I was sure. It felt uncomfortable being there with them; it was more of a very rough and tough situation going on around there.

They were looking me up and down as though I

was nothing but fresh meat. I looked at them, locking my eyes in theirs, to let them know, "Nigga, you've got the wrong nigga!" there were four guys who were in there, and they had been brought in for robbing a young girl. One of the guys was the ringleader of the guys who actually took the girl's purse.

The other three guys were just scared young boys. They spent most of their time there crying. They were scared to be in there. They had nothing to do with the robbery, yet they had been brought in. The boys were barely seventeen or eighteen- year-olds. The ringleader said to them, shaking them up, "If I go down, we all go down!" They remained quiet, too afraid and too shaken to say anything. They just wondered what it would be like, having had the dismaying experience of going to actual jail at such a young age.

I just listened to them telling the story of how they were going to tell their story to get out of it. I believed that they did not have anything to do with it. They did not know that he stole the girl's purse because he was trying to talk with her and ask her out on a date.

But he decided to steal her purse instead and run off with it.

Despite all of that, I was not scared. I was not worried, no. I was ready for anything. After all, I was as innocent as a shoelace.

As I sat there, closely listening to their story, a wave of sudden anger and madness rushed into me. It was some kind of madness that had complete and absolute control over me for a time long enough for me to jump to the boys' help. I said to the ringleader, "No, you can't do that. You can't make them go down with you because of what you did."

The youngest one looked at me and stopped crying. Sooner than I had expected, he started to smile, and it felt good to me, as though I had done something quite good. I said to the ringleader, "You are going to tell the judge it was all you and that you are going to apologize for your ruthless and shameful act. You are going to do that, and you are going to say that you will never ever do it again."

He put his head down, too ashamed, I presume.

"Yes, you're right, sir," said the ringleader. As soon as that happened, I prayed with them in the holding cell for them to have favor with the judge. I believed that they were right in their hearts and that they could be saved and born again.

Monday came very slowly, and the judge heard my case. He found out that it was my ex-wife who gave a false report. I got out and ran to the first sandwich shop I saw. Can you guess what I did? Yes! I got myself the biggest sandwich of all time! I didn't eat anything in that holding cell; the food was disgustingly nasty. I could never ever eat that stuff.

Athaliah came to pick me up, and she was too happy and relieved to see that I was out and alright. She sighed and said to me, "Don't you leave me like that ever again, Peace!"

A week passed after that. Out of the usual and sudden, there was a knock on our door at 2 in the morning. Athaliah and I woke up and looked at one another, "Who could this be?!"

We both went to the door and asked, "Who's

there?"

"Police," we heard them say from the other side of the door. "Is Mr. Reece Peace in this apartment?"

I just replied, trying rather hard to keep my calm, "Show us your badge through the peephole."

Upon seeing their badges, I pulled the door open. Athaliah stood beside me through it, standing up for me when she thought it was the best of times.

"We have an arrest warrant for you, Mr. Reece Peace, for a stolen car," they told me.

"This has to be a joke," I said to myself, trying not to say it out loud. "Y'all have to be kidding me!"

"Why?" I asked out loud in a petty rebuttal. "I just got out of jail last week for that, and I don't even have the car! I did not commit the crime, and I was proven innocent the last time."

They replied, "You need to come with us, sir. We are bounty hunters for the law, and we have a warrant for your arrest."

Athaliah jumped up to my defense, "He met with a judge about that already. His crazy ex-wife put a false arrest warrant on him and said he stole her car, but the car was his."

They were not to be shaken, and there was nothing I could do other than go into the station with them until I met with a judge. After all, I could not have run. I never committed that crime, and I was being bullied for it. So, I put my trust in my God, who watched over me, knowing that He was going to make things easier for me.

So, with my trust wholly in the God who sat in the heavens above me, I walked to the car, and we drove to the jail. I got put in the holding cell right back. It felt as though I was in a loop.

When I got to the cell, I found out that this time around, they would much rather have me in that orange jumpsuit that reeked of the word criminal. It felt as though I was the criminal, even though I was no one but a man of God.

While I waited to meet with the judge in a couple

of days that were to come, I met a person, a person who was being held in the holding cell, along with myself. He was a tall guy who was very distressed. While he paced around the cell in worry, I could see tears rolling down his face in a stream that made me believe that he was, just like me, there for a crime he did not commit. Or perhaps it was just the side of me that wanted to see the good in people around me. Well, he cried, and he kept crying about himself being in jail. "They have the wrong guy," he kept repeating, as though a track on loop with just those five words.

Throughout his time there, he kept on reciting Bible scriptures. Even then, he seemed sad, almost as though he was on the verge of breaking down. Was the Bible not helping him? Was the fact that God was there for him not enough for him? I did not know. Perhaps we were all sad in our orange jail jumpsuits. Well, he just kept walking with his crying and Bible recitation. I was feeling sad for him, and I wanted the brother to be at peace even though we were not surrounded by the best of circumstances, yet there came the point that I was just tired of him. He kept crying, and I was just trying to get some sleep.

I knew something was extremely strange about the tall guy. Knowing all the Bible scriptures, he still kept crying and being sad. What were the most reasonable things to do? With him knowing every single Bible scripture, I thought that he should have been stronger in that holding cell. Having the gift of being introduced to the Bible and memorizing it would make the worst of us happy; it would make us believe in God's greatness even in the worst of times.

"Are you born again?" I asked him. "Have you accepted Lord Jesus Christ as your personal savior?"

"No," he replied. "I never confessed it. I know it to be true, but I never really said it out loud, I guess."

"Confess Jesus Christ as your personal savior," I advised him. "Do that, and you will be saved. You will not be worried or sad anymore." I gave him the repentance prayer, and he confessed to Jesus Christ as his savior with tears rolling down his eyes.

"I feel good now," he said almost instantaneously. It was soon followed by him running around the cell. He rejoiced in a way that made me happy, along with all the people around us. He was shouting, calling out Jesus's name in a manner of love and passion. It was then that I got to know that I really was not going to get any sleep that night, none whatsoever. But I dared not say anything, noticing how the spirit of the Lord came in him. "Everyone..." he cried out, "let's dance."

I said to myself, "Dude, please stop!" But it was soon followed by another thought. I finally really saw the spirit jump in a man. He was sad to the point that he was crying. He was distressed, and he could not stop crying. I had seen how worried he was before. And now, he was happy. He was jolly. He was dancing and having a good time, placing all of his trust and faith in Jesus Christ. I saw it, and I was happy as well. I really did want to get some sleep, but I was happy, too; it was bittersweet. How I saw it was that he was as though an expensive sports car without an engine to sync and match with the fancy exterior. So, by him confessing to Jesus' power and authority over him, I had helped put the engine in him, making him as good on the inside as he was on the outside. So, I just looked at him running around with joy that was filled to the brim in his jail clothes in the jail cell.

The next morning, I was scheduled to meet with the judge. They brought me the courthouse in the same orange jumpsuit, cuffs around my wrists and ankles as though I was a monster who was eager to break out and eat them all alive. They had treated me like a criminal, even when I was not one.

The judge asked me, "What are you doing back here again?"

"You tell me," I replied with a rebuttal. I was angry. "You're the judge, your honor, aren't you?"

"Watch your mouth, young man!" the judge scolded me.

I replied, "The police came to my house at 2 in the morning and arrested me for the same charge that I was proven innocent of the last time I was here."

The judge asked, "Is this about the false report from your ex-wife?"

"Yes," I replied.

The next thing I heard him say was to the sheriff. "Let's put a warrant on the ex-wife's arrest for a false report."

The judge then asked me, "What did you do to her? Why's she after you this badly?"

"Nothing!" I replied instantly. "I did nothing. I just divorced her because she had a demon in her. Also, she purchased two guns and tried to kill me! I never did a thing."

"I'm glad you got away while you still could," the judge laughed.

"Your honor," I replied, laughing back, "You think that's too much? That's not anything! My first wife tried to have me killed too!"

The judge laughed harder than he had in a long

time, holding on to his stomach. He asked me, "What did you do to her?"

"Nothing," I replied to his rather innocent question. "Even then, I never did anything bad! I was a good husband to her too, and I never disrespected her."

"Are you married now?" he asked me, much curious.

"Yes," I replied with eyes that shone brighter than the stars themselves.

"You need to watch out for this one," replied the judge. "She might try to kill you as well!" He had made a joke, and I was sure to catch up on the pattern of my misfortune when it came to marriages. I was not offended, though, so I tried to follow behind on the judge's joke.

"I hope you have your running shoes on," added the judge. While he was still laughing, cracking more and more jokes with the passage of time, I had stopped laughing; it was not because he was not funny; he was. It was just that I was too tired and hungry, and I could not eat that jail food. Even a little movement would lead to a stomachache that could make me burst out into tears and scream. So, before I knew it, they released me and let me go home respectfully, even though they treated me no more than a low-life criminal back when I was in the holding cell.

After that and for quite some time to come, we only had one car. So, Athaliah used to drop me off at work, and she would go to hers. Later in the day, when she would get off, she would pick me up, and we would go home together. Time passed, and we were two weeks away from our one-year anniversary. Just then, something happened, something that altered the course of events. Two more weeks from our first- year anniversary.

It was one morning, a rather casual and usual day, and I went to work as I usually did. As soon as I walked in, my supervisor handed me a letter. A few questions emerged in the back of my mind, and I was sure to open them up right before I became too curious. It was a letter from child support.

I opened it, and it said that they would be taking 75% of the money that I had earned from arrears and payments owed to Doris Scott. The letter also told me that I apparently owed $45,000 of back child support and current child support. This was my little girl's mother, the one I had a child with back when I was 20 years of age. I called Doris right away, telling her that I had gotten a letter from child support, elaborating everything that it had said. Perhaps I wanted to hear from her that it was just ridiculous and that I should just ignore it. But for a little while there, I had almost forgotten how big of a snake that woman was.

When I told her that child support sent me a letter to my workplace, she replied, "You're hell right they did! I want me some money! I want all your money! I want your life to be destroyed!"

"Why are you doing this?" I asked. "I thought we had an understanding about our daughter. You know I love her more than anything in the world. And you know that I have wanted to be with her since day one. How can you do this, ask for back child support money plus current child support? I thought you were rich with a wealthy husband! You said all I need to do is has a relationship with my daughter and give the best I can since I started a new life in Atlanta. You know that I'm trying to get a record deal."

"Yes," she replied. "Once you get that record deal, I'm talking all that money as well. I want you to suffer for leaving your daughter."

I replied to her, "God wanted me to leave California."

"Boy, stop lying!" Doris cried. "God doesn't just talk to you like that! You are a sinner, and the devil is your best friend."

I asked her, "How can I live with 75% of my paycheck going to you?"

"You better get three more jobs or die working your ass off," said Doris, being the indifferent person that she had always been. "Either way, you're paying me back my money."

I was so hurt. I was furious. I was broken. Just as

I hung up on that wicked call, my heart raced. It pounded against my chest, hurting, aching, warning me that it would burst right out of my chest, breaking my ribcage apart as though nothing but caramel strands. And so, I wondered how I was going to live my life. I wondered what the next years of my life were going to be like.

So, I called the Child Support Division. I told them who I was and the case number. I asked them, "How could she do this and get paid when I have a relationship with my daughter?"

They replied to my concerns, "It's the law, and we are coming after every deadbeat father and man who doesn't pay us."

"So, I have to pay you?" I replied, "What about the child and the mother?" See, the caseworker had told on herself when she had said that. "It's about the money in the child support system's pocket and not the child or the child's family, is it? How can you get back child support if I was with my child?"

The caseworker replied, "Just pay what you own," hanging up the phone without any further discussion.

This world is evil, and there was nothing that I could think of other than that very thought. One thought led to another, and one feeling led to another. Before I knew it, I was having suicidal thoughts in my mind, all thanks to that very conversation. I wondered how people so very evil manage to sleep at night, knowing that they are destroying life's afterlife. So, I did what I did best. I did what I knew just how to do. I said to myself, assuring myself, "Peace, be still. Remember one thing. Remember what God has told you about your future. Be calm, and let God make it better for you. Trust Him, and it's all going to turn out just fine."

I saw my beloved Athaliah that night, and I told her about the child support. I told her everything that was troubling me, each thought that I was thinking, each saddening feeling that was giving me a hard time. She was very upset, and she said to me, "The devil is attacking you because you are about to get this big record deal and help people around the world through your music."

I got my next paycheck, and it was much smaller than what I was getting before. It was smaller than that which I had desperately and wholly deserved. I could not afford a happy meal, and it made me think about each decision that I had made in my life, each decision that led me to that point in my life, wondering how things could have been different if I had done something or the other a tad bit differently. I cried, tears dripping down from my shivering chin, "God! God, help me!"

Athaliah had to help pay most of the bills, and that did not make me feel any better. Sooner came out the first anniversary, and there was sadly nothing much that we could do because of the lack of funds. We just drove to the mountains and rented a cabin to celebrate the auspicious and respectful occasion. I was very upset, and I could not really celebrate. Though I was happy that I was with the woman of my dreams, I was still sad that I was not at the best stage of my life.

During the whole celebration and the time that I spent there with her in that cabin in the mountains, I was still thinking about how I was going to pull everything together, how I was going to get my life back on track. I was thinking about how I was going to support my wife and myself, how I could have a family and be the backbone that I was supposed to be, the backbone that I wanted to be.

A part of me wanted to lose hope in that record deal, the one that I thought was my destiny. Yet, then again, there was the other part of me that prevailed. I could still remember how God had spoken over me, telling me that my record deal was coming and that it was coming very soon. I reminisced the loving and warm memory of the three white ladies, or maybe they could have been three angels, speaking over me. I could see Reverend Lite Benjamin telling me that I was going to see great and big things in my life. Just then, I said to myself, "It's going to be alright. I will win this battle. I am going to win this battle." Athaliah had told me the same thing, "You going to be alright. You're going to be signing a big record deal with First Lady Benjamin very soon." In her words, I had found comfort, and I was sure to believe her words. She had believed in me even in the worst of times, and I was happy to have her in my life. I was happy to be her husband.

Athaliah and I were clueless about the fact that First Lady Benjamin was not going to sign me. So, in the mountains, I decided to not waste the beautiful time and an even more beautiful occasion thinking about the things that were going to worry me. Instead, I tried to think about the love that she and I had shared. I was happy. I just wanted to have some fun, and I was ready to do that. So, though the trip, we did some fishing and grilling, and we went to go Roaring Rapids on big tubes on a river in the mountains. I was still trying to hold it together. I was very weak, and there was barely any joy in my spirit, but I wanted to be happy for Athaliah. While Athaliah and I were playing in the river with the tube, a guy came up to us.

"Do you need any help?" he asked me, quite closer to me in the water. I have never seen a man so beautiful. The brown of his hair fell in waves, and the white of his skin was one to adore. He was about my size, but he had muscles and a body that was more of an epitome and nothing less. It was quite like you could wash dishes on his stomach. He was handsome – to put it simply – just beautiful. He was prettier than my wife, despite the fact that he was a man. He had a funny southern talk, and there seemed to be no cons to him.

He kept asking me, "Do you need help?" and I kept replying with a no each time, almost losing my patience and calm.

"I'm going to help you," the pretty man replied.

"Help me on what?" I asked him yet again. Just then, I noticed that the waters in the river were really tossing and turning really hard. All of a sudden, Athaliah flipped over, and her tube got away from her. All I could see was how her feet were over the water. She was upside down in the river water.

Finally, she came up above the water, asking, "What the hell happened?" I could not stop laughing, and so the laughter kept growing as though a viral infection.

"You went down headfirst in the river," I answered her question.

Athaliah said, "Yes," and the waters started moving harder. At that point in time, I could see fish swimming by my head, barely troubling me at all. I said to her, "I believe you were down there with the fish. It looks like you just got baptized by John, The Baptist," I was laughing as hard as I possibly could, making all sorts of jokes.

Her hair was all wet, dripping down all over her. She was still trying to figure out how she had twisted upside down in the water. It seemed like an anomaly, an alienated thing to happen out of a sudden. I was still laughing, and there was no way that I could stop. That laugh was stretched out for quite a long period of time. Each time I would think about it, I would burst out into laughter, and it would be rather hard to make me stop. Athaliah did not think it was funny, but I did. I just could not help myself from laughing at her. I guess what happened to her made my day, perhaps even the week.

In the meanwhile, I tried to think about that guy who wanted to help me. Where did he go after saying that he wanted to help me? Was that an angel who made the water roar like that? Perhaps he did that just so that Athaliah could twist upside down in the water to make me laugh for days and days straight. I would never know; it's a mystery, an enigma that needs not to be figured out. The Bible does say, "beware who you entertain. You may be entertaining angels unaware."

At least, it had me not think of all my issues. It was a great distraction for as long as it lasted, and perhaps there is nothing that would bring such colors to my life. But sooner before I knew it, I was questioning myself over all the hell that I had been through in my first year of marriage.

Am I in the right state? Am I at the right church? Or am I with the right wife? But I heard God… or did I hear the devil?

I believe it was God. But for this first year of marriage, it said, "Hell on Earth."

Chapter 8

My Beautiful Queens

The years to come were full of surprises, yet not in the way that I had expected them to be. I found myself in many circumstances and more situations that were really only there to break me down to pieces, shattering the world around me. Yet, was it enough to make my faith in the Lord go away? Not a chance!

Through all of it and more, there were two things that were bringing me to peace. There were only two things in the world that were ever worth holding on to. First of all, through all of it and more, I had trusted my God. Through every bad thing that came my way to show me that life was but a torturous series of events, I had my faith in the God above me. I trusted Him with every single thing that happened, every single thing that was there to make me think otherwise. Second, I knew that I had on my side the love of a good and pious woman.

Despite what the mind would wander off to at times, I knew it in my heart that God had chosen this woman for me, and that was more than enough for me. So, though all the bad things happening ever since our marriage, I had Athaliah by my side. And I was happy.

So, the two of us would go to church with one another. For the two years after, we were still praying, making our daily confessions, still trusting God that He would get me my multimillion-dollar contract. Child Support Services were still only leaving me behind with no more than one-fourth of my paycheck, and that was causing more and more problems with my financial status. The bank was dry as the Sahara Desert, and there was nothing much that I could really do about it. My wife and I had a small car that we were driving to get by, and we could not get a bank account together. When we did have a bank account, Child Support Services swooped right in, leaving us practically bankrupt; most of the money from the savings was Athaliah's. I felt sorry that she had to go through all of that with me, and I felt rather bad that she was struggling along with me even after she had done nothing wrong, even after I had done nothing wrong.

Still, despite all of that, our trust was with the one who had made us, the one who had loved us through all of that. Our trust was with our God, and that fact was more than enough to let us sleep somewhat peacefully when the night would fall.

But then again, I was the man of the house. I was the one who had the responsibility of providing for the house. And all I could do was try and hold on. It was quite sooner than I started washing windows again, the profession that I once thought I would never really get back to. I was doing that just to make a few extra bucks. I was mowing lawns and cutting yards, pressure washing houses. I was trying to do more shows and find any producers from a major label to sign me. I was just hoping that something good would finally happen. I was just hoping that something good would finally come my way. Yet, perhaps to my bad fortune or to life's eventual continuum, there were nothing but closed doors to be seen. Each place I would go to, having hope in my heart and dreams on my mind, there would be nothing but a bunch of doors banging shut right in front of my face.

Still, each time that life would show me what it had in store for me – something bad – I would look up to the skies and cry into a question and then a few more.

God, some kind of help? Any kind of help?

Am I not in your will? Am I not in the right state?

Am I not going to the right church? Do I not have the right wife?

I did all you wanted me to, so why is all this happening to me?

2004 came around shortly after, and with it, some good news, good enough to make us sigh for a short moment. Despite the financial downfall from my side, we were able to buy a house, our first one as a couple. It was a place that I looked forward to calling home, one that would embrace me in all the good times and the bad. Even with all the bad luck that was going on, we had gotten there. Yet, I really could not put it in my name because of Child Support Services, and my credit was not too handsome. But God had blessed us with our first home, and we were excited about it, perhaps a little too much.

Sooner came Thanksgiving, and along with it, the excitement of my wife finally meeting my family. It was time for Athaliah to meet my family in California. Before that, she had only ever talked to them over the phone, never in person. It was time to change that. And so, to make it happen finally, we flew out to California. She finally met my family, and even though she could not wait to meet them, I could not see that she was too excited about it. Still, she was nice to them, my mother, my sister, and my nieces and nephews.

My sister could not believe that I had married such a nice woman, and so she jokingly asked me, "Where did you find her? She is quite nice, too nice for you."

And I told her where I had met her. I had taken pride in it, and I said to her with my chin held high, "I meant her in my church."

My sister replied, "Well, she's very pretty. She's not like the normal street gangster-like women that you used to date or were married to!"

That was enough to make us laugh, though it was something that had made me sad, the way my other marriages had ended. I had not deserved that, and I had certainly not deserved working all day to get paid for an hour due to child support on the top of my head.

My mother knew she was my wife and had made me very, very happy. She treated her with respect, knowing she was the woman I had wanted to spend the rest of my life with. She treated her with love, but she was my mother. I had known her, and that was enough for me to know that the look she had on her face was one that told me that she was not the happiest about it. Perhaps she knew something that I did not know yet. She knew that there was something not right about this woman who seemed to be rather too good to be true.

There, in California, she also met my first daughter Brenda and her mother, Doris Scott, the one who had put me back in the unnerving claws of the Child

Support System. The mother of my daughter, though, did not start any unwanted drama, and the Thanksgiving day went by rather smoothly. The turkey was, as always, perfect. However, each time Athaliah looked at Doris, she had a look on her face that told me that she was ready to eat the woman alive. "You bitch!" her looks said, though she tried to keep her calm. So, naturally, she just did not talk to her. Doris, on the other hand, had her pretentious face, and she came over to Athaliah to say hello. She even hugged her, and that was something none of us were really expecting. Athaliah, the love of my life, in turn, put on her fake smile and looked over at me, whispering to me that she wanted this woman to go away and afar from her.

Later, I showed her around Los Angeles, all the beautiful beaches and everything else that it was known for, including my stomping grounds. But she got sick, and thinking that she was homesick, we thought that we should certainly head back to Atlanta. We said our goodbyes to my family and got back on the plane.

It was on the plane that she told me something.

She said to me, "Wow, Peace, you come from a rough family." She had said that with a frown on her face, and I wondered if she did not like my family at all. As we got back home and a few days passed, Athaliah put a letter on my dressing table, and I wondered what it said. I opened it, and my world changed. I opened it to read what it said.

She was pregnant. She was pregnant with two of my baby girls. I was going to be a father to twin girls, and I could not be happier than I was. After a few rough and troublesome years, God finally listened to me. He was about to bless me with two baby girls at once, and I was so very excited to welcome them. As I write these drafts, I realize that there is not a plausible combination of words or phrases I could ever try to write that would ever do justice to the happiness that I had felt, the feelings that went on in my head and heart.

I, then, understood why Athaliah had felt sick in California; it was because of the pregnancy, which none of us knew about back then. And just like that came the next year – 2005. Athaliah was going to her gynecologist for her regular checkups.

It had been nine months since Athaliah had been pregnant. I was at work when I read my wife's name on my phone; she was calling me. It was then that I heard her say something that shattered the world around me, swiping it away and afar from right under my feet.

"Get here fast, Peace," she said, her voice trembling beyond any possible explanation. "One of the baby's heartbeats stopped!"

I ran to the hospital and talked with the doctors. They said to me, "We have to do an emergency operation and get the other baby alive out, stat!" It was the only option, and all I could do was pray to God to let my other baby live. I had to touch Athaliah's stomach and pray for God's miracle power. I had seen miracles happen before, and I knew that God was going to show me a miracle. So I had to trust God when they were about to take my girls out. I prayed to Him to let them both live, despite whatever plans He had for me. I wanted them both to come out crying and breathing.

I was in the operation room when they pulled out

my baby girl, who was alive first. Right after her came Vision, the daughter of mine who was already with God, happy and at peace. I had tears rolling down my cheeks, no less than a waterfall itself.

As my first daughter cried just like babies are supposed to, I knew something. It was a bittersweet moment, but I knew that I would conquer the world for this one. I knew that I was going to do anything for this girl.

Though the delivery was, as always, grim and arduous, I knew that it was inevitable for me to endure anything and everything for the daughter that was going to be my little princess. Athaliah had been nurturing her inside her body for the past nine months, and I knew that she would do just as much for her as I would, if not more. And so, as she held on through the pain, I knew that Athaliah was happy for the one daughter who had made it out alive, a miracle indeed. Through the hurt and aching of delivering a child, let alone two, Athaliah had held on to the hope of life getting much more beautiful than it had ever before been. She had hope, and she dared to hold on to it. She held on to the happiness that was about to come along with the child. And so, she waited. She waited for the moment when she was going to hold her child in her hands for the first time ever. The weather was warm, yet she shivered. At that time, she was quite unsure what had her trembling like that. Was it the fact that she was giving birth to a child for the first time, knowing it was a responsibility greater than any other? Was it the fear of the future of the child or the fear of her own self?

The nurses finally wrapped my first daughter in a blanket and placed her rather carefully in Athaliah's arms, taking Vision to the back. With that sight, I knew that Athaliah was strong, perhaps even stronger than any person I had ever met, and with tears in my eyes, I was thinking about the ways she would go for my child over and above and beyond boundaries. I was thinking about how she was willing to cross each limit there ever was for the wellbeing of the girl, and she was happy.

I still had my faith. So, I asked the doctor to bring my daughter, Vision, to me. I wanted to see if I could bring her back to life. They had her wrapped in a nice baby blanket, and I held her. Tears started to roll down my eyes again as I prayed to God. "Let her live," I said and repeated. "Let her live, oh, my Lord. Please let her live!" After about 10 minutes of begging God, I could see that there were no results to be seen. And just then, I knew that God takes the best of us first because He does not like to distance Himself from them. So, I knew that God awaited her quite eagerly.

There were counselors who had come in to talk with us. I said to them, "Vision didn't know any sin. She went to be with the Lord before she came out of the stomach. She was just my precious seed to God."

I looked up, closed my eyes, and sighed, "Lord, I dedicate Vision to you."

Athaliah had to stay at the hospital for a while. I went home to get the house ready for the arrival of the woman I had loved, the mother of my child, and my child herself. As I came home, I came to see that there were two cribs. My heart splintered into a million pieces, never to be mended again. I had to take the other crib down, and I was too weak to do that, too torn up in my heart.

My buddy, KC, came over to hold me up and help me. I was sad, still not over my daughter's passing, my beautiful Vision. We went back to the local store with one of the cribs. So, while KC and I were walking to the front of the local store, two white doves flew on my shoes. I stopped and looked at them. KC cried to me, "Man, Peace, look at those doves on your shoes! Pick them up and take them home."

"No," I replied, and they later flew off of my shoes. Those doves were there for some reason or the other, or perhaps even out of utter coincidence, and it gave me some hope. I knew that everything was going to be fine. I knew that despite all the good and the bad, life goes on.

A few days later, I brought Athaliah home with our new baby girl, Victory. It was a feeling that was unmatched, one that was too good. I had the house cleaned and prepared for both of them, my wife and my baby, Victory.

A week passed, and we had a Homegoing Service for Vision, our gift to God. Athaliah's family came into town, and some of my friends were there. My family from California did not come, but they sent love, cards, and money. The Homegoing Service was wonderful, but there was one thing that had all our attention. There were the two butterflies flying around Vision's casket. Then they flew by me and around me, but they did not fly around Athaliah. They flew away shortly after, leaving me wondering. It was as though God was showing me, through different signs, that everything was going to be alright. It was as though He was telling me to hold on to the better in life, the better that was yet to come.

To shatter all that hope and good things came Vicki, the quite evil sister. She asked me, "Where's your family? Are they not here from California? Where are they? I don't think I've seen them around so far!"

I already knew what she was trying to do. She was just there to damage my spirit. So, I just walked away from her, being the bigger person by not replying harshly to her, even though it was something that she deserved.

A little while passed, and Athaliah had lost her job because it moved to Denver, Colorado. We were not moving out there. So, at that time, I was working overtime to pay the bills. I was alright with it because it was my family. I had the responsibility of supporting them, and I was happy to do it. Athaliah was not working for about 10 months. During that time, one day, I decided to go look for a job for her. I went to the labor board in Atlanta. I came to find out that one of the airlines was hiring. I received information to give to my wife. Athaliah applied for the position for the airlines and got the job within a matter of hours. All glory to God; it was some quick favor from the Lord. I was thanking God for directing my steps to help me get my wife a good job. I was happy, and so was Athaliah.

My daughter's first birthday was here, and we decided to celebrate it with our loved ones. So, we invited many people. It would have meant a lot for us to have them there for the joyous and auspicious occasion, and we were too excited. Victory was growing too fast, and that was amazing. Most of them, however, for some reason or the other, never showed up. So, when it was time to say happy birthday, I invited everyone at the park to sing to my daughter the happy birthday song and to eat cake and ice cream for Victory. My buddy, KC, wanted to barbecue the hamburgers. So, I was telling him how to light the fire. But KC stopped me by grabbing my hand and told me that he knew how to start a barbecue fire. I then excused him, letting him do the barbecuing.

I went back to enjoy my wife, daughter, and her friends. A little while later, I went to go check on KC; he was getting the fire ready for grilling. I had a feeling that there was something wrong happening back there. I went up to him and looked at his face; there was something about it that looked a little different than before. All his hair was burned off. He had burned off his eyelids, eyelashes, and mustache.

I naturally asked, "What happened to you?"

He replied, "I put lighter fluid in the coals."

I said to him, "KC, man, I told you. I tried to tell you not to do that. It already had fluid in the coals. Well, now your face is bald but face-headed."

We started laughing at the man's misery, and it was something that lightened up my mood rather dearly. He had no hair on his face; it was all burned off. KC was looking so different without hair on his face. He did not have the usual KC-look on his face, and it had come off as rather weird. So, I took over the barbecue and let him put water on his face. During all that time, and despite the time passing me by, there was nothing that I could do to stop the laughter. It was hilarious.

With that, the party ended, everyone went home, and life continued on. Three years had gone by, and during that time, we had brought to the world another little child, another girl, another queen, and another beautiful lady to bless the world with her mere existence. The delivery was just painful as it was supposed to be, but, very fortunately, there were no issues during the pregnancy or the delivery itself. Athaliah had made it known to me that she did not want to have any more children, and I didn't respond to her.

"This is our last child," Athaliah said to me. "I'm

not giving you any more babies. This is my body, and I just want to take care of it."

"God's choice, my love," I simply replied. "Whatever He decides will be done."

"You have all that Child Support Services' debt that you need to handle," my wife added, "and your credit is bad. How are you going to travel around the world when you can't get a passport because Child Support stops you from getting one?"

There was a long pause, and she broke the silence by adding, "When you met me, you told me that you had good credit."

I replied, "Yes, I did, but that was until this Child Support came into my life. I had nothing to do with my credit being bad. It was all right on track before that! What can I do about it? It's not really my fault."

Athaliah had an attitude, and I could see that she was not totally happy about it. I did not want to fuss with her; I was merely trying to figure out how to support my family and the lovely place that I had the privilege of calling my home. I still believed in God about what He had promised me and with every single thing that He had said to me.

I did not worry. I was starting to see the light in all the hell that I had been through along these years. Perhaps, by me having a family that was going through so very much, God was seeing that I was doing what made Him happy and that I was nothing but a good husband to my wife and a better father to my daughters. I was still hoping that the multimillion-dollar deal was coming soon to help me support my family and pay off this Child Support Services debt that I had found myself in.

I called the Child Support Services to see about any kind of program or help to reduce the payment that I had apparently owed them since I now had two daughters and a wife to support. The receptionist said to me rather harshly and quite unprofessionally, "You should have tried not to go out and have a family with all the money you owe us. The only thing you can do now is pay us." My heart just crumbled, the pieces falling down the floor, so weak that I feared that they would be taken away by the next breeze that came. She had said that and had come off as too mean, yet there was nothing that I could do about it. I just replied, "Wow! Really, lady?" And with that, I hung up on her, knowing that there was no way out, knowing I was caught up in a crime that I had nothing to do with since the very beginning.

I was still towing cars and washing windows. Sooner, I started a cooking show, and I named it "Peace Party Kooking Kitchen." I would cook, and I would dance. I was a great chef, and I always made nice dinners for my family. Ranging from Mexican dishes, soul food, to the Asian cuisine, I had known it all. I would dance while I was cooking, and I would put the recorded tapes on social media.

Sooner before I knew it, a producer from Hollywood, Los Angeles, California, saw my video and flew me out there to do a show. Yet, I came to find out that there was just another door that closed in my face after the Hollywood show. I was trying everything to help my family and pay off this debt that was getting ridiculously high. I was trying to use all the talents that I received from my Father above. It was quite sooner that I finally grew tired of all this stress that my life was revolving around.

See, each day I opened my eyes, there was nothing to be done other than the worry of providing for my family. Yet, there was nothing to be done about it. Life was not cutting me any slack whatsoever, and all I could do was wait. But then again, I had been waiting for the past seven years, and there was nothing good to be found.

So, I flew back to California to talk with a Child Support judge, asking for help. Now that I have a wife and two daughters, I thought that I could get some kind of relief. Doris Scott showed up, my first-born daughter's mother.

The judge said, "The law in California and all the states are to pay the debt and the arrears."

"What about my wife and two daughters?" I simply

asked.

"It's the law," he replied, "and the only thing you can do is see if Doris Scott would like to forgive you of the debt and your arrears."

I asked Doris, "Please, will you just forgive me?" "You are married now," she replied.

"You did this because I got married," I said to her. "You were mad because I got married? Just forgive me."

"No," said Doris Scott in front of the judge. "I will not forgive you. You are married now. So, you may ask your daughter, Brenda, if she would like to forgive you." See, Doris had already taught her not to forgive me.

So, I asked my daughter, "Brenda, will you forgive me?"

"No," my baby girl replied, "I will not forgive you." I did not blame her. I knew that it was the doing of the evilly wicked mother, the woman I had once thought I loved.

The judge replied, "You need to pay up, Mr. Peace."

"You guys, this law is wrong," I replied. "This law is wrong for all men who are going through this. This is wrong."

I was mad, and I was sad.

The judge replied, "Come down, Mr. Peace. It's the law."

"No," I replied. "It's not the law! It's about money! It's about hurting the poor!"

I was back on the plane sooner after that, and I had found myself all alone, feeling like I just got my ass whooped by the system. It was the system that had manipulated and taken advantage of the poor while trying its best to give to the rich. Had they not seen Robinhood? It was supposed to be the other way around.

As I got back, I knew that I really needed to have a talk with First Lady Benjamin. I had to get status about where I was standing on the million-dollar deal that I had deserved too desperately. When I tried to approach her, she frowned and turned her head. She did not want to speak to me. At that time still, I did not know what was happening. I did not know why she did not want to talk to me. And I wondered, thinking of no reason bad enough for her to treat me like that. I had done nothing but attend the church religiously and respect her just as much as I had respected my own mother.

Sooner, there was another time that Reverend Benjamin had a book signing at the local store. I purchased a book and went to get it signed by him. I also wanted to maybe get a good word from him. I was in line, and his bodyguards were familiar with who I was. They asked me, "What's up, Peace?" Then, they said to me, "You are about to get another good word from Reverend Benjamin."

My whole heart smiled, and it was rather evident from my face. So, I replied to the bodyguards, "I really am in need of that."

When I got up to get my book signed, Reverend Benjamin just signed the book with a mean look on his face. Without anything else, he cried out, "Next!"

I was so surprised. There was no kind smile on his face, and he had not even said, "Hello, Reece Peace," like he used to.

"That's funny," said the bodyguard who had just come up to me. "He did not say anything to you."

I replied, "I know."

The bodyguard said to me, "Maybe he did not recognize you."

"He recognized me. I know that," I replied. "No worries, I had my family and the word that God gave me. But now, I'll learn to keep my eyes on Jesus only. I know that the prize comes from God and not the man."

Despite all that, at least, I was a father to my beautiful queens. And that was something good enough for me. That was something good enough to let me hold on to all the good things that life had in store for me. I did not know what was about to come.

Chapter 9

The Record Deal

The hopes for my record deal, presumably the multimillion-dollar one, were just as high as ever. Keeping my faith in my God, I was moving forward and further, but there was no sign of the deal that I had deserved with First Lady Benjamin. But not just that, there was no sign of any deal, and I, with each day that passed, was growing frustrated. I had been sending my music to everyone, but when it got to it, each door would do nothing other than being slammed shut, right in my face, too indifferent to however that would make me feel.

It was 2011 that had come around, the second of the new decade, and everything had been going right according to routine. Everything was fine with the family. We were still going to church religiously each week, and the jobs were going just fine. But then again, that's not what life really likes – being predictable – does it?

So, before long, I would see First Lady Benjamin, and I would know that I had come a long, long way. I would know that things had changed rather drastically. From seeing my face and having a smile on her face that would light up the room, she had gone to frowning. She would not speak to me anymore, and each time she would see my face, she would turn away. It was as though she just could not bear the sight of me, and I kept wondering why that was so. I could not, however, figure out the reason, and that made it much, much worse.

As if that was not bad enough, life happened. The job – that was one of the very few stable things in my life – was resulting in my slipping and falling. I kept getting injured. The first of my falls happened one time when it was snowing in Atlanta, GA. The snow had come, falling all over the place and getting stuck in the canopies, adding much beauty to everything that looked good covered in white. For the cars, however, it was not that much of a treat. To my fortune, I was in a business that revolved all around cars.

There was ice all over the ground, and I was pulling a car out of a ditch from the wrench suspended by the tow truck. There was a little too much ice on the ground. As I took a few steps, I found one of my feet swinging forth, closely followed by the other. Before I knew it, I was hovering in mid-air, and it felt as though everything had happened in slow-motion. I saw the world around me shiver as I fell unto the snow right on my back. "Ouch!" I cried.

For some time, I was on leave from work due to the same back injury that I had suffered at the hands of my towing job. Sooner than I had gotten better and naturally back on my feet, my management started acting up. They had expected me to show up at work despite the back injury that I had suffered, and they were rather indifferent about that fact. Yet, each time I would go to work, my back would hurt rather badly, and in my legs, I could feel excruciating pain. Regardless of my suffering that they could very well see, they forced me to work, telling me that I was not hurt, implying that I was lying by faking my injury.

I got better, but sooner came another injury, and then another. There was a series of injuries, and they could not believe that it was possible. They could not believe that I was hurt, and they wanted to fire me because of the miseries that I would find myself in, one after another. Sooner, I went to see the doctor because the pain was just not going away, and the doctor found a little Arthritis in my back and my left hip. I could still function with the painkillers that the doctor prescribed, a momentary relief. Yet, the pain would come back at the end of the day, and there was nothing to do about it but take those painkillers all over again.

Quite sooner, I found myself without a job. The Child Support Services' debt had been piling up. The medications were costing me a fortune as compared to my situation back then. Before I knew it, the IRS had started to come my way, too, inquiring about the taxes that had gone unpaid. After all, they were doing their work. But even in that case, how could I ever possibly explain to them that I had found myself between a rock and an excruciatingly hard place? All I could do was cry out in front of the Lord, who sat in the heavens above. "This is too much!" I cried. "My Lord, My God, please give me a break! Please, show me some mercy. Please, give me a break, just enough to catch my breath."

A little while passed, and I got a mysterious call. I picked up, and the person on the other side of the phone told me that she was from Trouble Music Records. She was the A&R (artists and repertoire) Representative for the company. For those who do not know, an A&R Representative is a person in a record company who is responsible for finding promising new artists for a record label or music publisher to sign. Anyway, that woman had come to see one of my videos on social media and thought that I had a talent that was worth being represented. She had found me promising, and it was something that was quite pleasing to hear, music to my ears.

The woman went on, talking about how she had wanted to sign me to the label. I could not believe it. I just could not believe it. It was finally happening. There it was… my break, the one that I had asked God for. And so, still trying to really wrap my head around the call that had come to me, still not able to believe it, I asked her, "Really?" Athaliah sat right next to me as I talked to the representative on the speaker phone.

"Baby, that is the multimillion-dollar contract deal," said Athaliah, "the one you've been waiting for all this time long." On her face was the smile that brought the world around me to happiness and peace, for she was, in fact, just as happy as she was on the day that we got pronounced as man and wife. Athaliah was smiling. She was happy, perhaps just as happy as she could have ever possibly been. My heart beat faster and faster with each second that passed on the phone call, and I was just as well, too happy.

The A&R representative said to me, "We are going to send you a contract. You're going to have to pay two thousand dollars as your signing, and we can take things from there. I will give you thirty days to think about it. Talk about it, and give it a thought. I will give you a callback, and you can let me know your answer."

"Sure, alright," said I, "I'm going to do that," trying too hard not to sound desperately happy.

"And before I hang up, Mr. Peace," said the woman from the other side of the phone, "I want you to know that you are a very talented individual. You have talent that is hard to find these days. I can say that I haven't gotten many opportunities to come across individuals as talented as you. Keep that in mind, will you?"

"Yes, I sure will keep that in mind," I said right before hanging up.

Athaliah screamed and jumped just as I tapped the red button over the phone. She was screaming out loud in happiness that was just too good to be ever given words to. She was just so excited that she could find no other way to express it other than hugging me.

"Baby, let's do it," said the wife. "I'll pay the two thousand. And I will do that because I know that right after you record with them, your music will sell big time!"

"You'd do that?" I asked, a little surprised as to the lengths she was willing to go for me – or so I thought.

"Peace," she said, "you have talent. You can rap quite well, and that was one of the many reasons I fell in love with you."

I jumped up. But it did not make sense to a part of me. So, I thought it was right to speak my mind. "I thought God told me that I am going to sign a multimillion-dollar contract deal. But it is us who's paying them, Athaliah. It does not really add up if you ask me. Why are you so willing to pay them for me?"

Athaliah said, "The $2000 is just the seed to your millions. It's just the first step, and there are many more to come. It will give you a head-start, the one you needed so badly. So, let me do this for you."

"Let's do it!" I replied, for she had convinced me rather nicely.

It was that very week that we received the contract. I signed it, and Athaliah paid the fee. Her faith in me was much higher than the faith I had in myself.

Athaliah said to me, "Now you can pay off all that child support debt. You can pay off the IRS. And you can get your passport. Do you know why?"

"Why?" I asked.

"Because," my loving wife cried, "My baby, Peace, is going to be traveling around the world, blessing them with the rap that he makes and the music he creates!"

To me, that sounded like the biggest and most relevant compliment anyone had ever given me, the best I had gotten so far. And I was happy. Things were seemingly going the right way, and I could not complain about any of it. It was all rainbows and sunshine, and I felt that it was how life was going to work for the better for me.

Trouble Music Records (TMR) was in another state, and they wanted me to come out there to record. I, on the other hand, wanted to record in Atlanta, GA. You see, TMR was not quite good at making good beats, and their engineers were just fine. I needed money and faith to record in Atlanta.

I was trying to find anything to make money to record in a studio in Atlanta. I needed around 1,800 dollars to record and pay the singers, musicians, and engineers. I said to myself, "Why not start pawning jewelry and other stuff that I own from the house? There are quite a few things that I have not used anymore, really." I had one necklace in my possession that my second ex-wife had once given me as a gift. I thought to myself, "Let me sell it for 40 dollars before I pawn it." I got to find out whether or not this necklace was a fake and whether or not anyone would want to purchase it from me. So, I decided to pawn this necklace, and I headed to the pawn shop to do that.

I gave the necklace to the lady who seemed to be the owner of the pawn shop. She asked me how much money I wanted for it, and I replied in my street talk, "You know somethin', somethin'? I don't want to say too low or too high. So, I'm thinking, maybe around 40 bucks should do just fine."

The lady weighed it and checked to see what kind of gold it was. I said, "My ex-wife gave me this necklace as a gift. It's probably fake gold, you know?"

The lady came up to me with a look in her eyes that was much too serious, and she said to me, "I'll give you 2,600 for it."

Hearing that, I almost fell to the floor and passed out. I was trying to hold my peace, but my face suggested that I was not really doing a very good job at it. Being really cool and as calmy as I humanly could, I replied to her, "Aight! Wow! Was this necklace real?! I don't believe I almost sold it for 40 bucks!"

I put the 2,600 bucks that I had just gotten safely in my wallet, and I ran home on tenterhooks, much too breathless. I told Athaliah what happened, and we started praising God in the house. There was nothing possible without Him, and we had known that all too well. So, too happy, we were just thanking Him for all that He had been doing for us all this time long. We now knew that God was all in this contract deal, and that came to be a rather soothing thought, one that provided calmness to my soul, one that made me breathe anew, just as I had asked from Him.

So, I knew that this was the multimillion-dollar contract deal that God had once promised me. We started the recording, and everything went quite well. I flew to TMR to do my photoshoot, and I looked quite handsome – I have to tell you. During all that time, I could not help but thank God for my wife's faith in me and her work at the airlines; I flew for free through a "buddy pass."

As I finished recording with many of the producers, singers, and musicians, my album was a success. It was called "CONTROVERSY – Rap, Rhythm, & Rock." My music, my album, and my CD had Rap, R&B, and Rock n' Roll. My music was Rated-E for everyone. I wanted everyone to buy this CD, every ethnic group, every color, and every race.

Athaliah, my ever-loving wife, was telling everyone about it, and the excitement could be seen in her eyes, mere reflections and gateways to the happiness that she had held on to in her heart. She told her friends, the co-workers at her job, and the church, crying to them, "My husband has just signed a multimillion-dollar contract deal!" She even told her family and her sister,

Vicki.

Sooner, there was a day that I received a call from Vicki. She had called me up to congratulate me, and I could not believe it. Perhaps there actually was some good in her heart – or so I thought. But then, she said to me, "I always believed in you. I knew that you could help our family and many people. My sister has a very good husband to herself, and I feel happy for her, Mr. Peace." And I knew that she was being just as fake as she ever was. I did not smile even once as I heard her say all those nice and unicorn-y things. I wondered what she was expecting to get out of all the compliments; I never really understood for quite a long time. And so, I just mouthed, "Eh, that's my fake ass sister-in-law!"

Athaliah was very proud of me; the expressions on her face were as though she had fallen in love with me all over again. She was being too loving, and it was my motivation to keep doing better and better. It was my motivation to be the best version of myself – if not for myself, then for the love of my life. Each night, there were fireworks happening in the bedroom; the love we had been making ever since was quite awesome, leaving me too weak in the knees. It was as though I was her king, and she was my queen – nothing less.

The news was spreading around like fire in the forest. It was fairly sooner that it got to the church and even to Reverend Lite Benjamin and First Lady Benjamin. They now knew that I had signed a multimillion-dollar contract deal. I did a testimony with some TV producers at Planet Dome Church.

In that testimony, I talked about my journey to the record deal. I started off by talking about how God, Himself, told me to leave California. I then talked to them about my struggles and the sad times, how I was sleeping in my car, telling them how all those sad and desperate times mended me into the person that I once aspired to be. I told them how the struggling times were much too important in getting so far. I then talked about finding the right woman who God had sorted out for me and getting married to her, also mentioning how happy I was when I became a father. I thanked them all, my family, my struggles, and my God, for taking me thus far. All that, I told them, was what led me to this massive record deal with Trouble Music Records.

Reverend Lite Benjamin and First Lady Benjamin saw the video that the producers made of me signing a big record deal. It was the beginning of a new era, a new life for me, and I was just as happy as I ever could be. The Reverend and First Lady also heard that my album was coming out September of 2012. And when they finally got to hear it, they fell in love with it. The next thing I knew was that my testimony was being shown around the world. It also included Reverend Lite Benjamin speaking over me all those years ago, back in 2001, about the success of my life, the record deal, and my last name being Peace.

Now that I was fairly and somewhat famous, Reverend Lite Benjamin and First Lady Benjamin had started speaking to me again, and they were back to smiling at me once again. After all, I had just signed a multimillion-dollar contract deal. Or that's what they thought because I talked about it so very much, and my wife had been running around telling everyone. But they never knew that it was all by faith and Athaliah paying the company two thousand dollars.

Despite all that, I had my hopes. I was believing. I was holding on to my hopes. And along with my wife on my side at all times, I believed in the album's sales and success. I knew that it was going to be somewhere in the millions, and I knew that it would soon come in, flowing into the account as soon as the album was released.

September 11th of 2012.

I waited desperately for this date, as it was one when my album was going to air, and I could not be more excited. I had to promote my own shows and direct and pay for my own music video shoots. The first major music video I did for my album was one of my singles, "Put That Gun On Up." It was quite nice, and I played my part in helping to stop gun violence. People, friends, Reverend Lite Benjamin, and First Lady Benjamin were still smiling at me, and I guessed that they were waiting for me to sow millions into the church. But I was waiting on God to sow millions into my life first; that was the only way I could ever possibly sow millions into the church, right? I started performing shows and selling CDs, and for quite some time there, I was on top of the world.

Some weeks later, I could not believe the news while I was watching the TV. There was breaking news about the firm's founder, CEO, and son of Trouble Music Records, and it prevailed all over the headlines. They both were arrested on eight felony charges and one misdemeanor charge that accused them of embezzlement, extortion, and racketeering.

"Oh, hell no!" I cried, though no voice came out of my throat.

"When it rains, it pours."

I knew then… the record deal was a hot mess – nothing more, nothing less. Yet another lesson to learn.

Chapter 10

Arthritis

Two more years I waited, and there was nothing. With the influx of 2014, I found myself right back from where I had started, and it certainly felt like I had hit rock bottom. What went wrong? I thought to myself, not finding any answers. And the question would just remain in my head, unanswered, always popping up, reminding me of all that had gone wrong in my life, all the ways in which my life had gone erroneous.

There was no real contract deal, let alone the one that would provide me with millions and millions of dollars. I had been fired from Double-X Towing, and child support was still taking much of everything that I was left with. Along came the IRS, also wanting their money. To top that off, if all that was not enough already, Arthritis had spread from my left hip to the right hip, from one bone to another, and there was no more cartage around the bones. To think that I could just go through the pain was not really a possibility… not a chance.

And to add to all that, all that was a little more than too much. I had a wife who was getting angrier and angrier with each night that passed and each day that would come to life. Why? Well, mainly because there were no millions in our accounts; in fact, the case was quite the opposite. When I would see her, she would not talk to me happily.

We would quite often talk about the record deal, and she would ask me about whatever happened to it. I could sense the taunts in her tone, the sarcasm that it mostly revolved around. I could see that the sympathy she had for me was turning more and more into anger with every single minute of the day. And it did not feel good. So, I would just say to her, "God told me that I was going to sign a multimillion-dollar deal. I tried to explain to you, Athaliah, that this was not it. I told you that I was not getting the feeling in my heart that I was supposed to get prior to the big deal. But you thought it was. That was why you put money into it. I told you we had to trust in

God's timing. Something about it always felt out of order, out of the usual, and I told that to you, but you believed in the money probably more than you believed in my better judgment."

It was as though I was not the man she had fallen in love with; I was much rather a liability to her – as it seemed. I had started picking up weight; my stomach was turning more into a beer belly with each day. I was looking like I was pregnant with triplets, just about to go into labor. I was walking like a zombie everywhere I went, and I was not too proud of it. Trying my best to hide it off with oversized clothes or holding my breath for longer periods, there was nothing that I could do much about it. I was on medications, and some of the medications were very strong, but it was all just to ease the pain that felt too excruciating.

Victory, my beloved daughter, would put socks and shoes on my feet before I would go outside, just because the pain had increased so very much that I could not bend down to do it all myself. Dressing myself up would take much more time than it should have, just because the pain was too much; I would need to get up an hour, dedicating every minute of it to the many tries it would take for me to get ready. Everything hurt – all of it. To walk a little better, to numb the pain a little, and to try and please my wife in the bedroom, I was getting my hips pierced every four months with needles to receive steroid shots.

Sooner, I got to notice that she had been pulling away from me. Even walking into the house, she started to avoid walking across from me. There were no sorts of affection, verbal or physical, let alone hugs and kisses. Quite sooner than I could imagine, she had stopped wearing her wedding ring, the one I had gotten for her with much of all that I had at that time. Was I dead? Was I the one who was at fault? I think not. And all for what? Had she not promised to be with me through thick and thin? Had she not promised to love me and care for me through all the good things and the bad ones? She was the only worldly thing that was keeping me going, the only thing that was giving me hope for a better future. Now that everything she did said otherwise, what was I supposed to do? Now that every single thing that she did told me that she believed in me no longer, that she wanted to be with me no longer, how was I supposed to carry on? Was I supposed to give up? Everything around me did encourage me to give up and give in to life, even though that was the coward's way out. I did not know what to do, and I was having a harder time believing any of it with each minute that came to pass.

And to add to all that – as if it was not enough already – people still believed that I signed this big deal and had money rolling in. They did not know that there were just a lot of bills of debt, one right after the other. It was high time to look for a job. Even though my back and hips did not allow me to walk or even sit, I knew I had to work. I went to a local restaurant, asking for a job opening. I had parked right beside a fine, luxurious, and expensive car. When I faltered into the restaurant to get an application, I saw someone, and I could just not believe my eyes. I saw First Lady Benjamin standing in the restaurant by the door, laughing with a lady friend of hers.

The restaurant host asked me, "Can I help you, sir?"

"Yes," I replied. "I need an application. Are y'all hiring?"

"Sure," she said. "If you'll just follow me to the cashier area."

When First Lady Benjamin heard me tell her that I needed an application, I saw on her face a fit of rage, one that told me that if I did not get further from her, she would push my face through a wall – then I would not only have a useless back and hips but also a broken face.

And so, as soon as I could, I followed the host to the cashier area, and I saw Reverend Lite Benjamin and his friend; they were paying for their meal, the same one that they had just finished with First Lady Benjamin and the other gentleman's wife. Just as Reverend Lite Benjamin saw me getting an application from the host, there was an unusual and confusing look on his face, one that told me that he was confused himself.

Just as I got the application, I ran to the restroom,

and just then, there was this feeling that just found its way to me too inevitably. I was feeling embarrassed, and I confirmed to myself, "Both of them just saw me looking for a job. Let's just wait for them to leave the restaurant. I'll walk out when they leave." And so, I waited about ten minutes and then faltered out of the restroom and grabbed the application, thinking that I could just fill it out in my car.

Reverend Lite Benjamin was still standing outside, talking to people. Perhaps people saw him and wanted his autograph or a photo with him; he was much of a local celebrity around the town and also around the whole world, and there was no wonder about it. I walked up to him, patted his back, and nodded, "Hello, sir."

I went to my car to work on my application, still feeling quite so embarrassed by them seeing me in the circumstances that I was in. While I was working on my application, I looked out my rear-view mirror, and it was First Lady Benjamin; she was walking toward my car. As I saw her like that, I thought to myself, "Perhaps she's going to come to talk with me, checking what it is that is going on, why I am looking for a job. Or perhaps she wants to sign me now. It could be that." I didn't know. But then I got to find out that the fine, luxurious, and expensive car that I parked next to was First Lady Benjamin's, and she was just getting into her car.

She saw me sitting in my car, all sad, filling out my application for a job that would pay me not at all as much as I needed to go by at that time, with child support, IRS, and everything else. All that was just on my mind for a very long time, and I just rolled down my window and asked her, "Can you pray for me? I lost my job, and my record deal did not work out right. I have Arthritis in my hips, and I cannot walk right or do anything right."

"You'll be alright," she said to me with a greatly unkind, cruel, uncaring, and callous look. Just after that, she got into her car and screeched away.

"Wow!" I mouthed, not knowing what to feel just at that moment.

She did not pray for me, but I knew that God had loved me through all of it regardless. I was going through a lot, sure, but I was more than a conqueror.

She and her husband were in separate cars. First Lady Benjamin, when she got home, was waiting for Reverend Lite Benjamin to get there, and just as he walked in, she said to him, "You saw that fake-ass rapper, didn't you?"

"Yes, I did," he replied.

"He did not sign any big deal, let alone a million-dollar one," she told him. "We spent all this money on projects around the church, thinking he was going to bring millions into the church. Lord help, but that little rascal needs to leave the church before I remove his neck from his body."

Reverend Lite Benjamin replied, "Yes, honey. I agree. He needs to leave, that little devil. We just spent millions on so many projects. I'm mad myself, honey. I saw him getting an application for a job. Peace is just as broke as a joke. We will get rid of him soon."

The next day was a Wednesday, and quite enthusiastically, I decided to go to a Bible study. It was an early morning service, and I was excited about it. Just as I entered the church, I got to see that it was First Lady Benjamin who was teaching. I did not mind that, but there was something about her that showed everyone that her mind was a bit too preoccupied. I, like all the people present there, did not know that she was just mad at me, and that was why her teaching was not as good as it used to be. She seemed like she just could not get into the spirit, all because she was pissed off at me. I do wonder now. What if she had just talked to me about it? What if she had just asked me how much truth everything that she knew about me had held? Back then, I did not know much about it. Even after all that, though, I did not leave the church.

I did not hear God telling me to walk away from the church and never go back, so I stayed there and just trusted in God. I believed in what He said to me.

2016 came around with a bit of a relief – just a little, but enough to make me hold on for a little while longer. I got a job at Hospitality Airport Shuttle Service. It was a really cool job: I helped the guests with their luggage, and I had always been the one to help. It was not as bad as the towing job, and I did not hate going there. I used to take the guests to and from the airport. Even though my hips were still hurting, helping the guests got my mind off my hips and other issues in my life, all the pains that I was still going through. I had to take painkillers before I would go out to cut the yard, play with my daughters, or just go out with my family on outings.

I still went out to try and do shows at clubs, events, and colleges, still believing in what God Himself once told me. I was booked for a show at my daughter's Elementary school. My performance was horrendous: I could not walk or dance across the stage. The teachers and the school children noticed that there was something quite wrong with me, and I could see it from the sympathetic and pitiful looks that they had on their faces, their eyes reflecting what went on in their heads, "This poor rapper guy." They looked like they wanted to throw food at me, and with the frowns on their faces, I could see that they wanted to call the paramedics to come and get me off stage before I dropped dead. I was just worried about my daughter getting bullied about it when the kids and teachers would discuss my saddening performance.

I was still praying for healing every day. I was saying my healing confessions each day, speaking God's word over my hips and my back and all the other intangible things that inflicted unbearable pain upon me. Some people advised me to get an operation, but I refused without even giving it much of a thought. I was afraid. I was scared to cut my hips open. But then, I thought about it. "What if an operation is the only option I'm left with?" That led to many hours spent with research on people who got a hip operation. Some people gave out good reviews, while some gave out bad ones. I was just waiting on God to heal me; I still had hopes, and I was willing to see how God was going to help me. I knew that He was going to help me, of course. There was no one else who could help me if it were not for Him and His divine will.

Just then, Doris Scott, my first daughter's mother, moved from California to Atlanta, GA, with the rest of her family. We met a few times, and she liked me a lot better than she did before. She was happier, and I had always been a good ex-boyfriend to her and a good father to my first daughter. We were getting along better, both walking in forgiveness and love. I still had that child support debt, and that certainly was something that I just could not keep off of my mind. She and I never talked about it, but she knew about it just as much as I did. She knew that I was still paying for it, along with the interest that had piled up over it, summing it up to a hefty amount, much more than I could actually afford to pay. And with each payment, one would think that the debt would see a downfall, but I never could get it down: the interest was going up and up, not wanting to come back downward, not even a little.

There was one time that I took all my daughters and my wife out to dinner. It was pretty, and it felt pretty to see that all of them – my first-born daughter by my baby mama, Doris Scott, and my two other daughters from my marriage to Athaliah – getting along. They had the sibling time that they had not gotten before, and it was just a sight for sore eyes. At that moment, I was so full of love that I could never put into words that would ever really do justice to any of it.

Athaliah, however, was quiet, just enjoying her food while my three daughters and I were taking photos together. My younger two daughters thought it was cool to have another sister, a big sister. Athaliah did not want to be in the photos, and I wondered why she was angry. Things went around her head, things that I would have certainly feared if only I knew what they were. Yet, I did not know. I wondered, but I never knew.

A little while passed, and my Arthritis problem had ranched. It had gotten so bad that it would now take me much longer to get dressed. Instead of one, both of my daughters had to help me put my socks on because, again, I just could not bend down. The pain from my hips was hitting my whole body, and I was not sure what to do about it other than pray to the Lord above me. He was the only one who was there for me, the only one who seemed to care about me, out of all the people in the world, besides my daughters – as it seemed. So, I wondered. Where has my lovely wife been through all of this? How has she helped me?

A little while later, we all went to New York for Vicki's 25th anniversary with her husband. I did wonder how she had gotten to her silver jubilee without eating her husband alive. At the party, Vicki noticed how I was walking very slowly, and that was when she went on and asked Athaliah, "What's going on with your husband? Why he can't walk properly?"

Athaliah, just then, took Vicki to the back. And there, she told Vicki something that I never expected her, of all people, to say. "I'm tired."

"Tired of what, Athaliah?" her sister asked.

"Peace has Arthritis in his hips, and that's why he's been walking slowly," said Athaliah. "Vicki, let me be honest with you."

"Okay… go on," replied Vicki.

"He can't perform sex right," my loving wife added, "due to his hips."

"How's that contract deal going?" asked Vicki,

triggering my wife more. "How is it going with his music and all?"

"The firm's founder, CEO, and son of Trouble Music Records were arrested on eight felony charges and one misdemeanor charge that accuse them of embezzlement, extortion, and racketeering," replied my loving wife. "He's not selling anything. No CDs. No shows to perform. No fans. Not even a rooting audience. Trouble Music Records didn't use the money right to promote the artists."

"That's bad enough," replied Vicki. Perhaps she was happy at the sight of watching me fail. I was sure of it.

"Do you know?" added Athaliah. "Peace has an older daughter. He owes over $45,000 dollars in child support and arrears. And it's not just that! The sad part is that I have been paying all the bills!" Vicki's mouth was wide open as she was left speechless, all without a word to say.

"And Peace has been married two other times," added my beautiful wife, the same one I had loved much too dearly.

"What?!" cried Vicki.

"Yes, girl." Athaliah added, "His two ex-wives even tried to kill him, but they didn't succeed."

With eyes all big and a mouth wide open, Vicki could not believe that it was all being said to her.

Athaliah added to her sister, "And... he used to be a male hooker with all the women he has had sex with."

"Shut up!" cried Vicki. "I thought that Peace has been a church boy all his life! No, not Peace!"

Athaliah replied, "He used to be in the streets, trying to gang bang and sell drugs. From his family in California, no one ever went to college. Most of the male family members are dead or in jail, and you already know that."

"No, Athaliah," sympathized her sister. "I'm so sorry. My dear sister, are you sure that God told you that Peace was supposed to be your husband, your man of God?"

Athaliah replied, "I thought God said it. Maybe I was just hearing things or was tricked by the devil. I believe Peace is a curse. The devil has him, but not me. I'm blessed! I never had any issues in life! I have never struggled with anything in my life, not until I met him. Everything went down the drain ever since I met him."

There was a small pause just then, both of them not sure what to say next. Athaliah interrupted that silence that was much better than all that they were saying.

"Vicki, I believe I'm sleeping with a demon."

"Athaliah," said Vicki with an eerie look on her face,

"it's time to have fun!"

"What do you mean?" asked my wife.

"You have only been with one man," implied Vicki. "Go out and have sex with another man. Then after that, divorce Peace. Then we'll get you a new husband, a much better one, a Jamaican husband this time. I told you already that American men are lazy, and they have no brains."

"I can't divorce him," replied Athaliah, not too disgusted by the idea that her sister had put forward. "A divorce wouldn't look good for me. It will just make me look bad."

Vicki then told Athaliah a little secret. "I've been cheating on my husband. I have a lover now."

"Shut up!" my beautiful wife cried. "You have a good husband, Vicki. Why are you cheating on John? He's a good man, and this is your 25th anniversary with him!"

"Well, what can I say?" she asked rhetorically. "Girls... they need to have their fun."

"Yes, girl," cried Athaliah. "It's time to have some fun."

There was a pause in which my wife thought through a decision she was about to make, and she whispered to her sister, "It's time to have fun... and its starts now."

Chapter 11

A Plot to Kill

Her eyes would roll in the direction of each man she saw, and I realized that they had been rolling away and further from me. But I could not understand why. I could not understand the reason all of this was happening to me. Still unaware of the fact that my faithful and beloved wife was no longer on my side, I was thanking the Lord for the company of an amazing woman by my side. I was thanking the Lord for the beautiful lady that He had blessed me with, and I could not be happier. But the circumstances that I had found myself to be surrounded by, within and without, seemed to not help my case at all.

There was not much that was going quite fine in life. And to top the worries off, Athaliah remained on my mind. She was no longer the support system that kept me from falling apart. Her thoughts were no longer the peaceful ones that remained on my mind. I was worried about her. What I did not know was the fact that she was now willing and ready to look for extra-marital affairs; what I did not know was the fact that she was looking for lovers, all behind my back.

And so, while she was out without me, her eyes would focus on every other guy who would walk past her. Using those adorable eyes and the soft, calming voice, she would lure the men toward herself. Trying to find the right person to fulfill the desire, the thirst, the adventure of sin, she watched television shows and love stories religiously, especially the ones with tall and good-looking men. What I did realize was the fact that she was moving further and apart from me, and there was no remorse about it that was to be seen in the eyes that I had fallen too deeply in love with. When she was not watching her television shows, she was reading novels that revolved all around complicated and sinful love stories, those that you could never really talk about in front of your children. I was not proud of that, but even then, I was there for her. I trusted her with all my heart.

Though, at times, I did wonder.

She was growing apart from my music. She was not much excited about my rap or even my genre of music. Whenever she would get into her car, gospel music was not what she was looking for. She was looking for music that turned her on, all the sexual types of music. She had it all in her playlist from one artist or another, and I could do nothing but sit back and think about how my wife had been drifting apart from the religion that we so perfectly loved. It felt as though the Jezebel spirit had walked right into her, and she had welcomed it with arms wide open.

Each place we'd go, I would look at her, and she would look at the men who were in the surroundings. And when she would look at them, it was as though no voice in the world could pierce through her ears, no voice that could ever bring her back from the land of her own fantasies. She was in her own imagination each time, and I would just try to gather what she was thinking about. Ever too unsure, I would then ask her about the thoughts that would go through her mind right at that time, and she would just reply, "Oh, no, honey, I thought that it was just some famous basketball player." If not that, if she thought that the basketball player card was being overused, she would simply go for, "Oh, no, honey, I thought it was just some famous celebrity I saw on the TV show I've been watching for some time now." While saying that, she could just not maintain eye contact with me, and I knew her to be lying, but I thought, "Okay, she would not lie to me. Why would she lie to me?"

Sooner, she came up to me one day and told me that she was joining a book club and that she would need to go out with her friends on certain nights... to read. I was suspicious.

As time passed, I saw a pattern in her eyes. I looked at her, stealing looks at the two guys who lived next door with their mother. One of the men was in his late thirties, and the other, his older brother, was around his early forties. She had been watching them each time they were around. I wondered why. Perhaps they really were her type. Perhaps they were what she had always been looking for. Perhaps I was never the one she had loved. Thoughts went around my head, and I felt as though I was slowly going insane.

The men, however, were nothing like me. I was a responsible man who had taken care of the ones I loved and of the ones who depended on me. They, on the other hand, worked at the car rental company, and they would bring different girls to the house almost every other night for sex.

Each day, they would pull over in exotic cars, different girls and different cars each night, and all the girls would always act up as though they were the kings of the world or something of the same sort. They did not take care of their mother's home; they did not cut the grass that had really outgrown on their lawn; they would not do the household chores. 'Heathens' was the word that popped to my mind each time I saw them, and it had always fit them too perfectly.

Athaliah, on the other hand, would peek out of the window at the men, and she liked what she saw. So, each time the sound of an exotic exhaust approached, she would be ready, moving the drapes to the side so that she could have a look at the men. Sooner, her wish, it seemed, came to life.

She met the younger brother at the gas station one day. Brian. Treating her like a thing, he was just flirting with Athaliah even though he knew that she was married to me, even though he knew that I lived right next door. Perhaps that was the reason he was flirting with her in the first place. "Your husband, Peace," he said to her, "is he taking care of you?"

My wife did not reply.

"I noticed that he can't walk," he said, looking at her body in a much philander way. "So, does he take good care of a woman such beautiful as yourself?"

She clenched her lips and shook her head sideways,

"No."

"What's up?" asked the man.

"My daughters are in school," said my loving wife. "Peace is at work."

Brian said, "Let's go to your house. I can't wait to see more of you and all of you."

So, that was what they did. Just like that, while I had been nothing but honest and devout with her, my loving wife had cheated on me. She had – with keeping my trust and heart in no regard whatsoever – gone to bed with another man while she had vowed her loyalty and faithfulness to me. She did not care about the family that she was breaking apart while breaking her vow to me, the same vow that she had made in the presence of God and the Holy Spirit.

Sooner, as expected, the younger brother went home to tell the tale of him having sex with the neighbor to his elder brother. Bobby, the elder brother, did not hate the idea of it.

He, too, had sex with my loving wife, and my wife had no shame in doing that. To her understanding, girls need to have fun every now and again.

It was one day that Athaliah had come home with a wrecked car and a broken windshield. I asked her if she was alright or if she had gotten hurt, and she told me that she was just fine. So, that very day, I, Peace, the husband, went and got the windshield and car fixed for her. I did that so she would not have to go to the mechanic and all the trouble that came along. I just wanted her to rest. I just wanted her to be fine. I thought to myself, "Wow, thank you, God, for keeping my wife safe. Nothing happened to Athaliah, my amorous wife. That's very strange, but thank you, God." What I did not know was the fact that while I was out, Athaliah had called her sister, Vicki.

"Vicki, girl," she said, "I had sex with another man." "Way to go, girl," Vicki cried.

"I am having sex with two brothers," my wife added.

"It's about time you had some fun," Vicki was happy for her. "But don't do that with two brothers, Athaliah. You should have all the fun that you want, but don't have the fun with two brothers. When I told you about having fun, I did not mean that kind of fun. You can get a disease, or you might get in trouble that way."

"Okay, sister," said Athaliah, agreeing with the

sister who knew nothing but wickedness and trouble.

"Are they Jamaican, these men you've been having sex with?" asked the wicked sister. I had called my wife's sister "wicked;" it suited her just right.

"No," replied Athaliah.

"Girl, come on!" groaned the wicked sister. "Stop getting these American men! They're nothing but lazy. You need to have some real Jamaican fun. You will know what sex is all about when you take a Jamaican man, girl! I told you that."

"Okay, sister," said my caring wife.

"And you need to divorce Peace," added the wicked sister.

"I can't do that!" cried Athaliah, whispering as if someone could hear her. "Our daughters will be upset and miss him. Plus, I don't want another woman romancing him over his pretty eyes. I don't want no woman cooking for him either. I don't want him to be with another woman. It will also make me look bad with friends and family if I divorce him."

"That's true," said the wicked sister. "What do you want to do with him then?"

"I don't know," said my devoted wife.

"Maybe we can take him out," implied the wicked sister.

"What do you mean, take him out?" asked my ever- loving wife.

"Like…" the wicked sister paused and then went into a whisper; "You know, kill him. We can kill him."

"NO!" said Athaliah, laughing harder than ever. "You have to be joking."

Vicki said, "Do you love him?"

"Uh…" my very loving wife thought about that question for a good couple of seconds and replied, "Not anymore, no. I'm not in love with him, either. I don't think I ever really loved him."

"Let's kill him then," said the wicked sister.

"No," my wife, my savior, interjected. "You know, he would divorce me if he knew I was having sex with another man. Or more than one man. But if that happens, many people will find out and put me to shame. I cannot have that. I don't know… I need some time to think about it, what I want to do with him, but I ain't killin' him! Nobody's killin' nobody!"

I was still motivated, wondering about the ways in which I could provide for my family. I was looking for ways to make sure that my wife was happy with me. I was still going to work early in the mornings, even though the pain never lessened in my hips. Athaliah would take our daughters to school right before I would leave for work. Right after dropping them off at school, the time for her shenanigans would be there, and she would look for places to quench the thirst she had for sex. At times, it would happen over at my house, and at other times, she would go over to their mother's house.

Sooner, Athaliah got bored of the men. She did not want them anymore. She had found out that the guys had worked at a rental car company and were living with their mother, and that was how she came back to her senses. Away from God, still moving astray from His ways, she remembered what her sister had said to her. She recalled her sister saying, "Stop getting these American men! They're nothing but lazy. You need to have some real Jamaican fun. You will know what sex is all about when you take a Jamaican man, girl." She knew that American men were lazy after hearing it from her wicked sister. She broke it off completely, whatever she had with those two brothers, and she stop having sex with them after finding out how they were getting the expensive cars – they were renting them!

After that, I would see her walk out of our room, and she would be all dressed up – from head to toe. She would look pretty, and I was sure to compliment her. But whenever I would ask her if I could possibly go along with her to wherever she was going, she would cry, "No! I'm just going to the grocery store. I have to run some errands. You stay here. I don't want you worried." With that, she would pace out of the house as if she was being suffocated while she was inside.

Out there, her "errands" were to find random partners and fulfill her sexual needs. She would have sex with coworkers at her airport job and the strangers she would meet at the grocery store. She would also meet up with college guys she had crushes on back in her college days. Back in college, however, she was a good girl, and that was why she never had sex with them back in college. So, now that she was married, she had no remorse for doing all that, catching up with her sins, the sins that she used to refrain from back in her youth.

And when she would come home and go to bed with me, she would be all tired out. When I wanted to have sex with her, she would push me off, saying, "I'm tired. Not tonight." I sure would wonder what was happening to her, but I never saw all of it coming. She would come to bed covered in clothes so that I, her loving and faithful husband, would not touch her, the person who had waited two years to have sex with her. Be it summers and a burning 110 degrees, she would be fully covered from head to toe. "Honey," I would ask her, worried, "why are you in so many clothes? It's so hot; you're going to catch a fever or something."

"No," she would reply. "This is the way I go to

bed all the time."

"You didn't use to," I would reply.

"I'm cold," she would push me away.

In my mind, I would say, "You cold, alright!"

Even then, I trusted her. But it changed a little one night. It was something she said that made me think about what was going on, something very strange. That night, she wanted to have sex with me, and I could never say no to her. So, while we were having sex, she moaned out, "You are the best I have ever had!"

"Say what?" I asked.

She just dismissed that, telling me to continue. But in my mind, all I could think was, "I'm the only one you've ever had!" At that time, it sure felt very strange that she said that. I kept thinking about why she did say it. That was when I started to worry.

May 2018 was when I let go of all my fears. I knew that I needed hip replacement surgery, and I was ready for it now. I was still scared, but what kept me calm was the fact that I would have my wife there with me through the process, holding my hand. Athaliah, my loving wife, however, dropped me off at the hospital and took off, giving me an excuse that I do not even remember anymore.

I got the operation, and I was in the hospital, recovering for 3 days. I was there, all on my own. And when the doctors and nurses would ask me if I had someone to take care of me, I would reply to myself, "Yeah, my wife's just a bit busy."

The surgery was a success. From the hospital, we came home to a leaking pipe in the kitchen. We called the plumber, and he came to the house with so much cologne on that I literally shook my head sideways to let the smell go away and afar from me. I said to him, "I smell roach spray." The plumber did not like what I said. But then again, someone had to tell him the truth. When he saw me walking with a walker in the house, he said to himself, "This good-looking woman has a man that can't walk. That sounds like a plan." He called Athaliah into the garage to explain what was going on with the water leak; I knew it was a ploy, but I could not go to where they were.

And from where I was, I could not hear them talking in the garage. I could not see what they doing or talking about. I believe that he was flirting with her, although I possibly couldn't tell. He was a Jamaican guy with dreadlocks that suspended and dwindled, finally being tackled by his sturdy shoulders. He gave her his number to my loving wife, and she was much happy to take it. When he told me what he was charging her, I simply said, "Thank you for having a look, but we will just call someone else. This is too much." In a fit of fury, he stormed out of the house, banging the door behind him. He was not too happy with me.

A few nights later, Athaliah came home late from work, and she was talking to her sister. Over the phone, she said, "Vicki, I have news."

"Tell me," her wicked sister from the other side of the phone.

"I found a Jamaican man," my loving wife replied.

"It's about time, girl!" cried the wicked sister. "Leave these American men alone; they have no brains. These black men only want to be rappers or become professional basketball players, and the white men play golf and drink whiskey all day. That's what Americans do."

"Very true," replied my wife.

"Where did you meet him?" asked the wicked sister. "How was it?"

Athaliah replied, "It was the plumber guy who came to check a pipe leak in the house."

"Did he fix the leak?" asked Vicki with a little smile, making sure Athaliah knew that she was talking about her having sex.

"I'm still trying to find the right guy," said Athaliah. "He was okay. He was very much like a spoiled child. He got mad every time we hung out. I noticed he had skeleton bones hanging up from the ceiling of his apartment. That creeped me out."

What she did not know was the fact that the man

Athaliah was having sex with was a warlock. She did not know that she was having sex with a devil. I found out later on this matter, and when I did some research, I found out how the devil or demons can get into people close to you to harm God's chosen ones. The devil can use your closest friends or your family members to destroy you.

Anyway, Vicki told Athaliah, "There's a real nice and tall guy I know. He's my friend and has houses and properties in Jamaica, New York, and Atlanta. He's a businessman who is in the pharmaceutical business. He is very rich, and, to top it all off, he's a Jamaican."

"Ooooo… he sounds tasty," my wife replied, knowing that he matched her type completely.

"Let me introduce you to him one day," replied the wicked sister. "His name is Darius Dog. He is in New York with me now. He is a very nice guy, so don't let the weird name fool you. Look… your husband's name is Reece Peace, but there's no peace in him. And he is not sweet like chocolate peanut butter candy." They shared a good laugh, and I remained unaware of all of it and more, still thinking of ways to make my wife happy while she was doing all of this.

Vicki introduced Darius Dog to Athaliah the next day on a three-way phone call. Darius Dog flew to Atlanta to meet Athaliah. My loving wife made excuses to me so that the two of them could hook up at different hotels to have sex. She did not even know Darius Dog or any men before well enough, and she was just giving up on her husband, who was worth many fine jewels, for these unworthy and half-assed pebbles.

Reece Peace had to wait two years to have sex with Athaliah. Now, all the men she was having sex with were getting her on the first night because she just wanted to explore. Darius Dog was giving her money, and Athaliah was enjoying the money, the sex, and the type of guy he was – her type. He was tall, and he was a Jamaican man who had businesses. Sometime later, they hooked up again, drinking wine, and Darius Dog put drugs in her wine to get Athaliah high. She was high.

During that time, they were having conversations. Darius Dog explained to Athaliah how he needed medication drugs delivered from Atlanta to Jamaica, Jamaica to New York, and so on. "I can pay you a lot of money," he said. "By you, Athaliah, working for the airlines, you can go through the airport very easily without being searched."

Athaliah replied, "That's true. No one searches me. But I don't know about the drug part… it seems very scary."

"Let me take care of the fear," he said, reaching down to his duffel bag, grabbing a thousand dollars, handing all the bills in her hand, and kissing her all over.

"You're beautiful," he told her. "You have that honest look. You talk very nicely, so no one will ever suspect you."

He gave her another grand, took her clothes off, and they started having sex. Athaliah was so confused; he was getting her to bring drugs from one country to another through the airport; she was scared. She did not want to get into the drug business, but the man just seemed too appealing to the love of my life, my loving wife. She thought that she was in love with him. Darius

Dog asked Athaliah, "How did you get that good job… working for the airlines?"

Athaliah replied, "God is with me. The job just came to me." She knew that she was lying. She knew that her husband, Reece Peace, went out and found that job for her. That crossed her mind, but she shook off the thought, placing her undivided attention on the man.

The next day, Athaliah talked with Vicki on the phone about what Darius Dog proposed to her. Hearing that, Vicki confessed to Athaliah, "I work for Darius Dog. I package the drugs in our pharmacy store in New York, the one that we own. I still do my management job at the hospital. How do you think I'm buying property, houses, and all of it?"

Not being able to believe what Vicki was saying, Athaliah said, "I can't do that! I'm a good girl. I'm a girl who goes to church!"

Vicki laughed at Athaliah and said, "Girl, please! You're having sex with different men."

Athaliah replied, "I'm righteous in the path of

God. I don't sin. God will love me if I sin or do good. Nothing bad will happen to me."

"Where did you get that from?" asked the wicked sister.

Athaliah said, "Reverend Lite Benjamin preached on the grace of God. My sins have all been forgiven. I wronged no man. The grace of God is with me, and God loves me. I had sex with many men, and God is still blessing me. I'm going to be alright. God wants me to have fun. God knows my husband is cursed. Look at all the stuff Peace did and all the forgiveness he got from God."

The wicked sister replied, "Athaliah, I thought he did all that stuff when he was a sinner and wasn't saved back in California."

Athaliah froze up, not able to say anything. She then found her words and said, "Well, Vicki, you go to church and do all this bad stuff. You direct the church choir. You council people in the church."

The wicked sister countered, "God loves me too.

I can sin, but in the end, God will forgive me.

Athaliah said, "I'm not smuggling drugs through the airport!"

She was sensible for the first time in a long time, a little hard to brainwash.

Six weeks had passed since my first hip replacement. I was healing fast with the divine grace of God. The surgery had taken place on my left hip, and I had gone back to work, but I was working with light stuff, all the things that did not require me to carry or pick up heavy stuff. I was just watching the cars in the parking lot, doing security with a radio in my hand. I was just making sure that no one came into the lot to steal some cars, and I was doing a good job at that. For me, in my mind, with what little I knew, life was falling a little bit back on track.

Another day came to keep me in the dark about all that was going on right under my nose. I remained unaware of what my wife had been up to. I was at work, and Brian, the neighbor, the younger brother, came knocking on the door. Athaliah opened the door and was surprised to see that it was the ex- lover that she thought she had gotten rid of. "What are you doing here?" she asked, looking around to see if someone was looking at the two of them talking. "Don't come into my house like this!"

"What's up?" asked the younger brother.

"What's up with what?" asked my wife, knowing what exactly he was talking about.

"You're not receiving my calls," he complained. "You're not replying to my texts. What's going on?"

"Yeah, I was a bit busy," lied my wife. "That's alright," he replied.

"What's up?" asked Athaliah. "Why are you here?" She was getting worried.

"Let's have sex," he moved closer toward the door behind which she subduedly hid.

"No," she cried. "I don't want to have sex with you anymore. Whatever happened is in the past now. I'm trying to work it out with my husband, and I don't want you knocking on my door anymore."

"I lost my job," he said with his head kept down. "I need some money."

"Go and run to your mother," said my wife. "You're a mommy's boy, aren't you?"

"Well, Athaliah," he replied with a mischievous smile that prevailed on his face. "I know something that your husband doesn't. I know how you've cheated on him many times with two brothers and probably many more people too. So, if you don't give me 500 dollars by the end of each week, you're going to have many more problems than just having a husband who can't walk. I'm going to tell him."

"Get the hell out of my face," she yelled, gathering the attention of all those who were in close proximity for a while. "Get away from my house," she added, slamming the door in his face.

Athaliah, panicking and chaotic, paced around the living room, wondering about the course of action that could be taken. Innately, her mind wandered off to the memory and thought of her sister. So, she called her go-to person, no matter how bad the go-to person had always been, even since the day she was born.

"Hello?" said the woman on the other side of the phone.

"Let's do it," cried my wife.

"Let's do what, sister?" she asked, genuinely confused as to what my wife was talking about.

"Let's…." Athaliah stumbled with her words. "Let's take him out. He needs to die. We need to kill him."

"Okay, okay, okay," the wicked elder sister tried to calm down the younger one. "Slow down. Slow down."

"He is cursed anyway," the wife did not slow down. "He can't walk. His hips still don't work. He's in debt. He has no money to his name. He can't even get a bank account. He can't get a passport. He is nothing but a fake. I'm the real Peace. God has blessed me. I'm a good woman, and I'm a woman of God. I'm one of God's favorites. Peace is not that. Peace is none of that. We gotta take him out. He needs to go."

"Okay," said the sister. "Perfect."

"How will it go?" asked my wife; perhaps she was concerned for my well-being.

"We'll get X-ray, Filter, Skillet, and Maniac to do it," implied the sister.

"Our crazy Jamaican cousins?!" exclaimed Athaliah into a question.

"Yes," Vicki replied. "They're drug dealers and gangsters. You know that, right?"

"Yeah," Athaliah replied.

"Well, they've been helping me to deliver for Darius Dog. And throughout this time, I believe that they can be trusted with something so important. But because they are good at what they do, it's going to cost you at least 10,000 dollars."

"His last two wives," the wife said. "They tried to kill him, but they failed. They are not me, though. I am different. I am better. I will not let him go this time. I will kill him. Peace is going to die."

"That's the spirit!" exclaimed the wicked sister.

"I will miss his pretty eyes, though," my wife told her sister, the very and only thing she liked about me. She did not have a second's regard for the work I had done for her. I had helped her find a job. I'm a great husband to my wife and a good father to our daughters. I clean the house, cook, and still work with my hip recovery from an operation. She had no care for the fact that I was still hurting, that I could still not walk properly. She was unaware of the fact that I was going through a very rough stage of my life. She did not know how it hurt all the time that I found myself in need of walking. She just could see the material things, and there was nothing that I could do about it.

Perhaps that wasn't really her. Perhaps there was some part of her that did not want me dead. She did not know what I was going through. So, perhaps it was a language barrier that prevailed. Athaliah had been sleeping with Darius Dog and other men until one night, a thought crossed her mind. "If Peace finds out, it'll hurt him too much," she thought to herself. "He really does love me, I think." Just then, her mind wandered off to the fact that I would – while making love – keep telling her how much I loved her. Even while we were making love, I was focused on the love that I had for her and how good she had made me feel. So, she wondered and thought to herself, "If he finds out, it'll hurt him. He loves me so much, and if he finds out about me, he will be too hurt. He will be so hurt, and people will find out about what happened. They will find out about my business, and the word will then spread out to everyone. My daughters will know about what I did, and that will not be a good sight to see. I, in the end, will be put to shame. My name will be put to shame. I can't let Brian tell Peace that I had sex with him and his brother Bobby. I can't let him tell Peace that I had sex with any other man."

She voiced all of her concerns – all her thoughts and all the things that she was overthinking – to Vicki.

"Since you are going to have him killed," suggested the wicked sister, "Get a puppy. That way, when he's dead, your daughters can be comforted by the puppy. Hopefully, the puppy will have pretty eyes too.

Hopefully, it'll have prettier eyes than Peace does."

Athaliah said, "That's ideal… getting a puppy! It'll work too well in comforting the girls."

The following Saturday, Athaliah went to a women's meeting at the church. The speaker was First Lady Benjamin, accompanied by many other women. In that place, there was God present. Yet, in that place, there was also a woman who had the worst of intentions and the most extreme of issues, though disguised behind a face too pretty for the disastrous world to see. Nobody knew.

Athaliah was walking to her car after the meeting. She had faded off into thoughts of her own, created carefully by her mind to reflect upon the type of person she was and how her heart felt. She was brought back to reality by a car's incessant horn. A beautiful white Bentley had driven up. It was First Lady Benjamin who sat inside.

"Hello, how are you, Brother Peace's wife?" she remarked as she pulled down her window.

Athaliah was taken aback when First Lady Benjamin approached and actually talked to her. "I am fine, thank you," said Athaliah. "How are things going for you?"

She remained silent with a grimace on her face. "Follow me," urged First Lady Benjamin.

My wife got into her own car and did exactly what the First Lady advised her to do. They drove into a secluded area.

"What is going on?" the First Lady inquired.

My wife suddenly began telling her everything. "Peace is neck-high in debt. We cannot open a bank account because of his child support obligations. The last time we got one, they took the money that was in the bank account as well. It was not my fault that he had married before and did whatever he did. He cannot fly abroad either since he cannot get a passport. He cannot walk. He's been married two times before me. He has sold drugs. He has been to jail and served time. He has been with many women. He is no Peace. He keeps talking about how God told him that he was about to sign a multimillion-dollar contract deal. The truth is that he is just too old to rap, but he's too oblivious to that fact. He would be rapping with a cane soon. Rappers retire at his age, but Brother Peace is still talking about starting his career. He is also talking about traveling around the world to help people by doing his rap thing. He can't even help himself."

As she talked and kept talking, the First Lady just listened. Tears rolled down my wife's eyes, though no one but herself knew whether or not they were real. "I'm tired, First Lady Benjamin," she added. "I'm just so exhausted. It's been too much on me, and I cannot take it anymore. I don't think I can."

"Tell me just one thing," said First Lady Benjamin. "Yes?" my wife scrubbed away her tears.

"Do you love him?" asked First Lady.

"No," replied Athaliah instantly, almost abruptly, without even thinking.

First Lady Benjamin said, "Well, to tell you the truth, we lost a lot of money because of him. What happened to his multimillion-dollar contract deal that everyone was talking about?"

Athaliah explained how the CEO and many were arrested for embezzlement, extortion, and racketeering. "They were not paying the artists," said Athaliah. "Peace had been talking that mess for years... about his multimillion-dollar contract. He told me that he talked to God, and God told him that he was signing a big deal. God doesn't speak to him. He is a fake! He is not the real Peace! I'm the real Peace!"

"How so?" asked First Lady Benjamin.

"I never go through anything," replied my wife. "God has been blessing me. I get so many raises at my job, and I work hard for them. I get what I deserve. I have God on my side, and I know it. Peace doesn't have God by his side, but he is just too insensible to wrap his head around that fact. You see, I believe in sowing and reaping, and that's why I'm so blessed in my finances. I believe my husband is the devil, a cursed and a con man. Peace is a wolf in sheep's clothing. 'Peace' is not even his real last name; his last name was changed to 'Peace' from 'Barnes.' He has been saying that God changed his name for the end times to help the lost ones, the lost souls. He is not real. I believe God gave me my true husband now. He is rich and is in the medical field; he is from Jamaica, like my family's roots."

First Lady Benjamin was at a loss of words. Her brain stuttered for a moment, and her eyes took in more light than she had expected, every part of her going on pause while her thoughts caught up. She placed one hand on Athaliah's shoulder, "Well, Sister Peace, my husband, Reverend Benjamin, and I have a plan to play his testimony on our broadcast around the world three times a week. Did Peace also do a "Stop Gun Violence" rap music video called "Put That Gun On Up"?"

"Yes, he did," replied Athaliah.

"We are going to show that on our broadcast," said the First Lady. "We are going to make him famous, then the next thing you know, Bro Peace will end up dead. And we do a "Go fund me" for him and ask for donations for you and your girls. And just when we see millions coming in, we can share it together... you and

I."

With a certain image of dollar bills in the back of her head, Athaliah just smiled. She liked that plan. Athaliah said to First Lady Benjamin, "I have some gangster cousins. I'm flying them into Atlanta to have Peace killed."

"You already have plans to kill your husband!" she exclaimed, surprised. "I like that enthusiasm!"

"But there's a problem," complained my wife. "What?" asked the First Lady.

"It's costing $10,000," said my wife.

First Lady said to my wife, "Athaliah, you have nothing to worry about. I can bless you with half of that amount. Just give me your number and stay in touch."

"I sure will," said Athaliah, stepping out of the car.

Just as she stepped out, First Lady Benjamin said, "And need I mention… not one word to anyone."

"Of course, Lady Benjamin," my wife assured

her that she would keep her mouth shut.

"I need you to wait a bit," added the First Lady. "Don't go through with your plan just now. I'll give you the green light when it's the right time. You may do it then. Let's start playing the video of his testimony first."

Athaliah said, "Okay," and they both departed, going their separate ways.

Athaliah, of course, had to keep Vicki in the loop, so she called her and told her about all that she had discussed with First Lady Benjamin, ensuring that she left out no detail.

"Girl," Vicki said to Athaliah, "I told you. I told you that God is with you. You even have First Lady Benjamin helping you. This is God's help. This is how God works. Lady Benjamin is a woman of God, and she is helping you. So, I can say that God's way of helping you. Peace is the devil, and we have to take him out."

Athaliah needed extra money as sooner as she could because of Brian next door, worrying that he might tell me about her. So, Athaliah called Darius Dog and told him that she would help bring the drugs through the airport. She had accepted his offer, becoming a part of a story and crime much bigger than herself – a cartel. She asked him how much she would get paid, and Darius Dog gave her a very green answer. "5,000 dollars every time you take it through."

Darius Dog said to Athaliah, "We need to take your husband out. He will be in the way since we need to bring the drugs in bottles to your house."

Athaliah said to Darius, "We already have it handled.

The plan is in play, and it will all go down soon enough."

"That's my girl," said the man, who was too happy to hear that answer. "I heard. I talked with your sister, Vicki, about how you ladies are thinking of taking him out. My gangster bitches!"

Athaliah said, "No. I'm a good, devoted Christian woman."

Darius Dog laughed it off, "Anyway, you only

need to have sex with me and not that little buster."

"You're right, baby," laughed Athaliah. "When will I see you again?"

"This weekend," replied the man.

"I need you to have that beautiful pussy of yours wet and wide," said the Jamaican, "We need to put balloons of drugs inside it."

Athaliah cried, confused, "What do you mean?"

Darius Dog replied, "It's safe, Athaliah, baby. It's completely safe."

"Okay, babe," replied my wife to the man, "I trust you."

Athaliah had sooner gone out to get the puppy that she had been thinking about - my replacement. The moment she set foot in the house with that little puppy pressed tightly in her hands, the girls adored the puppy, and the puppy adored the girls and Athaliah as well. But for some reason, the puppy did not like me. It was scared of me. If I went downstairs, the puppy would rush into her tiny cage area. Athaliah did not like it when her puppy went into the cage every time I came downstairs. She seemed to prefer the puppy over me. Perhaps that was what had become of our love over time.

In the December of 2018, I got my right hip replacement surgery done, and this time, things did not happen much differently. Athaliah just dropped me off at the hospital for 3 days, and I was, again, asked if I had someone there for me, someone to take care of me while the hospital staff attended to their chores or other patients. I just told them that the loving wife just had some stuff to do, which was why she could not be here for me. In my mind, I wondered if she actually ever cared about me, if she still did.

The three days passed excruciatingly and slowly. There was nothing to do but lay there on the hospital bed with the smell – that I never grew a liking for – thinking about all that I could do with my wife when I was well and walking. Oh, how delusional I was!

As I got out of the hospital and got home, it did not take much time for me to recover fully. I was happy, and I was motivated to be well. I was motivated so that I could make my wife happier than I did when I could not walk. During my recovery period, there was an unusual knock on the door one evening. I received a box from Hospitality Parking Shuttle Service. It was from my job, and when I opened it up, there were some cookies and a note that said, "Get well soon, Mr. Peace." It felt too good to know that people at my job, much unlike my own wife, actually cared about me, that they were thinking about me. It felt too good. My wife, on the other hand, was taking care of her new puppy better than she was taking care of me.

Athaliah's father and his new wife soon moved to Atlanta. We had a little get-together, a housewarming party with a few of my in-laws, my daughters, and, of course, Vicki! Once again, my loving wife was nowhere around to be found. Everyone kept asking me where Athaliah was, but I did not know, in all honesty. I said to them, an excuse that would last only so long, "She'll be here after work." Little did I know! Athaliah was out with Darius Dog; Vicki knew it, but she did not reply – she simply smiled and chuckled each time I would say that.

Every time that Vicki was behind me, I could sense the presence of an evil spirit, as though my surroundings were damned ban dusted because of this presence. I knew that it was Vicki, the evil one, and I would turn around to her and just look at her, wondering what it would take for a person to become that bad. Each time I would look at her, she would move her eyes toward me, giving me a look that made me confused. That woman could literally chop me up and throw me off into the ocean in all its glory. I saw a demon in her face.

My daughters and I got home that night from Athaliah's father's get-together party. I asked her why she didn't show up, and Athaliah replied, "I had to work overtime again. Someone needs to pay the bills around the house, don't they? And since it's never you, it has to be me."

I said, "I work to help and provide for our home and family. Even when I couldn't walk, I was still bringing money in – cutting yards, pressure washing homes, or cooking for a party. Why are you talking in this way to me? I'm the one who helped you get that job that you are boasting about right about now. Did you forget what it took? Even when you had to go out of the state to train for eight weeks, I had to take offs from my job for a while to watch the girls as a stay-at-home father while you pursued your career. Do you have anything to say about that?"

Athaliah, without the courtesy of a reply, just ran downstairs to watch her TV programs that were clearly, very clearly, more important than I could ever be. This time around and for the time to come, I sensed a change in her. There were not just the emotional changes that I was endeavoring with her; there were also the physical changes now. She was looking different. There was just something about her face, her body, her expressions, her walking, her talking, and her mind that seemed too different, as though there was something that was holding her back, something that was making her sure to never talk to me again.

She already had a dark tone of the skin. Even though she was dark and beautiful, she had this dark aura on her face. She was looking older and getting darker.

Athaliah was watching a lot of television. The one that made me ponder was a TV series in which people endeavored to get away with murders. She had all of the episodes taped. She even had all of these crime episodes recorded and was watching them. When I came downstairs while she was watching her shows, she had her neck out like an ostrich.

"She genuinely enjoys these shows," I would tell myself. Now here I was, attempting to record my shows, but every time I attempted to watch Marriage Ministries, cheating shows, or the Healing Show, the recording was destroyed. I would question her why she kept removing my shows whenever I had great hopes and a strong want to view them. She would just say, "Oh, I don't like those shows."

Perhaps she did not like it because she herself was cheating on me. Perhaps that was a wound too open to put salt in. So, I would just crave for her to take my hand so that I could go to her and talk nicely... like the old times. Or perhaps by her not doing the things I liked, she was letting me know that it was not worth it, that it was not going to amount to anything good in life. Or perhaps all of it was just a reminder from God who wanted to tell me that I was not in the right place or with the right person. Perhaps he wanted to warn me and let me know that Athaliah did not have the best of intentions for me. She also mentioned that we did not need marriage counseling.

"Okay, then, what about the Healing Show to believe in me, aiming to walk and do all the chores again?"

Athaliah replied, "You are getting old. Your age is catching up with you. Nobody is going to sign you a multimillion-dollar rap contract deal... or any deal for that matter."

"It's over with you," she said to me.

"NO!" I yelled. "It's not! I'm called by God; I heard God about what He told me. I heard his voice as clear as day. I don't care what it looks like. I don't care what it feels like or what I hear! I'm Peace! I'm chosen!"

Athaliah just listened, and my heart broke. Yet, she just stood there, cold, feelingless, without emotion, and she just listened to me yelling and crying, holding back my tears. "I rebuke you, Athaliah. What's coming out of your mouth? I need to stop playing."

While I was going through my healing, it was time to crank up my faith with peace and with shalom.

Chapter 12

Shalom—Studying the Word 'Peace'

People gain a better, bitter, and deeper understanding from their life experiences. Having a variety of positive and negative experiences helps us develop our way of thinking; it broadens our perspectives and teaches us valuable life lessons that we must implement in the future. Life is lovely, and every moment is a celebration of being alive, but one must constantly be prepared to confront difficulties and obstacles. A person who has never faced problems in life will never be successful. Life is lovely, but it is not always simple; it has issues, and the task is to face them with bravery, allowing the beauty of life to work as a salve, making the pain tolerable during difficult times by bringing hope.

Memories fade away with time, someplace deep within our hearts. They never abandon us; they only keep themselves out of our sight for our own benefit. It must have happened to you randomly, catching you off-guard. That is it; those memories from deep within strive to claw their way into your memory. This is what it is called as time passes, situations change, circumstances grow, and life goes on. But there was still this one aspect of my life that I could not understand all too well. There was something about my life that was troubling me deeply, and there was nothing much that I could do about it. There was not much that I had power over. My wife. My dear, loving wife. Athaliah.

Child support was still taking its money from me, cutting my cheques in half. The IRS would come right after, collecting payments of its own, cutting my cheques further. I was still recovering from both of my hip replacement surgeries. The pain was still there to some extent. I was getting sympathy from no one. My coworkers were somewhat sympathetic and understanding, which came to be quite the surprise; my wife was neither sympathetic nor understanding, which also came to be quite the surprise.

And to make the matter more sadly interesting, Revered Lite Benjamin and First Lady Benjamin were still not talking to me. I, at first, thought that there was something wrong with them. But I was confused. At this point in time, however, there was no confusion. It was all evident and clear; they were not trying to conceal the fact anymore, the fact that there was something about me that bothered them, something about me that they did not like. I still did not know what I had done wrong. They were not acting right when it came to me; all else was just normal and routine.

Life is unpredictably unpredictable. Along the road, there are ups and downs. Many of us want to believe in God. It might feel easier when times are good. But it is much more crucial to trust God when situations are challenging. When circumstances feel wobbly and unpredictable, God's constant character may provide us with a solid foundation. For a time, life may appear to be going well. It was the same with me. My employment was fine, my life was entertaining, and my objectives, finances, health, and perspective all appeared to be positive. Then, out of nowhere, life had thrown a curveball. I had lost my job. I was betrayed by everyone I cared about at that time of my life. Things I once felt comfortable in were becoming unsteady and unsure. In these situations, I wondered.

How do you believe in God?

How do you believe that God is good?

How can you trust Him when you do not comprehend what is going on?

When you cannot see a way out?

Just then, my mind would take me back to the fact that He was there all along, watching, smiling, waiting, and planning. I remember Him talking to me. I remember what He had told me all that while ago. I remember how He had been the only one who was actually there for me.

So, I trusted God. I really trusted His word. And I had done that as a priority, over and above every single thing in my life. I knew I had heard God for myself. That was enough for me. That was more than enough for me.

The word that God told me was for me only and no one else. I knew it to be a spiritual battle, for we wrestle not against flesh and blood, but against principalities, against powers, against the rulers of the darkness of this world, against spiritual wickedness in high places. I had wanted my 'Peace,' so it was time to go to war, pray, and win.

I am a person who has always looked for ways to learn and has left behind no chance or opportunity that might end in learning or bettering my knowledge, be it from a man or from a dog on the corner of a street. I was a controversial guy who would much rather tell the truth, speak the truth, and want to hear about the truth, even if the lies may have sounded prettier and many worldly things may have come off of them. One thing I remember was how Reverend Lite Benjamin had prophesied over me. I did not know that he was prophetic lying, but I sure did take those words to heart, how it seemed too beautiful, and so, I kept it all closer to my heart. What I remember about that day was much more than just compliments that he did not mean; it was the fact that he said, "Wow, what a great name! Listen to it: Peace. Study it."

What had I to lose? So, I wondered, "Let's see what my name actually means. Peace. Shalom." So, I grabbed quite a few of everything that I could have my hands on. Dictionaries and Bibles were the least of them. I got Strong's Exhaustive Concordance books. I got Hebraic and Greek books. I got historical and religious books. And I really went at it.

What I came to learn was the fact that "Peace" wasn't just about being away from war or conflict. What I learned was the fact that you may be in a war to get to Peace. No matter how life is going, you are in the right place of shalom. Life is complex, and when one part of your life is out of alignment because of sickness, loss, a broken relationship, or anything else that may trouble you, your 'shalom' or 'completeness' break down. So, it is something that needs to be restored.

'Shalom,' as a verb, means 'making complete' or

'restoring.' 'Peace,' in Hebrew means, 'Shalom,' the exact translation of an English (Peace) to Hebrew (Shalom); it is the way the Jewish people greet the other person, a means to say "hello," "have a blessed day ahead," "have a prosperous day," "goodbye," or "may your day be blessed." It is a spiritual and ancient Hebrew greeting. When you say Shalom to someone out of your mouth, you are telling them to have a blessed and safe day. In Judaism and in the Hebrew language, when you say Shalom, you bring the blessings of God into your conversation or meeting.

Shalom is taken from the root word shalem, which means "to be safe in mind, body, or estate." It speaks of totality, completion, or a form of wholeness that inspires you to give back – to generously repay something in some way. There is no power in just saying hello and bye, but when you say shalom, you are speaking from a position of strength to a position of the same strength – not physical strength, but more spiritual and moral strength. So, then, I looked in the mirror and saw how this one five-letter word, Peace, in Hebrew, simply implies the entire six-letter word, Shalom. It was much as though a diamond, reflecting light in several ways, much more than the brain could humanly perceive.

Well, apart from that, shalom has multiple other meanings. Let's talk about them, shall we? The word, as I found out from the books and hours of research, talks about fairness, favor, comradery, greatness, goodness, health, and perfection. It was more of a means to say, "be at peace." As a word, it talks of Peace and prosperity, restfulness, safety, holiness, appeal, niceness, congeniality, agreeableness, satisfaction, pleasurableness, making ends meet, finishing, giving, selflessness, goodness, paying, repaying, performance, recompensating, reward, deliverance, offering, rendering, restitution, surety, restoration, wholeness, happiness, and much more.

It was at that instance that I realized what wholeness felt. It was as though a pie, sliced into eight, sitting peacefully over the kitchen counter. If there's a slice missing, the pie is not whole. So, for us to be whole, we need everything that is missing in our lives back in our hands, and that makes us whole. And that is how we like it. That is what makes us feel better about ourselves, being complete. Nothing missing. Nothing broken.

Then I went a bit deeper into my last name. I came across another meaning. It told me about how the word revolved around the destruction of the authorities that caused chaos. Whatever causes chaos in your life, 'Peace' is to destroy it – with the saying of shalom. But that happens not just by saying the word into existence but by actually and truly believing it. I went a bit deeper into the word shalom, then. I got to know that in Hebraic, you read the words, phrases, or sentences from right to left, not like we do it in English, from left to right. SHIN ש looks like teeth to crush or destroy. LAMED ל was a shepherd's staff voice of authority. VAV ו was a nail to hold things in place. MEM מ was the water moving the chaos and destruction away, destroying the authorities that connected to Chaos שלום.

The word, at this point, piqued my curiosity. I had just wanted to do good in the world and with my life, and that was why I had chosen the word Peace to be my last name. I had chosen it because God had told me to. But boy, I did not know what I was in for! So then, naturally, I went much, much deeper into the Hebraic word shalom, used in numbers to reveal a word. Then I saw something. '300' is hidden in shalom.

With SHIN, 300 means 'redeemed from death; you can't die, and no one can hurt you or kill you.' But wait a minute! I noticed in the Bible, Judges Chapter 7, Verse 7:

"The Lord said to Gideon, "With the three hundred men that lapped I will save you and give the Midianites into your hands. Let all the others go home.""

Gideon had 300 chosen men from God to defeat the Midianites of 120,000 men so that God could get the glory and not man. It was God's doing, just to use 300 men. But then, I remember reading about how Abram had 318 men, which meant the Gnostic Value of Christ and the famous. Abram defeated the four kings of the north with 318 trained men. He had trained all those men by himself, and Abram's name was later changed to

Abraham. Yes, it was changed because of his calling... just how my last name changed from Barnes to Peace! Because of the calling! Then I said to myself, getting more and more curious with each passing second, "Hold on a minute... King David had three mighty hound warriors who defeated eight hundred men in one encounter!"

As I was thinking about all that, it hit me out of the blue, "Hey! My birthday is September 30, and 30 means spiritual awakening and spiritual growth! That means... I'm ready to take the next step on my spiritual journey, and the angels are with me every step of my way!"

It was after that I realized that so many people's names and birthdates can mean a lot about what their future is going to be like, all determined to be by their names. By your birthday, you can find out who you are. Anyway, I then said, "Okay, then. I remember something else my mother told me."

When I was in my 30s, my mother told me this story when she found out she was pregnant with me in her old age. My mother was going to have an abortion. When she was about to do it, she heard God's voice, and He was the one who told her to not do it. "That child in your stomach is chosen. He has a calling for his life. He is redeemed from death."

It was at that point in time that I realized that there was still hope for me. With all the studying and the story that my mother once told me, I guessed that I would be alright, that I was going to be just fine, and that life for me was all going to be alright.

Numbers 6:24-26:

24: "'"The Lord bless you and keep you;

25: the Lord make his face shine on you and be gracious to you;

26: the Lord turn his face toward you and give you Peace.""

Jeremiah 29:11:

"For I know the plans I have for you," declares the Lord, "plans to prosper you and not to harm you, plans to give you hope and a future."

Isaiah 26:3:

"You will keep in perfect Peace those whose minds are steadfast, because they trust in you."

We create plans, but the Lord has the last say. We may believe we know what is right, but the Lord is the ultimate arbiter of our motivations. You will succeed if you share your plans with the Lord. Everything the Lord does has a purpose because of cause and effect. God can wait you out to see if you will repent and change your ways. If we sincerely love God, our transgressions will be forgiven; if we respect him, we will avoid sin. When we satisfy the Lord, even our adversaries become our friends. It is preferable to be honest and impoverished, rather than dishonest and wealthy.

John 14:27:

"Shalom I leave with you; my shalom I give you. I do not give to you as the world gives. Do not let your hearts be troubled and do not be afraid."

And that was when I realized. "WOW! The word Shalom is powerful!" Right now, I'm just giving you a taste of what I learned then by me studying and meditating on the Hebrew word shalom. I started seeing the results of the name Peace. Shalom is not just for me; it's for you just as much as it is for me. So, when you speak shalom out of your mouth, you are calling out the Lord to bring out better things in life. Shalom is for me. Shalom is for you. Shalom is for everyone. It is E-rated.

That understanding was followed by betterment in my life, all the downs slowly transforming into ups. It was getting better; my hips had been recovering at a better pace, and, therefore, I was walking properly. I was making the gym a part of my daily routine, and I was surely getting in better shape with each day that came to pass. I had resumed my much- awaited dance routines, and I was back at writing songs and making music videos that fit just well with the songs that I wrote.

I even wrote a song for my job titled as "Do The Hospitality Parking;" it was a tribute and means of appreciation for those who had remembered me in the hardest times of my life even though they were not entitled to do so, even when the law did not ask them to do so. They had sent me cookies that were too lovely and too heartfelt, and that was something worth thinking about, something just enough to make me happy and put a smile on my face that stayed there for quite some time.

During my healing process, I came to watch this TV series. In that, one of the characters had a record label and a smoothly-run business. It was a little drama and had gangster- type scenes, but, to me, it came as much of a means of inspiration and motivation. By watching it, I was compelled to have my own record label. It was a thought that seemingly crossed my mind and stayed there... on my mind. I was not able to forget that thought, and I kept thinking about it. Even if it were to come true, it would take some time.

Anyway, a few weeks passed, and life was surely turning for the better. It had previously knocked me down so very hard and left me with so many emotions and feelings of loneliness and destitution that coming back to normal felt like a supreme feeling, a feeling that made me think of myself as elite and God's chosen one. Well, my credit was getting better. I had paid off my taxes with the IRS, and that hefty burden was off of my shoulders. There was still the child support thing that hovered all the time over my head, yet there was nothing that I could do about it; I knew that it would stay there for quite some time.

With faith in my God, I decided to treat myself to a nice new car, something that I would love. I had seen this perfectly black Chrysler 300S, and it resembled the Batmobile way too much. With tinted windows and rims that sat seamlessly over the tires, the car was one to adore. It had a nice sound system, and that was something that I had surely looked for in a car. With favor from God and the dealership, I bought the car, and it sure seemed like it was the nicest car in the whole wide world. I modified it a little to my own taste – something that was necessary. I added a panoramic sunroof to it right after I brought it home. And just when I brought it home, I got compliments about it from everyone around, anyone who'd lay eyes on it. It was surely a feeling that I would never forget.

It was perhaps because of that car that my

relationship with my wife had gotten better. As soon as I brought it, her mouth dropped wide, and she loved it too, just like the rest of them. She loved sitting in it. It was perhaps due to the fact that she really actually liked that car or because of the fact that it made her look filthy rich – blinded by my love for her, I never really knew.

Soon after, I went to the DMV to get my tags. I was talking to the clerk, and I told her how badly I had wanted to have "Peace" on my license plate. She told me that it was already taken, and that made me quite sad. "Wow," I sighed, "I really wanted that on my car's license plate." Then, with faith and high hopes, I asked her, "Do you have 'Shalom?'"

She typed it in her system, and she browsed for a minute or so. I had my fingers crossed, and they uncrossed when she replied to me, "We have 'Shalom' available. No one has that nameplate."

"Really?!" I exclaimed, almost not being able to believe it. She told me that it was true.

I thought to myself, "All the Jewish and Hebrew people who live in Georgia, yet nobody has Shalom?

That's strange!"

"No one has it," she added.

"Can I get it?" I asked, too happy to hide it.

"It's all yours," she replied.

The devil shouldn't have ever let me get this license plate, yet I got it. So, now, I rode around and about with confidence and grit seeped into my veins, confidence, and grit that knew no ends and had no bounds. And, to sum it up perfectly, I felt as though I was a superhero straight out of a comic book. I was happy and jolly, and it was about time that I had some break from all the bad things that had, for so very long, prevailed in my life. With the blessed plate of 'Shalom,' I felt invincible and honored.

As I write this, I recall an instance that felt quite weird and miraculous to me. One time, I was driving around, going about the daily errands that I just could not escape. On the driver's side of the car, something came running and bolted into the window. It was a coyote. It kept trying to bust through my window, and there was nothing holding it back other than God's divine hand that had helped me in much too many ways and circumstances. Its sharp talons and teeth kept trying and trying to pierce through my window but to no avail. It once hit the window, fell down, and died. "Jesus!" I exclaimed out of exhilaration and relief. I pulled over, and a guy walked over to me, just ensuring whether or not I was all good. I told him that I was, in fact, all good. He asked again, still shaking, "Are you well, sir? A coyote just attacked you! Are you all right?" With a smile on my face, I told him that I was at peace because, in my heart, I knew that I was good. In my heart, I knew that it was God who was protecting me at all times, who was always there to look out for me. Well, since I had Him, whom else would I ever need? So, as I look back on that day, it feels like it was God's sign to tell me that He was looking out for me because I had my windows rolled up. It might not have been this good if my windows were down. Quite surely, if that had happened, I would not be here today to write this book.

Some time passed, and I took my daughters to a

birthday party – it was Vicki's mother-in-law's birthday party. Athaliah was supposed to join us right after work. We arrived at the place, greeting one another. Family and friends looked for her and kept asking me, "Where's your wife, Peace?" I assured them that she was about to be here right after she got free from work. In the meanwhile, Vicki called Athaliah to check in on her, too curious to know where she was and what had kept her for very long.

I, on the other hand, without a care in the world, danced all night with my new hips. My hips were better, and I could move my legs all that I wanted to.

"Darius Dog is in town," replied my wife, stressed out a bit. "I'm out with him."

"Okay," replied the wicked sister. "What's going on?"

"He has me bringing in drugs through the airport for him," replied my loving wife. "I had to keep the drugs in my vagina so that airport security cannot detect them. Darius Dog is such a smart man!"

"But I'm a bit scared," added my loving wife. "This is scary. But well, the money is quite good, you know?"

"I'm still upset that you couldn't make it to my mother- in-law's birthday party," replied the wicked sister. "Family and friends were looking for you with your family."

"Well, what can I do?" asked Athaliah. "Yeah," replied the wicked sister.

"Anyway," replied my loving wife. "Just keep an eye out on Peace. Keep me updated. Tell me when he leaves, okay?"

The wicked sister said just then, "Oh, I see Peace! His legs and hips are quite well. He's on the dance floor, shaking it up. And he is not stopping. He looks really good, I see...."

"Just text me when he leaves, please," Athaliah said to Vicki in a hard tone, hanging up the phone in her sister's face.

See, that night I noticed that Vicki was watching

me a lot. She was stealing looks at me, and I was weirded out by that, not sure what to think of it. Now, I was still trying to reach out to my loving wife on her phone, but she never answered any of my calls. I was growing worried about the whole situation, yet there was nothing much that I could do other than worry about the whole situation. Her family and everyone else kept asking me if Athaliah was coming, and I kept assuring them that she would be here shortly. I kept telling them that she was still stuck at work, but it sooner got to the point that it just felt like I was lying to them. So, time passed, and when they kept asking me again and again, I just told them that I did not know whether she was going to be here or not. I, on the other hand, decided to forget about it. I knew that she was a big girl and that she could take care of herself. And so, I did what I was supposed to do. I had a great time there, dancing with my new and replaced hips. That was something that I had looked forward to doing after I had fully recovered — dancing. It had been a really, really long time since I had done that.

The party was over, and I made it home with my daughters. Athaliah's car was in the garage, and I was shocked to see that. Why was she not picking up my calls? I walked into the house and went upstairs right away. I saw my wife there, and I asked her what I wanted to ask her, "Athaliah, honey, why you didn't show up for the birthday party?"

"I had to work overtime," Athaliah replied. "There were so many delayed flights, and I was caught up with that." Oh, if only I could figure out that she was lying to me. For some reason, I trusted her so much that whatever she would tell me, I would believe it right away.

"Are you all right, my love?" I asked.

"Yeah," she replied almost instantly. "I'm just tired, and I need to go to bed."

"Okay," I replied. "You do that, and I'm going to tuck the girls into their beds."

I leaned in to kiss her goodnight, but for some reason of her own, a reason that I did not know, she frowned when I kissed her. The next morning came, and I had woken up quite early. Since my legs were working just fine now, I decided to cut the yard and make it look good. While I was cutting the yard that I saw a car going really fast up my street. I saw two ladies in the car; one was driving the car, and the other in the back seat looked just like First Lady Benjamin. After I finished cutting the yard, I went into the house and said, "Athaliah, I think I saw First Lady Benjamin passing our house."

Athaliah looked strangely at me and exclaimed in fury and confusion, "No!! That was not her! You're just seeing things. You've gone insane!"

"What?" I thought to myself; I was startled, and I did not have any words to say. In my mind, I knew that it was First Lady Benjamin who was sitting in the backseat of the car.

Like any other, that week, too, passed. This week now, my neighbors were being put out of the house for some reason. It was the two brothers' family – Brian, Bobby, and their mother. I walked over to their side of the house and asked them, out of goodwill and courtesy, if everything was good if there was anything that they needed from me, any kind of help whatsoever. Brian and Bobby did not talk to me; they did not reply to me, and ignoring my existence, they walked away.

Without a mere word. I thought that interaction to be strange; I had never harmed them in any way. I just thought that we were cool; there was no bad blood between us, but then again, people are strange, aren't they? They are funny. How? They love you one day, and the next day, they try to stab you in the back.

Anyway, I just went into the house and said, "Athaliah, honey, the two brothers and their mother are being put out of their house."

"Yeah?" asked Athaliah with a wicked smile on her face, a smile that showed me just how happy she was. I, trusting her with my life, decided not to think much of it. Perhaps that was my mistake.

I said to myself, "My wife is not the same church girl anymore, is she? I really need to pray for her."

So, at the end of the night, I found myself praying

the word Shalom over everything. I knew how powerful the word shalom was supposed to be. But Jesus is our Prince of Peace. He came to restore peace within us. I knew that He was our Prince of Shalom. And that was enough for me. So, with all my hopes and faith in Him, I prayed the most heartfelt of prayers ever for my wife, the most beautiful of prayers. I prayed for her betterment. But then I prayed the Shalom, to destroy the authority that caused chaos.

Chapter 13

Assassination Attempts

The life that I had been entitled to live had changed. For the time being, it felt like it had changed for the better. Perhaps it was the calmness before the storm. Perhaps it was the silence that was followed shortly by the chaos that remained too unimaginable and too wicked. I did not know.

I had started to walk better. The gym was a major part of my routine. I was taking care of myself to the best of my ability, doing all that I possibly could. I was working my job full-time, and I was giving my all to it as well. I was also working on my music.

I felt as though I was a man born anew. It was as though life had turned around 180 degrees for me, and there was nothing wrong with it. I knew that it was what God had planned for me, what God had kept in store for me. Surely, I was feeling like a new man. Victory, my daughter, was rapping, too, following her father's footsteps. And it was when she would sing and rap that I would hold my chin high and my shoulders wide: she was that good! Surely, my baby girl was making me proud with each word that came out of her mouth in the perfect synchronization of rhythm and hymn. It was not just music; it was art. From such a young age, she was the artist that others – people much older and more mature than her – had only ever aspired to be. And so, she and I would spend most of our time in the studio, bonding. We would record her music there, and she was happy while making music.

I, as the father, was very proud of the girl that my daughter had been growing into. To make life better for myself and for those around me, those I cared deeply and vigilantly about, I was praying more and getting the revelation of peace and shalom in my body, mind, soul, and spirit. I could feel it with each step that I took to any given place. That was more than enough for me to hold on through this rather troubled course of life. Knowing that God was on my side was all that I would ever need, all that I ever needed. For that, I was happy.

It was just another day at work; I was at the Hospitality Parking at that time. I picked up two ladies from the airport, and I welcomed them on my bus. They told me that they were the marketing staff of Hospitality Parking, and I greeted them, telling them that it was quite nice to meet them.

I then said to them, "I have a rap song about our company."

"Okay," they replied, confused, not knowing what was just about to come their way.

"Check it out," I started the rap. "Yeah, yeah, here we go...."

They listened in closely, not sure how the song was going to be.

"Hospitality Parking is number one, now. You know, airport parking shuttle, we on the go...."

I kept rolling, and the words kept flowing, and there was no stop to the amazingness that they experienced on that bus ride. At the end of it, I could see that their mouths had dropped, and they were left in absolute awe at what they had just heard.

All they could say was, "Oh, my God, that is so very good!"

And so, they glanced at my nametag, and they cried, "Your name is Reece Peace...? Like the chocolate peanut butter candy!"

"Exactly," I laughed, and so did they.

"Do you have the words written to that song?" they asked me.

"Better," I said. "I have it written and recorded."

As the bus ride continued, we conversed and discussed all the possibilities that came with the song. We wondered about the things that we could do with the song. Hospitality Parking was talking about turning the song into a music video, and I was excited about that. How could I not be?

"Wow!" I whispered to myself. "Hospitality Parking is very well-known around the country and in many major airports across states. I am about to be famous! I am going to be famous!"

A few weeks passed, and I produced Victory's music video. That was something that I had been working on with my daughter, and she was making me prouder and prouder with each passing day. She did splendidly, and the whole song and video turned out to be amazing. The song was titled "Livin' Life." After all, that was what the two of us were doing, my daughter and I; we were livin' life. We were making music for people so that they could take some inspiration from the two of us, from the father and daughter duo, and live life a little. The song had a nice beat to it, and it came with encouraging words that flowed throughout the lyrics. So, quite naturally, it did well on YouTube; it had a lot of engagements and many likes. People commented on good reviews and liked everything about it. They praised my daughter for the song, and it was more than enough to make me happy.

Victory started doing shows and getting paid for it, and surely, I was proud of her, my younger daughter, Victory. Her younger sister was also happy for the big sister. Victory then recorded two more song in the studio. "Never Give Up" and "We Are Queens." But Athaliah wasn't around to support her. It mostly seemed like she was plainly jealous of us.

In front of Athaliah was too much success going about. She was watching how my life was turning for the better, and I, at the time, thought that she was happy about it. She could see that I was not just making a career for myself, but I was also managing and producing our daughter's music career. She could see that, and a part of me just hoped that she would be happy about it. Yet, despite the love that I felt for her, there was a part of me that rebutted to me about her happiness upon watching me succeed. There was a voice within me that emerged from the part of me that knew better; perhaps it was instinct, or perhaps it was a gut feeling, and it said to me, "She can't let you succeed. She doesn't want that."

Seeing the success in life that was coming my way in bits and pieces, she called her sister.

"It's time," Athaliah said. "It's time. We need to do it now."

"Do what now?" asked Vicki, the wicked sister, pretending that she did not know what her sister was talking about.

Athaliah ignored the question and added, "Peace is about to do a music video with his job. He is also working with Victory to get her a major deal. If he comes successful, the men I have been sleeping with will know who he is, and they will want to blackmail me. They will try to blackmail me and ask me for money to keep their mouths shut… you know, like this boy Brian who used to live next door. Also, if Peace gets famous, Darius Dog is going to leave me and also blackmail me for money. We need to do it now, Vicki. We are out of time, and we need to do it as soon as possible."

"What about waiting for First Lady Benjamin?" asked the wicked sister.

"I can't wait," Athaliah replied, getting eager and eager with every second that came to pass. "Let's do it now. Let's move forward without her. I cannot waste a second of my time knowing Peace is getting where he wants to be."

"You need to fly X-Ray and Filter to Atlanta with your buddy passes," suggested the wicked sister – it was more of advice from the wicked one to the one who was wicked in the making.

"No problem," Athaliah replied. "Oh, and I have the $10,000 to have him killed. I've made enough money with my baby, Darius Dog. I think that should be enough to get this job done."

"I need to get the guns to you," Vicki replied.

"Just mail the guns to my P.O. Box from New York," Athaliah replied. "I have a cute dog to take the place of Peace already. I would like for him to be killed before our 17-year anniversary. I have Darius Dog now. I have a new man in my life. I have the right man in my life, and he is my man. Peace wants to go to the beach with all of us – the daughters and me – trying to be a family man. We don't need him in our lives anymore. He is useless to us now."

At the end of that same week, Athaliah met X-Ray and Filter. She gave them the guns and the amount that she had been able to muster while working for

Darius Dog. This happened as soon as they had flown into Atlanta, Georgia. That was where a whole new chapter of my life began. This was where it all changed and when life's real twists and turns started to take place.

July had come, and it sure felt like God's gift. In the summertime, you could close your eyes, and you'd feel that the meadow and floral blooms were as much within you as they were around you, supporting your body upon the warm earth. In the late summer wind were the red flags of the poppy petals, a living masterpiece of nature. Though they would grow unnoticed by so many, they would be more to your eye than any artwork that would bring your likeness in beautiful strokes of the softest bristles.

It was 2019, and the year had been going smoothly for me – and seemingly, for everyone around me as well. The year, however, had come without any warnings about the year that was to follow after.

Back in the month of July, my daughters and I got into the car, and we headed to the editing company to edit and add the final touch to her music video. We came out of the garage, and we pulled out of the neighborhood. All the while, there was a little white car behind us, closely behind.

We arrived at an intersection. When we stopped at the red light, the white car stopped behind me as well. I saw two black guys at the light. There seemed to be something that felt wrong with the guys, but I was not too sure of it. I wondered what bad could happen in the middle of the day when everyone was watching.

The light turned green, and I headed forward to make a left turn. Soon before I knew or realized it, there were noises that grew louder and louder. It was as though a warzone; there was shooting all around. Bullets flew in patterns, and I jumped over my girls, trying to protect them before I could protect myself. With my foot jammed at the gas pedal, I shouted, "Get down! Get down!" My daughters' shouts and screams rang in my ears, mixed with the voices of the people who were around us, running in all and each direction, followed closely by the voices of guns that emptied with each microsecond. I screeched the car off of the road and got us to a safe apartment building around the corner of the block. "Are you all okay?" I asked my daughters, making sure that they were not hurt.

They were scared, yet they were strong. "Yes, yes, daddy, we're okay," each of them got up and replied.

I then got out of the car and checked for any bullets that might have pierced through the car. There were, fortunately, no bullet holes; I could not see any. Just then, after checking in on my girls and my car, I called 911 and said to them, "I believe a small white car just got shot up. It was behind me, and I sped away from the scene." Upon their inquiry, I told them the location of the happenstance, the place that felt like a mere warzone.

While waiting for the police to show up, I called some of my neighbors and asked them if they had heard that shooting within the timeframe of the last ten minutes. They assured me, confirming that they had, in fact, heard the sounds of bullets and guns going on. "It sounded like a warzone," they said.

We, however, did not let the bullets and the

trauma that followed let us hold us back. And so we headed to the video editing company. We told them about the distressing and Godforsaken encounter that we had come across just a while ago. With happiness and a sigh, we told them that we had managed to survive that. I told them how I believed that they were shooting at the white car behind me, but the behavior of the editor and his wife changed when they heard what I had just said; they were acting so very strangely because they were thinking that someone was shooting at me. But I knew they were not shooting at my daughters and I; we did not have those kinds of enemies.

We were editing my daughter's video, but the editor was going too fast; it felt as though he was rushing it. It did not look like he was doing it like he wanted to do it. It felt like his mind was preoccupied. He finished it sooner, and we left that place. The ride home was not too fun; everything reminded us of the warzone that we had escaped from earlier, and that was not a good thought to entertain. My girls were scared.

As we got home, we saw that my wife was not

home at that time; I texted her, "Hello," followed by another text that said, "My daughters and I came close to being shot during a shooting in the neighborhood. We are okay. We made it home safe."

Athaliah panicked as she looked at my text, far away from me. So, she ran to her confidant in crime; she called Vicki. She also called the shooters whom she had hired, X-Ray and Filter, her cousins. She was trying to see what had happened. She could not figure out what had just happened.

Athaliah cried and yelled, "You guys did everything wrong! My daughters were in the car! You could have killed my daughters! And what the hell, why in the hell is Peace still alive?! Just kill him! Where's the money that I paid?!"

The shooters hung up the phone; they did not want to deal with someone who was so very sensitive to the topic. Now, only Athaliah and Vicki were on the phone. Athaliah was still crying, upset about what had happened, and concerned about what was going to happen. She was unsure of the future, like any other person, still wondering how she was going to get me killed.

"What just happened?" asked my loving wife. "What now?"

"The guys don't know how they missed," said the wicked sister. "It was impossible to miss. They said that they both shot the driver's side of the car, and they were just six feet away. They are the guys who never, ever miss. They don't know how he survived or even how they missed the whole car. They didn't know, however, that your daughters were in the car. His windows were all tinted and dark, and anything inside could possibly not be seen from the outside. It just doesn't make sense."

My loving wife replied to her wicked sister's notions, "Praise God that they didn't kill my daughters. That's probably why Peace survived it: God was trying to save my daughters, who were also in the same car. God saved my daughters."

Had she not realized that in this aspect of her life and in this idea, there was nothing that related to God? Perhaps it was the dumbness in her that did not realize the fact that killing was not encouraged by God. In her selfishness and impiety, she had forgotten the fact that killing was one of the biggest sins known to man, that it was something that has led men and women to eternal damnation in hell. When she knew that her daughters were safe, she was being all religious. Perhaps there was a demon – or many demons – that had possessed her.

"I'll just wait for First Lady Benjamin's call," replied my loving wife after giving it a thought.

"Keep playing like you love him," advised the wicked sister. "If he wants to go to the beach and pretend like a happy family, do that. Go to the beach. Take photos with him. Play the role of a good wife. Play the good mother. Play the woman whom he fell in love with and the woman who fell in love with him. In the meanwhile, we will try and come up with something else – another plan, probably. We will soon try again."

Sooner, the beach trip's time arrived. Athaliah was distant, and she did not seem as though she was having a lot of fun. She was laughing a little less and smiling a lot less. She just sat on the beach chair, looking like a zombie with this big black hat and black clothes, looking like a witch. It was very weird, but I let that slide. I did not care about that. I had planned that day for fun and for family, and there was nothing that was going to hold me back. So, I decided that I was going to enjoy myself along with my daughters. I wanted to go swimming with my new hips, and I wanted to play with my daughters. I noticed that she kept staring at me with a look in her eyes that seemed so very strange.

It had been quite some time – a few days – since I had seen that same look in her eyes. There was something different about that look, but I just could not pinpoint what it was that was so different about it. I kept wondering, but I could not figure it out. There then came a time that I let myself move on from thinking about what that look meant and concentrated on having a fun time that my daughters and I were going to remember for too many days to come. I didn't pay it no mind. I just kept having fun with my daughters in the water.

Sooner came October of 2019, and the big music video shoot with Hospitality Parking had arrived closer.

When I got there, it looked like a major movie set.

"Wow!" I was caught off-guard. Surprised, I wondered if it was, in fact, the little song that I had written, rapped, and recorded that had brought all these people together. I wanted my daughter Victory to be in the music video, and that was something very important to me. I was repeatedly calling Athaliah to hurry up and bring her to the music video set. Apparently, there was some hold-up or the other that made her late.

Ms. Terry, the producer and chief of staff of Hospitality Parking, wanted to meet my wife. She had waited too long to meet her, wanting to see the hype since I had, for so very long, talked about her in the highest regard.

She asked me, "Is your wife coming?"

"Yes," I replied to her. "She's coming to drop my daughter, Victory, off. Victory wanted to be in the video for the longest."

Ms. Terry replied, "I just cannot wait to meet your wife and daughter! I have heard so much about them from you. I want to meet them in person finally."

With the passage of some time, my wife showed up at video shoot, and I took Ms. Terry to the car.

She and I walked up to the car, and Ms. Terry came to my wife. They hugged each other through the window.

Ms. Terry said, "Look at your husband… he's a big star and all! He's about to be famous! Are you proud of him?!"

"Mm-hmm…." replied my loving wife, just nodding her head up and down without uttering a word in agreement. I could see that there was a frown on her face, and I was sure that Ms. Terry noticed it too. That was something that made me wonder, thinking whether my wife was actually happy to see my success. I, at times, truly, felt like I did not have my wife on my side, and that feeling came along with thoughts of loneliness that pierced through my heart like many burning arrows shot at me – all at once.

Some time passed, and the Hospitality Parking

music video was a major and significant success. It was the start of my magnificent career. It was a rap and dance music video. And boy, did I dance!

I danced as though there was no worry that I saw in my life – not now and not ever. There was no pain in my hips, and I knew in those instances that it was not the treatment that had fixed me; rather, it was God who had really healed me.

There was a time through the day that we were shooting many takes. My hips and legs saw cramps, and I could not do any more dance moves. I tried to play it off, pretending like I was fine and that there was nothing hurting me. My daughter, Victory, noticed that there was something wrong with me; she noticed that I was not doing too well. She walked up to me and said, "Daddy, are you okay?"

"I can't move my legs and hips," I replied. "I have some kind of pain or cramp."

My beloved daughter had learned her ways of life from me. So, she put her hands on both of my legs and prayed to God, saying, "Lord, heal my father! Lord, hear my prayer: heal my father!"

At that instance, with a smile on my face, I just closed my eyes and just concentrated on what my daughter was praying for. After she finished praying, the pain was gone. It was as though it never even existed in the first place. I was healed, and there was no doubt that my daughter was gifted. There was no doubt that God listened to us from the heavens above.

I said to my beautiful daughter, "Victory, you have the anointed of God working around and for you. I'm healed, Victory! I'm healed!"

My beautiful daughter replied, "Yes, daddy, I believe in prayer the same way I watch you pray for people. They become healed right away, and that is my motivation when I pray for something."

I was so very proud of her. She and I hugged, and we went back to dancing for the music video. We worked through the day, and we worked when the night fell. The most important thing in our lives was that video, it seemed. It was a very hot day, and there was no sign of any thunder or storm. We worked through the day, and we progressed, making progress.

Later that night, a strong storm sought and threatened to damage the shoot and the whole setup. It began to pour rain, and the winds became tougher, harsher, quicker, and heavier. I yelled out as I peered directly into the clouds that held the storm, "Peace! Be still!"

Trust me, it was a matter of minutes before the storm came to a halt; there was no sign of it anymore. We were all sweating while we worked on the video shoot. The storm gave us a nice cooldown; we all needed it quite desperately. You see, the devil always tries to mess up the things that you have put your head and heart to. He always tried to make things that you love to go to waste. Due to prayer and a pure heart, what was meant for bad turned into something very good. The storm caused a nice cool breeze, and that was all the natural refreshment that we frantically needed.

Sooner, we were done for the day, and we went home to straighten our backs before we set out on the course of our lives with the beginning of the day that came next. When the video came out, it received many hits on YouTube. We even won the best AVA Digital Gold Award for Original Music in a Video Campaign.

The year passed, and it made way for the start of a new decade. 2019 did not end on such good terms, though we thought it did. We welcomed 2020 with arms wide open; had we known what 2020 was going to bring for us, we may never have been happy about its arrival. The pandemic was the most common and widespread news of the year, and it remained throughout. The filthy and untreatable coronavirus, Covid-19, had been killing people left and right, and there was nothing that could be done about it. No scientist was proving helpful, and no research was helping to save any lives. All that helped was staying indoors. So, because of the imposed lockdowns and economies that broke and fell to the ground, businesses were shut down, and people found themselves unemployed.

It was a scene of hell, and unemployment had skyrocketed. Then, the government started giving out $2,000 cheques to those who were unemployed. I, however, could not get one. I was one of the many men and women who could not get their cheques. Why? It was because of child support. This made me so very upset. I was unemployed, and I could not get a relief cheque from the government. I cursed this system, this biased and indifferent child support system; it was so unfair and prejudiced toward us men and some women as well. I was tired, and I was ready to give up this time. This time around, unlike the other times, it was not like you could just walk out and seek jobs around the place. I could not take it anymore.

My loving wife, Athaliah, would see me, and she would know that I was so very upset. She, however, had gone to her own level of indifference and inhumanity. She would never come to comfort me, let alone help me. It felt as though she never loved me. It felt as though I was not her husband, as though I was just a stranger whom she had daughters with – that's about it. Through all of it and more, she saw me struggling, finding it hard to hold on to dear life, and she let me struggle by myself. She did not even ask me if I needed a glass of water, and that came as quite a worrisome thought in my head.

I was tired of dealing with this child support system. I called them, and I told them that I could never get ahead. I asked them why they were doing this to me. I was seriously worried and confused, not understanding why they had been so unsympathetic and uncaring. "Why are you guys taking everything from me?" I asked them, on the verge of having a mental and emotional breakdown, still holding back my tears.

The caseworker replied, "You own the state money, and you own Doris Scott."

I replied, "How do I own the state money? I didn't have a baby by the state!"

The caseworker said, "Come down, Mr. Peace. The only thing you can do is see if Doris Scott will forgive you of the debt. Otherwise, you just have to pay the money that is asked of you one way or the other."

I hung up the phone and called Doris Scott. As she picked up the call, we talked about walking in forgiveness for my daughter Brenda. Doris Scott told me that she was never getting any payments; they had just stopped sending her the money that they were taking from me. That came out to be much of a surprise.

I said to her, "Child Support Services has been taking the money from me all this time. You were not getting any money?"

"No," replied Doris, "I thought you paid it all off."

"No," I replied.

I had found something immoral, and I knew then that Child Support Services were just evil; they were all about the money and did not care about the recipient or any of the children that it was supposed to help. Doris did what she had to do with the paperwork; she had forgiven me of the debt, and she had done that quite a long time ago. I paid the state their money, and yes, I was finally free from Child Support. I praised God with a sigh that talked too deeply of my relief.

The first thing I did was get myself a personal bank account and a corporate bank account. I was so excited about my new bank account. I would just go and hang out at the bank. I liked the way, when I walked in, the bankers would say, "Welcome, Mr. Peace." I was excitedly exhibiting my new checkbook to my wife. I asked her to support me in writing my first million-dollar cheque - all by faith. Her hand was shivering as she began to write, and she was unable to concentrate.

"Athaliah," I asked, "are you alright?"

With excitement and glee, I plucked the pen from her grasp and penned it myself. My wife did not appear to be in a good mood; she appeared to be sick or fever-stricken in some way.

"Babe," I advised her, "go lay down. It seems like you are about to pass out." I kept checking in on her, ensuring she was good.

With the passage of time, my credit score recovered significantly, and I established my own record label. However, when I was filling out paperwork for my company, Peace Vision Global, I heard the voice of the Holy Spirit declaring to me, "Add a movie label to Peace Vision Global."

I replied, "Okay, God, a movie label too? I'm moving on up!"

I was talking to my wife, and I told her, "Babe, since I got this record label and now movie label, I need a movie to think of and write." Athaliah, again, looked as if there was no reason for her to be happy. She looked as though my happiness was her reason to frown, as if my success was not her success, as if, in fact, it was her downfall.

Later that year, in October, I was chosen to be in a movie. I played a dancing bartender in the series, serving drinks. I had favor with the director of the movie, and the favor was a blessing when the director said, "Reece Peace," instead of "Action," when my part was played.

I studied the film crew. The set provided me with ideas and expertise. I studied the position of the cameras, and even the director. I said, "Yes, I can do this. I can write and direct my own movie one day." The next thing you know, I was applying for a passport. And, yes, I received it in the mail weeks later! I ran around the house like I had won the lottery that pronounced me as a billionaire. I was telling my wife that I could now go around the world. I was overjoyed, and I was delighted. I could even attend her sister's daughter's wedding in Jamaica, and that was something that I had been looking forward to.

"God did it," I exclaimed to her.

All over the house, I was worshiping Jesus. Athaliah was no longer smiling. "It's about time," she remarked simply.

Athaliah called Vicki again the next day, and she told her, "Peace got his passport. Now, he's talking about coming to the wedding in Jamaica."

"What?!" replied Vicki, not believing that it was possible.

"He can't," rebutted my loving wife. "He cannot come! Darius Dog is coming! Peace needs to die now! All these blessings are coming to him now! I can't let him succeed in life! He will find out that I cheated on him, and he will divorce me! I cannot have that happen.

I cannot let it. He might end up with another woman, having children with her in some big mansion, and living like a billionaire! He needs to die... now! Right! Now!"

Reverend Lite Benjamin's broadcast welcomed my testimony with open arms as November came. People I knew saw it, and they were in love with it. "Peace," they said, "we saw you on television about your testimony, and it's really good!" I said, "I know." It was true; the testimony was, in fact, really good. The testimony video, before I knew it, was playing around three times a week, and that was something worth mentioning. I was happy. Life surely was turning a corner for me.

First Lady Benjamin, around that time, contacted Athaliah, and she commented, "The time has come for us to do it. Are your guys ready?"

"Yes," replied Athaliah, explaining to First Lady Benjamin how she had already tried to have me killed.

"What happened?" asked First Lady Benjamin.

"My cousins didn't get him," my loving wife

replied. "They didn't know how to shoot right."

"What?!" examined First Lady Benjamin; she was not happy at that. "You already did it without my help? Is there going to be an issue this time?"

Athaliah said instantaneously, "No!"

That was enough to convince First Lady Benjamin that it was not going to go wrong this time around. And so, First Lady Benjamin gave Athaliah $5000. The rest of it was arranged by Athaliah herself since she had been working for Darius Dog, transporting drugs through the airport. Around that time, perhaps right around that week, my loving wife flew in Maniac and Skillet with the help of her buddy passes.

It was two days before Thanksgiving Day that I was out looking for some sweet potato pies. No store was offering what I was looking for, and that had me frustrated and exhausted. From one store to another, I kept looking, and I just went throughout the town, but there was nothing good to be found. Something happened in the last store I went to. As I walked out of the store, still frustrated at the fact that I just could not find my favorite pie, I walked to my car. As I was walking, I felt the shadow of a person walking right behind me. He was quite close behind me, and that was not the most comfortable of feelings I have felt.

"What's up?" I asked, turning around.

"We must be going the same way," he replied. "…towards our cars."

"We must be," I concurred. By that time, I had also noticed that the guy behind me was quite nervous and shaken. I was a devoted servant of God, so I did what I knew best. I turned around.

"Do you need a prayer?" I asked him.

"Yes," he screamed even without thinking. "Pray for me."

"Have you been born again?" I asked him.

"I can't get born again," he replied.

"Why?" I asked, curious.

"I worship a different god," he replied, and that was not enough to hold me back from praying for that person.

"Yes, you can," I contradicted. "You're about to know Jesus. You're about to be a Christian. Your life will lighten up in ways that you simply could not have fathomed before."

"Save me, sir," said the man.

And so I grabbed his hand, and while I was giving him the repentance prayer, there came a guy running toward the two of us. This guy had the same look on his face as the guy whose hand I held. In his hands, however, was a bag, and he was seemingly trying to pull something out of the bag. Skillet, the guy I was praying for, let go of my hand and embraced the other guy into a hug, saying, "No." He had said that out quite loudly, and I did not know what was happening around me. I was quite unaware of the magnitude of the events until sometime later.

Skillet said to him, "He's praying for me. He's getting me saved. I believe that you should get that too. You should get prayed for and saved too."

Maniac, the other guy, agreed to it, and I talked to them about the religion that I so devotedly followed and the goodness that Jesus had held, the goodness that remained to this day and would remain for the next to come.

There was another older guy who saw me praying for the two of them, and he joined us too. And so, instead of two, I prayed for three guys. Instead of my favorite pie, I taught the goodness of the Lord to two guys, and that was something that felt much better than the much-desired pie. That very evening, those guys received Jesus Christ as their personal savior.

Whispering to each other, the two guys walked away, and the old man went his own way. As I saw them walk their own way, I walked on my own, getting in my car. As I sat in the car, there was a sense of happiness and fulfillment that prevailed, a feeling that reminded me of the goodness of the fact that I had just helped three guys get born again. Happy and jovial, I drove my car into my garage and turned the engine off. Just then, I heard something extraordinary, a voice that was divine, a voice that did not exist in this world. I knew that it was the Holy Spirit who was talking to me and said in a much clear voice, "The guys you got born again, they were trying to kill you. They were after you, and they were there with the intention of gunning you down."

I jumped out of my car; it had all made sense now. That was why the guy was creepily following me in the parking lot! That was what the other guy was pulling out of his bag, a gun! And that was why he let go of my hand and embraced his partner in a hug and cried, "No," so very loudly.

"Oh, my God," I cried to myself. My Lord had saved my life through His own ways, and I could not be any more grateful.

Running inside the house, I gathered my breath, and I looked at my wife, eager to tell her how I had escaped the darkening claws of death yet another time – of course, oblivious to the fact that it was her behind all of it. As she saw me, she had this strange look on her face, almost as though she had seen a ghost, a paranormal being. The phone that she had in her hand slipped to the floor. She was sitting at the table with my daughters.

"Honey, I was almost killed today," I said. I told her the full story of all that happened – the guy who walked behind me, the guy who grabbed something out of his bag but was stopped, the older guy, how I prayed for all of them, and how the Holy Spirit told me that they were after my life.

"NO!" exclaimed my loving wife as she jumped up from her chair, almost tumbling down. She ran over to the kitchen sink; it felt like she was about to throw up.

Victory, my dear 15-year-old, ran to her, hugged her, and said, "Mommy, I'm scared."

My other younger daughter, at this point, had stopped eating, and she looked as though she was fear-struck; she was.

I, on the other hand, a man blinded by the shadows of love, thought that perhaps my wife had jumped and exclaimed like she did because she was worried that someone had tried to kill her husband. I thought that she had done that because she was happy for me to be alive because she could not have seen the daughters grow up without their father. I said to her, "Yes, honey, God saved me from being killed."

Athaliah just stared me right in the eyes, and teardrops started to trod down her eyes and onto her cheeks. She was staring at me with tears in her eyes, and I added, "Yes, honey, once again, God saved me."

The next day came, and I was simply happy to be alive, all at the divine mercy and grace of my God above me. Athaliah was, however, a bit too confused, still not being able to figure out how her husband had survived yet another attempt at his life. She wondered why and how the guys were just unable to kill me. First Lady Benjamin and her sister Vicki were trying to reach her, but she was not answering her phone. Athaliah was fasting and praying to God about the course of events now. She was asking Him for guidance on her blood-stuck journey, a mission of mayhem. Little did she know that her prayers were not reaching God because of the evil that was instilled within her heart, the evil that she harbored within her very self.

Sooner came December, and we, of course, as any other family, awaited Christmas and the holidays. It was December 2020, and I was still working on my music, aiming for the stars and beyond, aiming for miracles to take place. I could vividly see the presence and dominance of God in my life. I saw that God had blessed me in ways that I could not imagine, and with every beat of each song ever created, I would pay my utmost gratitude and heartfelt thanks to him.

At that point in time, I could tell that there was something that was going to happen to me, something big, something that I had always been looking for. I could just feel it in my bones, and that was something worth going through, that feeling. I knew that something extraordinary was about to happen to me. A record deal or a movie deal – it could have been anything. I knew something was coming.

I had started my own company, Peace Vision Global, and I was mainly just looking for a record label. But then, just at the right time, I heard the Holy Spirit say to me, "Add a movie label to the company." I didn't want to be signed by a company anymore; in fact, I was ready to sign artists and make movies of my own. I had amounted to something, and that was all because of God, all thanks to God.

I would usually tell Athaliah that I needed a movie, something big, something different for the world to see. Now that I knew that God was about to bless me even more, I wanted to go look at new houses so that I could set myself up properly in an office, a studio to record the artists that I was going to produce and manage, a place for the people, the community that I was going to work with. Amidst all that, my faith had skyrocketed, and there was nothing bad about it; I loved it.

I was seeing my testimony video being played on Reverend Benjamin's broadcast show. The Holy Spirit was urging me to have it stop playing since my name and business name was trademark. I called my attorney to have them not to play that testimony of my family and I anymore. Still not knowing what was really going on, my lovely wife, the one who's trying to have me assassinated, is on there with me. But the Holy Spirit knew what was going on. My attorney took care of business and had my video stop playing.

I finally resigned from the Planet Dome Church; I believed that my time at that place was up. God had chosen a different path for me, and He was showing me that. I had to follow that. And so, I followed his prescribed path to see myself with the greatness that no one had ever seen before.

I started going to a new church called New Chapel; there was a nice pastor there, and the church members were really good, honest, and modest people. At this church, there were more white faces that I got to see as compared to the black ones, but that was not a bother to me: I always believed all of us to be one family since we had all shared the same color of the blood that ran through veins. Athaliah also resigned from Planet Dome Church to join my daughters and me at New Chapel. But really, in all honesty, Athaliah was just keeping an eye on my comings and goings. The trouble was that, at that time, I did not realize that the situation was such. I believed that she was going there because she wanted to be with me.

A few days later, I was outside in the backyard, burning up all my debt papers from child support, IRS, and every other debt that I had to once suffer from. Athaliah returned home after work. She was staring at me while I was burning up papers in the barbecue pit in the backyard. She had a witchy expression on her face, as if she was not delighted with my happiness; she had been acting this way for a while. But I did not mind because I was out of debt from child support, and my credit was fine. I had a passport that allowed me to travel across the world. I was also looking forward to attending Vicki's daughter's wedding in Jamaica.

I went out to run errands and stopped at a petrol station to fill up my car. When I stepped out of my car, I noticed a large, hefty man holding the door open. As I got out of my car and started walking to the door, he walked in after me. I said, "Sir, you were holding the door for me all that time."

"Yes," replied the big guy.

"Do you do bodyguard work?" I asked him, and then I said, "You are a really big guy. I just started my record and film label, and I would love to have a bodyguard, someone of your size, around my company so that I know my business and I are in safe hands."

"No," he replied. "I don't do bodyguard work."

I replied, "Okay."

He had this Pearl color on him that made it hard for me to determine to tell what kind of race he belonged to. He had strong shoulders, which followed his huge neck. He looked like he was somewhere around 10 feet tall – he had to be.

He went into the store, and I went to pay for my gas. After I finished pumping gas. I thought to myself, "At least I should have given him my business card just in case he changed his mind about being my bodyguard." And so, I waited in front of the door for him to come outside, but he did not come.

I thought to myself, "He must be in there still shopping for stuff." I went back inside to give him my business card. I was looking everywhere for him. I was wondering where this guy had gone off to. He was the biggest guy in the store. No one can't lose him. I said, "That's weird! The biggest guy in the world, and I lost him inside this little store." I went back to my car. I set for a while to see if he was coming out anywhere. He never appeared. "That was an angel," I said to myself.

As life calmed down there for me, life in Jamaica was quite a bit different. There was something else going on. Darius Dog was mad; he was at one of his houses with his entourage, his gangsters, and his killers, breaking glass tables and trying to figure out why this little nigga was not dead.

"Let me show you how easy it is to kill someone," Darius Dog grabbed his gun that was tucked into the back of his pants. Right there, he shot and killed one of his men. All the other men jumped up in fear, their legs shivering.

Darius Dog added, "You see how easy that is?"

Right then, the man called for Athaliah, asking her, "Do you still have the buddy passes?"

Athaliah said, "Yes, honey, I have two more left. I already use 4 of them to fly the other guys to Atlanta from New York, those who failed to kill my husband, Peace."

Darius Dog replied, "I'm bringing my best guys, Heart Attack and Beast Boy. They don't miss."

Athaliah did not see that as a request, and she had surely placed her utter trust in that man. She, before long, got them over to the United States from Jamaica; it was not too difficult for her.

Athaliah and I decided to go have an early breakfast one day at the lovely restaurant in Atlanta, Georgia before we went looking at houses. I could tell that God was about to bless me with my dreams. There were simply too many miracles taking place for me. I realized how the windows of heaven had opened for me. I'm out of debt from child support. I had a personal bank account as well as a business account for my new company, Peace Vision Global. And, sure, I did have a passport that allowed me to travel throughout the world. God was planning something. He had some exciting ideas for me. He had some good plans that He kept in store for me.

Before we left, Athaliah texted the guys to let them know where we were and where we were heading. Athaliah and I had a fantastic time when we arrived at the restaurant. While we were eating, I was giving her my love rap speech, telling her everything she wanted to hear, all that sounded like music to her ears. I believed that she was happy.

Just then, I said something I thought I would never say in my life, "Athaliah, honey, I love you so much that if you had ever cheated on me with another man, I would still love you. If you have cheated on me, tell me right now, and I will forgive you."

Athaliah gave me an odd expression as if she was going to weep. "No, honey, I have never cheated on you, and I never will," Athaliah answered. I leaned across the table and kissed her.

Now, I think the Holy Spirit directed me to say that in order to give her an opportunity to repent and apologize to me, her lawfully wedded husband. I had no idea she was cheating on me or attempting to murder me; the Holy Spirit did.

We were shooting photographs together, but it was only a game for her to pretend she liked me. She would see crime and murder mystery shows and realized she may get images of me after I died. She had learned just how to hide her truth and act like she was truly happy with me. The photo would look like she did not have anything to do with my death.

As we finished eating and taking photos, we went outside to the car, but Athaliah rushed to the back of the car. Just then, I saw two strange guys bolting towards the restaurant, their eyes set on me; they were approaching my car.

I just stopped them right away and asked them a question that was going to change the rest of their lives, "Can I pray for you and get you born again? That way, you will receive Jesus as your personal savior."

"Yes, sir," they replied. "Please do that."

I prayed for them, and they received Jesus as their

savior. I hugged them, turned around, and walked to my car. The guys, too, walked away. I saw Athaliah, and there was something strange that went on with her face, the look on it. She had on her face this frown as if she was about to cry and break down. Perhaps she cared for me too much. Perhaps she could not bear the fact that there were people trying to kill me. At least, that was what I thought. And so, I ran up to catch her before she fell.

"Are you okay, honey?" I asked her.

"Honey, you are a good man," she replied. "I don't deserve you," tears rolled down her eyes. "You love getting people saved, and you love praying for them. You love telling people about Jesus."

I thought she was just crying to see how Jesus in me just saved those two men, but I didn't realize that those were Heart Attack and Beast Boy from Jamaica – who had come with the sole purpose of assassinating me in broad daylight, right in front the restaurant, in front of my wife, in front of all these people. I guess they were supposed to run off, and Athaliah was supposed to be crying over her dead husband's body. All the news was interviewing her, her wicked sister, Vicki, and First Lady Benjamin were ready to set up the GoFundMe to raise millions over her dead husband. Yet, the fact remained: God had saved me... once again.

But like I said, I remained oblivious to all that was happening to me. I did not know that they were supposed to kill me. I guess I was lost in the presence of Jesus.

We were driving out to go look at the houses after that, and Athaliah was very quiet. She didn't talk too much, and she was looking very funny, as though she had seen a ghost again.

Athaliah looked at me and just started crying.

I asked her, "Honey, are you okay?"

She just asked for some tissue, and I gave it to her.

I said to my loving wife, "God is good to your husband. He knows who I am." That was the biggest truth about my life.

Chapter 14

Revelation by the Holy Spirit

"Why did you not tell me that God is with him?!" the wicked sister cried out, yelling at the younger sister.

"I was blinded by the devil," from the other side of the phone, my beloved wife replied – finally, some truth. "I'm scared now, Vicki. I don't want to do lovers anymore. I don't like it. I won't ever have lovers now. I won't cheat. Besides, they always use me like a garden tool anyway, you know?"

Athaliah was frightened. Perhaps she had realized that she had made a mistake. Perhaps she had seen how badly all her attempts to kill me had gone. The world was on the verge of breaking down and crumbling to the very ground at that point in time, yet that did not scare her. She was scared of something else. She was scared of something more important to her, something of much more importance. She had realized that I could not die. She had grasped that God had not wanted me to die just yet. But most importantly, she had comprehended that Reece Peace was a man of God, a man whom God had loved too dearly. She got to see for herself that the Lord had His hands on me, and that was the thing that scared her the most, the thing that kept her up at night and worried during the day. She knew now that Reece Peace had a calling on himself from God. And so, to save her own self from any added trouble, she called everyone who was in on her plan, and she told them to stop trying. She told them what she knew to be true now. "God is with him," she told every single one of her accomplices.

"I'm going to get back with my husband," she continued telling her wicked sister. "I'm going to get back with my man of God. I will just love him, and I'll take care of my daughters just like I'm supposed to."

Vicki just listened to her talking, not knowing what to reply. She knew that there was nothing she could say about the circumstance that she had found herself in.

"I can't be with Darius Dog anymore," added Athaliah. "He's not my husband. He is not a romantic guy. He only cares about money and not me. Every time we had sex, he just got off and then got up and left. I don't want to be with a guy like that!"

"I found out something about him," interjected the wicked sister.

"What?" Athaliah inquired.

"Darius Dog is married to three other women and has many women on the side," replied the wicked sister.

"Why the hell did you not tell me that before?" cried my loving wife.

"I didn't know myself for a long time," the wicked sister replied.

"How did you find out?" Athaliah asked.

"Darius Dog told me," replied the wicked sister.

"You know…." mentioned my loving wife, not certainly sure if she should say it, "I saw many red sores on his penis and lips. I think he has a disease or something. He was always coughing and choking when he was around me."

"That's bad," replied the wicked sister, growing concerned.

"I messed up, Vicki," confessed my loving wife, her voice breaking down. "God, help me! Please, help me! Forgive me, my dear Lord. Forgive me!"

"He will forgive you," replied the wicked sister.

"I am not going to tell Peace anything about this," confessed my loving wife. "This is my little secret. Our little secret."

"I guess his name really does fit him... Darius Dog," the wicked sister thought out loud. "He's a real dog. I guess you should have stayed with Peace."

"I know! I should have!" exclaimed my loving wife. "And if it weren't for you and your devilish ideas, I would have stayed with him, loyal to him. It's all your fault, Vicki. It's all your fault!"

All Athaliah heard as a reply to her blames was the sound of the phone call being hung up.

"Forgive me, God. Please, forgive me!" Athaliah fell to her knees, crumbling to the floor beneath her.

Days passed, and there came a night when I was praying downstairs. Just then, I heard a voice talk to me. It was the Holy Spirit. The Holy Spirit spoke to me and said, "In the shooting that happened back in July of last year, the shooters were shooting at you. They were trying to kill you."

"What?!" I exclaimed, "Jesus Christ!"

"But the angel of the Lord blocked all the bullets that bolted toward you, too eager to kill you," God said to me. "The same angel you meant at the petrol station who had the door open for you."

In happiness and in agony, there was a scream that escaped. I had my daughters in my car that day. God forbid, what if something had happened to them? They could have died. It was not the normal kind of scream, not one of the lungs and throat. It was the kind of scream that came straight from the soul and right out of the heart.

I bolted upstairs to tell Athaliah, happy that my

daughters were safe and sound. I said to her, panting, "Babe, do you remember that shooting back in July 2019?"

With an estranged look in her eyes, she replied, "Yes, I remember the story you told me about the guys shooting the white car behind you. What about it?"

"No, baby!" I replied intravenously. "Athaliah, they were shooting at me! They were shooting at my car, my black 300. They were not shooting at the white car."

"How do you know that now, all of a sudden?" she asked, too curious.

"The Lord," I replied. "The Holy Spirit just told me that an angel sent by God blocked all the bullets!"

She did not reply. It was as though she was speechless. She just nodded, and I added, "I cannot wait to tell our daughters!"

Then, she responded. She jumped out of bed, crying, "NO! Don't tell our daughters!"

I replied, "Why not? Let's tell them, so they know God's angel protected us! They need to know!"

"No," my loving wife commanded. "You will not tell them."

Being the good husband, I obeyed.

With the passage of some time, Athaliah's behavior towards me varied. It was as though she was a whole different and new person. It was as though the wife I had known for so very long, the one who never seemed to love me, now had suddenly and certainly fallen in love with me. She would ask me to go shopping with her, and I would be much obliged to go with her. She would hold my hand in the crowds, showing me love in ways that I had wanted yet not gotten for so very long. Quite so often, she would tell me that she loved me, and that was something nice to hear. To be perfectly honest, though, I had grown out of it. The words felt rather unfamiliar now.

There came a day when she took me out shopping and said to me, "Honey, anything you want is yours."

In my heart and head, I could not believe that it was her. I asked myself, "Whose wife is this? This is not my wife! I have the wrong wife! I hope I'm not cheating.

This does feel like an episode of the body snatchers."

Each night now, she would want me to make love to her. The closeness that had vanished was now back again. She would lay closer to me, holding me closer. And when we would make love, I would give her the best she could get, not knowing that she had already tried elsewhere.

Now that I had good and properly working hips, I was giving her sex in the best way. With this new steal in my hips, I felt like I was Iron Man. But now that I would have sex with her, I could feel something change. There was something that did not feel right, something that just did not sit too well.

When I would make love to her, I would see other men sleeping with her. There was just a feeling in my heart, a voice that my head put forth. It just told me that I was not the only one she had been with lately. And that thought scared me. That thought made me wonder about things that I did not want to think about.

Since my hips were working, I started going skating at Skate Fast, getting the proper exercise for my body and peace of my mind; I really liked doing it. Frank was one of my friends I had there, and he would join me almost every time I went skating. Once, while we were skating, I said to him, too worried, "Man, I have something to tell you."

"What's good, homie? You good?" he asked carefully.

"I think…." I said to him. "I think… my wife of 18 years is cheating on me."

"No! Surely not your sweet Athaliah?!" he replied. "What makes you so sure?"

"I have this funny feeling about it," I told him.

"It's probably nothin', dude," he replied, dismissing the notion.

Perhaps he was right; I did not know.

I was keeping myself busy with the studio and everything else. When I would go to the studio to make new rap songs, the producers would read my face and know that I was quite preoccupied. And so, warily, they would ask me, "Are you okay, Peace?"

"Yeah," I would reply to them with a slight smile on my face, even though I was not okay.

You see, in my mind, I kept seeing my wife sleeping around with other men.

When I would work out in the garage, and she came home from work, she would always come and kiss me, always mentioning that she loved me. It was a good feeling, yes. But there was something different. The feeling that I felt was too strong. The voice within me had somehow made sense, and that was something that troubled me to the very core of my heart. And so, whenever she would tell me that she loved me, I would think to myself, "Oh, hell, no, something ain't right. It's either that this is not my wife, or she feels really very guilty about something she did."

I had no idea how right I was.

Some days passed, and something bad happened one night. Athaliah was having some bad cramps on the side of her stomach, and that was not natural. There was something wrong. So, I had to rush her to the hospital that night. All the while that I was there, I kept thinking about one thing. It just kept popping up in my head.

See, I did not take her to the hospital and drop her off there. I did not leave her there, all by herself. I stayed there for her, quite unlike what she had done with me twice when I had my hips-replacement operations. I walked in with her and stayed with her; as her husband and the man who loved her, I was supposed to do that. While she was there, she was scared and nervous about something. As she sat next to me, she kept trembling. It was as if I had left her in Alaska in December without a jacket to cover herself with.

The doctor then took her because he needed to ask Athaliah some personal questions. Athaliah walked out of the room and said, "Let's go, Peace."

Worried as expected, I asked, "You're not getting checked?"

"Let's go!" she yelled at me, her eyes turning red and her face swelling. She really was angry. "Let's get out of here."

"Okay, let's go," I did not inquire further, sensing

that she was not too comfortable with it. "These doctors don't know what they are doing or talking about. I'll make an appointment with my personal doctor."

Later during that same week, Athaliah called me while I was cutting the yard. She said, "Hey, Peace, honey, when I get off of work, we are going to drink wine, kiss, and make love all night."

"Yes, Athaliah, that sounds really nice to me. It's a plan even though I don't drink wine," I replied, my smile extending from one cheek to the other. We hung up the phone, and I got back to cutting the yard.

Still happy, there was the inner voice that spoke to me. It was the Lord, and He said to me, "Brian is one, and his brother Bobby is another."

Perplexed, I asked, "What, Holy Spirit?"

Just then, I looked over to the house next to mine, and I remembered how there used to live two brothers, Brian and his older brother Bobby; they lived next door with their mother.

I remembered how I had Brian's number still on

my phone's contact list. And so, I called Brian, and I got the answering machine. I left a voice message, "Brian, this is Peace, Athaliah's husband. Give me a call when you get this message."

Right after that, I texted my wife, "Athaliah, you know Brian and Bobby, who used to live next door?" I did not get a reply. I was expecting a reply from her because I knew that she had seen my text. There was no reply, though.

That night, Athaliah came home from work and pulled up into the garage. At that time, I was putting up yard equipment. She got out of the car and said, "Peace, I don't feel good anymore. Let's take a raincheck on spending time together tonight." With that, she just walked into the house. This time, she did not tell me that she loved me. This time, she did not kiss me. I knew the answer; I knew the truth now.

"Oh, my God!" I exclaimed to myself. "The Holy Spirit just told and showed me that she was cheating on me with Brian and Bobby, the guys next door!" I was sure of it now. The voice that kept talking to me, telling me that Athaliah had had extramarital affairs, was not lying at all!

I was sad, yet, at the very same time, I wondered. "Why am I not mad?" I needed more proof, and I needed to get to the bottom of it. Even though I saw the evidence and Holy Spirit just spoke to me, I needed to come up with tangible evidence to conclude that my loving wife had cheated on me.

Just then, I realized something important about marriage and love. You see, people have to realize that when you are married, two becomes one. You are not different people any longer; you are one – bonded by God and in front of God. So, when you are married, everything that one or the other does, the other one will know. In one way or the other, it is all revealed to the other. At the end of the day, that is how God's math works. In marriage, one plus one is one. So, since we are one, we know one another like we know ourselves. That's the beauty of marriage.

And so, later that night, I asked Athaliah, "Are you okay, honey?"

"Yes," she replied. "I'm better now."

I said to her, "Babe, I love you so much, but I know you are cheating on me."

"NO!" she exclaimed, jumped out of bed, and rushed out.

The next morning dawned, and there were a few days left in Christmas. There was still something that did not feel right, something that did not make sense. It felt as though there was a void in my spirit.

I knew that she was cheating on me and lying about it. The Holy Spirit already told me, and I trusted the God I believed in. I still needed rock-hard proof about it. Since something was going on with her body, I decided to go get myself checked to ensure that I had not contracted any kind of sexually-transmitted disease that she got from all the men she was having sex with.

So, the following morning, I made an appointment. My doctor asked me, "What's the problem, Mr. Peace?"

"I'd like to get myself checked for any sexually-transmitted diseases," I replied.

"Why?" he asked inquisitively.

"I believe my wife is cheating on me," I replied. "So I want to get myself checked for any diseases that she might have transferred to me."

The nurses came in and took some blood for the regular procedure and protocol. My doctor came into the room and told me that I needed to drink a little red wine sometime. I told her, "I don't drink."

She contradicted, "A little red wine will be very good for you. I'll know the results in a week, and I will tell you about them then."

"Great," I replied and walked out.

That night, I went to do my skating exercises at Skate Fast. Some of my friends were there too, and they could see from my face that there was something that was not right with me. They knew that I was going through something that I was not talking about.

"What's up, Peace?" they asked me.

"I'm here, getting my mind off of some stuff," I replied to them, assuring them that there was, in fact, something that I was going through.

They asked, "Where are your daughters?"

I replied, "They are wrapping Christmas gifts back at the house."

And while I was staking, my phone buzzed. I stopped, and I saw who was calling me. It was the doctor. I wondered and worried why she was calling me at 8 in the night. Naturally, my mind wandered off and told me that there was something wrong, that there was some bad news that I was about to get.

"Hello," I said, my voice shaking.

My doctor replied, "Hello, Mr. Peace."

"What's up?" I asked.

The doctor replied, "I need you to come back in and get some more tests done. We found something."

"What's going on?" I asked, "What did you guys find?"

She replied to me, "Come back in tomorrow morning. We'll talk about this then."

Just then, there was a fear that raced through my veins and sent chills to the core of my bones. I said to myself, "I have some kind of disease that Athaliah gave me."

I removed my skates and exited the skating rink. "What is going on, Peace?" my friends puzzledly inquired. "Why are you leaving? "Is everything all right?" I did not even stop to reply to them.

I was speeding home at 100 miles per hour. I needed to speak with Athaliah to find out whether she had infected me with some kind of disease that I never knew of. When I came home, I bolted upstairs and into the room. I slammed the door shut behind me. Athaliah was surprised, but she chose to conceal it. She inquired how my skating went, and I told her it was fantastic.

"Athaliah, Christmas is in a few days," I remarked. "Christmas will be wonderful for you, me, and the daughters. We're going to have too much fun!"

"Yes, honey," Athaliah said. "We're going to have all the fun in the world."

"Athaliah, I went to the doctor this morning and was tested," I explained. "The doctor stated I would find out the findings in a week. But today, when I was skating, my doctor phoned and urged me to come back in tomorrow for extra tests because they discovered something. They did not tell me what they discovered, but it sure was something. Gathering from her tone, it did not sound like it was something."

She seemed perplexed, despite the fact that she understood exactly what I was talking about.

"Now, are you cheating on me and giving me some type of disease?" I asked Athaliah.

"No, honey!" said Athaliah as she sprang out of bed.

"Swear to God," I said.

"I swear to God," Athaliah replied. "I'm not cheating on you. I swear to Jesus Christ!"

That was when my spiritual eyes opened. I saw

something unusual, something I had not expected to see. I saw an angel with a large sword poised to sever Athaliah's skull. I could literally see it and was terrified. It understood what was best for me, and Athaliah was not that. But then I saw another angel seize the sword from the enraged angel and say, "No!"

"No, Peace," Athaliah said, tears running down her face. "That is not something I would do to you. The devil is seeking to derail our Christmas celebrations. It's just his way of keeping us apart. Don't let the devil win against us."

"I have another appointment with the doctor tomorrow," I stated. "They came to discover something, and I don't want to go there to find bad news about myself contracting some disease because of you!"

I slept on the couch that night. The next morning, I awoke early, ready to return to the doctor's office. I got a call from my doctor's nurse, who said, "You do not need to come in. You are not ill or have a problem. You are just fine. The results of your tests came out great. The doctor, on the other hand, suggests that you start drinking red wine."

"All right, y'all read my mind!" I cried. "Seriously though, why does the doctor advise me to consume red wine?"

"Let's schedule another appointment, and we can talk about this in detail in that appointment," the nurse suggested. "Your blood and urine samples suggest you are fine for now."

I had a sense of tranquility and peace in my spirit. "Sweetheart, Athaliah, I am clear," I replied as I returned upstairs. "Thank and praise God, I do not have any ailments! I am fine. The tests came out all right. I would like to apologize to you, Athaliah, for believing you were cheating on me."

Though I said that, I still needed to find out more truth about her. That was what was going on in my head. That was something that was bothering me, and I had been doing so for quite some time now. I needed more truth to the feeling that I had about her – that she was cheating on me. You see, God had told me that fact, and so I believed it. I just needed proof for the world to see.

Now, since I was prescribed to drink red wine, I decided to drink a little too much one night. I was conversing with myself. "I am going to rock her world and give her some good sex tonight! Yes, I will show her exactly what she is going to miss out on by cheating on me."

Athaliah arrived home from work in the mood to make some good love. I had some slow jams playing and candles ablaze in the bathtub, which was filled with the bubble bath water for her. Athaliah was in a good mood after some sensual lover love. She lay nude next to me after the sensual bubble bath.

We began kissing and caressing each other on the body. And now we begin. It was time to do what I knew just how to do. Athaliah was having a great time with the Peace machine. With the Holy Spirit, Jesus had turned water into wine just like that; it was miraculous. What I did to her that night was just as well miraculous. With my brand-new hips, I was smashing that coochie. Athaliah was unable to walk once we finished. "Honey, Peace, my knees are numb," she explained. "I am unable to walk." Every time she got back up and tried to move, she fell down again. I assumed she was the one who really needed new hips. Yes, Peace, my Moby Dick did some deep-sea swimming in the ocean of Athaliah. I had just given her a true love story, too good to be true, too good to ever forget.

Athaliah had a doctor's visit two weeks later, on a Tuesday. I followed her to the doctor's clinic. She could not see me since I was behind her. She went in as I waited in the car somewhere close where she could not see me. I saw her weeping as she walked out of the doctor's office an hour later. I called her, pretending to be at home. I asked her how she was doing, dispelling any doubts about my close proximity to her. Everything was good, according to Athaliah. I went inside to speak with the doctor after she left the doctor's office, trying to inquire about how she was doing and if there was anything wrong with her.

"I am Athaliah's spouse," I explained. "Is everything all right with her?"

The physicians gave me a strange look and

stated, "Due to HIPAA regulations, we cannot share anything with you, Mr. Peace. You might inquire with your wife when you go back home. This matter is out of our hands."

When I arrived home, Athaliah said, "Peace, I need to tell you something."

"What?" I inquired.

"We will not be able to have sex for quite some time now," she explained. "I think I washed our clothing using the incorrect detergent."

I had a feeling she was lying again. Athaliah was required to take medicine. It may have been because she had sex with one of her partners. I was investigating whether she had been cheating on me, but the Holy Spirit had already revealed it to me.

I got along well with Athaliah's father. After work, I went to see him. Her father enjoyed telling me about his life experiences. So, we were talking about something, and he began telling me about Athaliah's mother, his ex-wife, and how she had attempted to murder him.

"What?" I exclaimed.

"Her lady friends would come over to the house while I was at work," he explained. "They would gossip about me for 8 to 10 hours while I was at work, earning money to support my family."

"That is truly unfortunate, sir," I concurred. "That is very sad."

"Once, she locked me up and scratched my face like a cat," he explained. "She genuinely wanted me dead."

"WOW!" I said, at a loss for words.

"Guess what?" he said as soon as he saw me dumbfounded.

"What?" I was perplexed.

"She was pregnant," he unveiled to me. "When she was doing all these things to me, Athaliah was in her stomach."

"My wife has a witch's spirit being harbored in her," I said as I leaped out of my chair, my eyes wide.

Chapter 15

Oh No! I'm Sleeping with a Witch

I was laying down sleeping next to my wife. I knew she had been cheating on me. I could see all the signs, but she would not confess it to me. I noticed she had been shivering in her sleep. I could even see this very dark complexion on her face. It wasn't the dark shine she used to have. She must have transferred sex demons in her. I remember telling her stories when we used to have prayer and bible studies together in our house. How we must stay faithful, because if one of us decided to step outside of are marriage covenant and sleep with someone else then those sex demons would be waiting to possess our soul and spirit.

I was thinking, "Like, damn, my last two wives used to shiver in their sleep. Wow they had demons in them too…"

I decided to go to the courthouse to file for a divorce or at least get the paperwork. I didn't let Athaliah know what I was doing. Maybe God wanted me to stay with her. I still remembered the time while we were having dinner.

"Honey, I will still love you and forgive you if you've ever cheated on me," I had said.

"No, Peace, I will never do that," she had said.

But she kept lying about it, and I believe God wanted me to know some more things. So, while I was getting the paperwork, something stopped me and made me wait.

"Peace, you are a good man," Athaliah said the next morning as she kissed me before going to work.

I spit and wiped my lips off when she left. I just didn't trust her. I went downstairs to make some breakfast. While I was frying myself up a vegetable egg omelet, I heard the Holy Spirit.

"It's your wife," said the Holy Spirit, "that's

trying to kill you."

I was like, "What did I hear, Lord?"

Then I started thinking how she didn't want my daughters to know about how the angels of God protected us from that shooting in July 2019. Then I started thinking about how she jumped up and said no when I told her about the two guys that wanted to kill me at the grocery shopping center two days before Thanksgiving. Even the way she was looking at me, like she saw a ghost that I was still alive, was concerning. Then another time at breakfast, the way she ran to the back of my car. When we were leaving the restaurant, I prayed for the two guys and got them born again. She was crying with tears in her eyes behind me. Even when I tried to get her name on a Peace Vision Global t-shirt, her name disappeared out the printer hand. As if an angel just took her name out.

It was the best disappearing act the printer and I ever saw... Wow this was really true. God, this bitch witch tried to have me assassinated three times! That's why she was watching that program How to Get Away with Murder, and other crime shows; Athaliah was studying them to kill me. I then got a text right after what God just told me.

The text read, "Child of God Almighty, I don't know you in person, but God knows you. God ministered to me in a revelation when I was on your profile to see things around you. I saw blessings, but spiritual attacks holding unto you, in prayer. I saw a woman in the realm of the spirit monitoring and plotting delay in your life with an evil mirror, and with motive to destroy you. But as I speak to you now her time is up."

I fell to the floor and said, "Oh no! I'm sleeping with a witch!"

Athaliah came back home. She opened up the door real fast. My heart started pounding thinking she was about to take me out. She came in and said, "Hey, honey. Good morning. I forgot my work badge." She walked over to me, gives gave me a kiss again, and said, "I love you." After she got her work badge from upstairs she came downstairs to leave.

"Honey, check this text I received," I said.

I read her the text after I finished the last line. "BUT AS I SPEAK HER TIME IS UP." Athaliah almost fell on the floor and kept repeating, "MY TIME IS UP MY TIME IS UP." Athaliah came back off her trance and said, "Let me see that text." After she looked at it, she said, "This is some BS!" And she was not talking about bacon and sausage. She just walked out of the house to go to work. She drove to work, thinking about the text I read to her. She still kept saying, "MY TIME IS UP, MY TIME IS UP." She called her sister, Vicki, to let her know the text I received. But Vicki didn't answer. Athaliah was scared and nervous. She started praying in the car while driving to work, telling herself she was going to be all right. I'm the righteous of God.

I got dressed and told my daughters that I would be back. I called my neighbor across the street from me, Ms. Deon, to keep an eye on my house while my daughters were home. Since the COVID-19 pandemic was still going on people were working from home, so my neighbor agreed to watch my house. I drove to the police station just to talk with a detective or anyone about my situation. I arrived to the station. Due to the pandemic you had to wear a mask and wait outside six feet apart. I got up in line and the officer asked me, "Can I help you?"

"Yes!" I said. "I believe my wife is trying to kill me. I believe she put three hits on me and failed."

The officer looked at me crazy and told me to come inside. He looked kinda afraid to be talking to me outside all in the open like sitting ducks. Since it was a hit on me, he wanted himself inside for his safety.

"What happened?" he asked me.

I told him all the times I had people shoot me. And the last two times failed because I prayed for them and got them born again. I told him all three attempts that I believed my wife had something to do with.

"Do you have any proof or any recording?" the officer asked me.

"No."

"Well," said the officer, giving me a case number. "Make a report and bring it back or email it with the case number."

"Okay."

I did some errands while thinking about how I could prove that my wife was trying to have me killed. I received a phone call and texts from Athaliah informing me that she was home.

"Let's spend time together," texted Athaliah.

I was like, "Hell no."

Then, an idea popped up in my head. I decided to go to the grocery store and get the videotape of the guys who were in the parking lot that wanted me dead. It was in the daytime so I remember seeing cameras. I believe they were working there too. I stopped at the local grocery store, asked the manager if he could give me the video from two days before Thanksgiving in 2020.

"I believe I was going to be attacked and killed in the parking lot of the grocery store," I said.

"I can't give you the video," said the manager despite his shock. "Only a detective can get it."

I went back to the police station and spoke with the officer.

"You can get the video from the store manager," I said.

"Okay," said the police officer. But he didn't really didn't pursue it.

"If this was a woman coming to the police station for help, you guys would have sent the whole army!" I thought to myself. "But because there's a guy telling a story on his wife trying to kill him, you won't even pursue it."

"How do I get the videotape for evidence?" I asked him.

"Just file the report and use the case number I gave you," said the officer.

"That's it?" I said, bewildered. I left the police department utterly disappointed!

"Maybe my wife is not trying to kill me," I thought to myself. "Maybe I'm just tripping. Maybe I just need some rest. Perhaps the pandemic was making people come out of the closet and go crazy. Or was the pandemic revealing the truth about the people of this world? Maybe she was cheating? But we have children together. She wouldn't go that far to have me killed. I was just hearing things and that message that someone sent me was probably fake." I headed back home. Athaliah was blowing my phone up asking to see me and spend time with me.

I arrived and went upstairs. Athaliah was laying in bed watching television.

"Hey, honey," she said. "How was your day? I missed you."

"It was good," I said. "How was work?"

"Slow," said Athaliah. "People are really not flying a lot due to the pandemic."

"Wow," I said. After a short pause, I said, "Babe, guess what I did today?"

"What?"

"You remember that time I told you about the guys who were going to kill me at the grocery store parking lot?"

"Yes, I remember the story you told me."

"Well, I went to the grocery store and asked the manager for the videotape so I can take it to the police."

Athaliah jumped out of the bed and said, "No! Don't do that! They will get you! Plus, you prayed for them and got them born again. Let God's grace be upon them. Just leave them alone. Don't go to the police."

I turned around and my heart almost fell out of my chest. I thought to myself, "Oh no! I'm sleeping with a witch! This holy bitch really tried to have me assassinated!"

I just walked out of the room real calm. But my insides were screaming trying to figure out what to do. Athaliah was calling me back upstairs.

"What you doing, honey?" she asked.

"About to work on some music in the studio," I replied.

"Come upstairs and give me some sex."

I started sweating like a Hebrew slave. I thought

to myself, "I am not going to sleep with a killer! I'm no fool!"

"Let me finish this song and I'll be upstairs," I replied.

"Okay," Athaliah said. "I love you." I couldn't run because we have daughters.

The next morning, after Athaliah left for work, I got up, went on the computer, and did my report on how I believe she was trying to kill me with the dates, times, and whereabouts. I went back to the police station with the report and case number.

"Thank you," the detective said, taking the report from my hands.

"That's it?" I said. "Are you guys going to investigate and start recording her and checking her phone and text records?"

"We don't have the kind of resources," the detective replied.

"In California they do," I said.

"This is not California," the detective said, bluntly.

"You can get the videotape from grocery store," I told the detective. "I know she did it, she's trying to have me assassinated." I started telling the detective how she jumped out of bed when I told her I was getting the videotape from the grocery store to show the detectives the guys who were trying to kill me.

"I need some more proof," the detective simply stated. I was a little upset.

"If I was a woman, you'd bring the whole army to the house to arrest the man," I told him. "But since I'm a man telling you this it's like you don't care or don't believe me in some way."

I left and went back home. I called the FBI after reaching home. The receptionist answered. "Can I help you?" she asked.

"Yes," I said. "I believe my wife is trying to have me killed."

"Sir, don't call here no more," she said.

"Lady, she is!" I said. "I need help." She hung up the phone.

I decided to look into Athaliah's secret box. There were a lot of bank receipts; she had a lot of money. I wondered if she was bringing drugs through the airport. Her sister, Vicki, with her husband, do own a pharmacy. I wondered... I called the airport police tip line. A lady answered the phone. "Can I help you?" she asked.

"Yes!" I said. "I believe my wife may be bringing drugs through the airport." The lady put me through to Sergeant Douglas.

"Can I help you?" asked Sergeant Douglas.

"I believe my wife is bringing drugs through the airport," I told the sergeant.

"Why do you say that?" asked the sergeant.

"Well, Sergeant, I believe she tried to kill me three separate times, but failed." I told the sergeant each time she had someone to assassinate me and how she did it.

"What airline does she work for?" the sergeant

asked.

"Flight Airlines," I answered. "She a gate agent, but they stopped the buddy passes they used to have."

"She's lying," Sergeant Doulas said, loudly. "They never stop their buddy passes. Does she have drugs on her now?"

"I wouldn't know," I said.

"I'm going to check her out and her history," Sergeant Douglas replied.

"Okay," I said, and we hung up the phone.

I was watching my step everywhere I went around the house. I hid all the knives in the house. Every time I slept, I had one eye open. Athaliah was still trying to be a good wife around the house. I knew she had been cheating on me, so I stopped having sex with her. But Athaliah didn't know that I knew she was trying to kill me or have me killed.

It was Sunday and Athaliah would be on vacation starting tomorrow, Monday. It was late Sunday evening, and Athaliah receives a call from her job asking her to come to work on Monday. "No, my vacation starts tomorrow," she said. I noticed she hung up. She came up to me and told me, "That's my job asking me to come to work on my off days, my vacation days. That's funny. My job never does that. They know I'm on vacation." I was looking at her. I knew why they called her. I had a strong feeling Sergeant Douglas was trying to get her to come to work to see what her routine at work to see if she was bringing drugs through the airport.

Days later, Sergeant Douglas and I were texting each other. But then I received a phone call from Sergeant Douglas. "Mr. Peace, you need to get out of the house," he said on the call. "You don't need to be there. It's dangerous."

"Why you say that?" I asked him. "Where am I going? My family is in California."

"Do you have protection?" he asked, referring to a gun.

"Yes," I said. "What's going on? What did you see? What do you know?"

"I'll get back with you," he said. I was cutting my yard.

I noticed I missed a call. I checked my answer machine. It was the FBI. I listened to the recording. It was Agent Eric Harris from the FBI. "I have a lead, a tip, from the police department about a female who works at Flight Airlines who I believe is your wife or significant other. Please call me." He left his number and wanted to know more information.

I called right away. Agent Eric Harris answered the phone. "Hello, Agent Harris," I said. "This is Reece Peace returning your call back."

"What's going on?" Agent Harris asked me. I told Agent Harris about the three assassination attempts. I told him about the first time when my daughters were in the car with me back in July, 2019. Then I told him about the second hit on me in November, 2020, two days before Thanksgiving. I told him how I was coming out of the local grocery store and how this guy was following me to my car.

"I said what's up to the guy," I told Agent Harris.

"He replied saying we just going the same way to our cars. I noticed he was like on top of me looking kinda nervous. I turn around to him and ask him if he needs a prayer. He said yes, pray for me, so I grabbed his hand. Then I asked him if was born again, if he believed in Jesus. He replied saying he couldn't get born again because he worshiped a different god. I replied yes you can be born again. I'm giving you Jesus now. There came another guy running up on us after taking something out of his bag. I believe it was a gun to have me killed in broad daylight. The guy who I was praying for let go of my hand and bearhugged the other guy. NO! He told his partner to get born again with him."

"What's born again?" Agent Harris stopped me to ask.

"When a person repents from the sins and becomes a new person in Christ Jesus," I replied. "His or her new birth is in accepting Jesus to be their personal savior."

"Very Interesting," Agent Harris replied. "I thought I knew everything because I'm the FBI."

I continued with my story, "So, I go on and I got them born again with another man, but the third guy wanted a couple of dollars. When I get home, it was revealed to me they were about to kill me. I go inside the house to tell my wife. She jumps up out of her chair, screaming no. She runs into the kitchen. My 15-year-old daughter runs into her arms and says, 'Mommy, I'm scared for daddy.' My wife was looking at me weird. Later, I found out she was the one putting the hits on me. I put the report in to the police station. I decided to go to the local grocery store to get the videotape. The manager said he could only give it to police. I then thought that maybe I was tripping and that my wife is not trying to kill me. So, I went home and told her how I went to the grocery store to get the video of the guys who wanted to kill me that day. I was going to let the detective look at it. My wife jumped out the bed and said, 'No, leave them alone. They will get you. You already prayed for them. Let God handle them.' I turn around and my heart almost fell out my chest." Then I told him about the third hit when I was at breakfast with her.

"We'll get back with you," Agent Harris said, seeming convinced.

"Okay," I said.

The next day, Agent Eric Harris called me. He wanted my wife's phone number and her bank details. I got into her secret box to get her bank account number. I told Agent Harris, "I couldn't find the full number. I only have four digits."

"All I need are the last four digits and the name of the bank," said Agent Harris. I gave Agent Harris the information and we just hung up.

I decided to go back into her secret box while she was still at work. I was looking at her bank receipts and wondered how she had so much money in her account. "She could've gotten me out of the child support system debt a long time ago," I thought to myself. I saw one bank receipt that had $13,000 in it. Then, in a week it was at $3,000. "Wow, she must have paid $10,000 to have me assassinated," I said to myself. "But she did it three different times... Wow, did she pay $30,000!? I need to find more receipts." While looking for more receipts I discovered she had two other bank accounts. I couldn't believe my eyes. Then I saw she had a life insurance policy on me for $20,000. "That's not enough money after I'm dead," I said to myself. I guess she was going to save money by cremating my ashes. Ashes to ashes, dust to dust.

I started reading her notepad. I was seeing notes that read, "God have grace on me. Lord, I'm tired of my husband. He needs help. It's time for me to have fun. Time for my time of glory." Then, I saw a rental car discount card. "I couldn't have been getting discounts on rental cars on our family trips," I thought to myself. "She never told me she had this discount card." That's right! Brian and his brother, Bobby, used to work at a rental car place. I picked up another notepad she had and my eyes got real big. I was seeing notes about having a GoFundMe account on me. I screamed, "Jesus, she really was going to have me killed and then raise money!" My daughters ran to my bedroom door when they heard me scream.

"Are you okay, dad?" they asked me.

"Yes," I said. "I'm just rejoicing in the Lord." I began digging deeper in that box of hers. "Okay, why does she have all these books about mercy and grace in this box and not on the bookshelf where the other books are?" I was talking to myself. "Wait a minute. Athaliah was asking for mercy and grace from God before killing me." This was premeditated murder. "This witch bitch is loco!" Athaliah was asking for mercy and grace from God before she would have me killed. She was hiding these books and reading them to herself. Later, I spoke with the police and the FBI and let both of them know what I saw.

I decided to call the good sister named Joyce, Athaliah and Vicki's older sister. I was trying to pull any kind of information from her. Joyce and I were real close.

"Hello, Joyce," I said when she answered the phone. "How you doin'?"

"Brother Peace," she said. "I can't really talk right now. But I want you to be careful." Then Joyce said something that I never believed she would tell me. What my ears heard had me wanting to eat liver with milk and cereal. And I don't like either. "Athaliah and Vicki have been trying to play god in your life." She was basically telling on her sisters, Athaliah and Vicki.

"What do you mean?" I asked her. Joyce just hung up the phone. I knew exactly what she was saying now. See, I was changing for the better. She couldn't support the new me. Athaliah was afraid of what I was becoming. I was becoming more like Jesus Christ. She couldn't let that happen on the earth.

Chapter 16
She Knows that I Know

The detective wanted anything I could give them to help with the case. I also called the FBI and left a message on their phone, and I had a word with the airport police. Sergeant Eric Harris had advised me to leave the house. I told him I didn't have anywhere to go because most of my family lives in California. He told me to get a small apartment or stay with a friend I trust in the meantime.

"Do you have protection?" he asked.

"Yes," I said.

Stay safe," he said.

He didn't tell me much, but with that little bit Sergeant Harris had told me enough. Now I really knew that I was sleeping with the enemy. That night I couldn't let her know that I know. I had to sleep with both eyes open. My wife wasn't the type of wife that liked cuddling. But now she wanted to cuddle. Usually when she cuddles with me it means she wants to have sex and I'll be ready. But not this time. I was ready to run. I used to hear a man can get it up anytime. But this night I'm keeping my homeboy down. I wouldn't want to have sex with her. What if she put a razor blaze in her vagina? I don't have time to get my homeboy cut off, I have things to do with it!

The next morning, she kissed me and went off to work. I got into her box to make copies of the information the police and FBI needed. But I couldn't send it from my computer. I couldn't take the risk of not do something right and her finding all the information and knowing that I know. I went across the street to my good friend James's house.

"Can I scan these papers and send them to the police station?" I asked.

"Sure," said James. "Is everything okay?"

"Man," I replied. "James, I believe my wife is trying to have me assassinated. I believe she tried to have me killed three separate times."

His eyes widened and he said, "No, not your sweet wife Athaliah!"

"Yes, my sweet wife, the church girl," I said. "That bitch."

I explained to James of the three separate times when Athaliah tried to have me killed. James couldn't believe it.

"This is the same lady who's so quiet," James said, still processing the information I shared with him. "This lady who doesn't speak to no one?"

"Yes, that one," I said.

I scanned and emailed the information of the paperwork to the detective and the FBI. I was feeling a little better now that they had it. I spoke with the FBI and the police a couple more times. I was thinking that they were getting the paperwork and arrest warrants together soon to apprehend everyone involved. Moving on during the days Athaliah was at home working on the computer and checking her emails. All of a sudden, she jumped up and ran around like a chicken with its head cut off. Later, in some days, I noticed Athaliah was acting strange, but she's been doing that for a while. I didn't know at the time that she found out that I was aware of what she did. She started talking to God saying, "Lord have mercy on me." Sometimes I will see some tears in her eyes, but she wouldn't really look at me. Every time I came in the room she would put the blanket over herself. When she would walk past me in the house, she wouldn't look at me in my eyes. She would just keep her head down. I would say to myself that she was feeling guilty and ashamed about cheating on me. I saw that now. She might finally even tell me the truth about it.

The whole week, I could hear her crying to God. She looked very worried. One night I got into my car and drove down the street. I called Vicki. She answered the phone and told me she was still at work at the hospital.

"What's up Peace?" she asked.

"Listen, is Athaliah okay?" I asked. "She's walking around the house crying and saying Lord God have mercy on me. She's been doing that the whole week."

"Let me close my office door," said Vicki. She got back on the phone. "Peace, don't tell her I told you this, but she's trying to kill herself."

"What?"

"I don't know," said Vicki. "You need to talk with her and help her. Show your wife some support and love."

"Okay."

I decided to drive back to the house. As I entered, Athaliah was leaving and told me that she would be right back. Athaliah drove down the street to call Vicki because she received an urgent text from Vicki to call her. Athaliah called Vicki, and Vicki answered the phone.

"Come down before Peace finds out," said Vicki. "Peace just called me and is worried about you. He said you're going around the house with tears in your eyes crying out to God to have mercy on you. You need to relax, girl."

"Stop it," Athaliah said. "It's all your fault all that's going on."

"It's your fault!" said Vicki, yelling.

"Peace knows everything," said Athaliah.

"About what?" asked Vicki. "That you cheated on him?"

"No," Athaliah replied. "About we trying to have him killed."

"Don't put 'we' in it! It's you. You paid the money."

"You suggested it, Vicki!" said Athaliah. "Peace went to the police and the FBI. I saw the report on one of his emails he sent out. I hacked into his emails months ago to find out what he'd be doing each day. When I saw this one, I couldn't believe it. I jumped up and screamed. I can't believe he could do something like this. I'm his wife. He's trying to put me in prison. He could have spoken with me before going to the police and the FBI. We could have worked it out. Why is he trying to have a single parent home with our daughters?" Athaliah broke into tears.

"We need to think of something," said Vicki. "Because they're going to trace all this to me as well, and our cousins. Athaliah, you're too emotional. You told on yourself and us. We just need to pray."

It was Sunday and Athaliah went to church early that morning. She wrote a big check to put in the church. She was thinking that if she gave God a big offering, He will forgive her and have grace and mercy on her sins.

She drove off crying…

Days went by and I was running up to the police station to find out what was going on. The detective advised me that the FBI had the case and it would take a while.

"When the FBI takes over, they'll get evidence," a lady officer told me. "Leave them alone. They know what they're doing."

"Well," I said to the detective and the lady officer. "I found out my wife is trying to kill herself. I'm being impatient because I'm sleeping with a killer who's trying to kill me and herself. My daughters and I are not safe." They did not say anything. "No kind of help? If I was a woman, like I said before, you'd send the army to help. But since I'm a man I can't hear a mouse pissing on cotton for help."

I walked out of the police station hurt and trying to figure out what to do. I went home, walked in the house, and saw Athaliah at the kitchen table on a zoom call with all these women praying. They sounded like witches praying in some weird voices. I could tell were many of them and her sister Vicki was there too. I could tell there were about seven to nine women on this zoom call. Athaliah asked me to join in the prayer and that the women would like to meet me. I said hell no! That's not no prayer. What kind of language is that even? They were not speaking in tongues of the Holy Ghost. It sounded like some voodoo prayer. I went upstairs to pray to God myself. I saw a battle, warfare with some witches of the dark side. I had no fear. I had the God of Shalom in my life.

"I have an idea," said Vicki to Athaliah.

"What?" asked Athaliah.

"Let's poison him," said Vicki. "I have these pills in the pharmacy that can stop his heart."

"Will it work and how did you get them?"

"Darius Dog," replied Vicki. "He makes them in Jamaica. It's called the kill pill. I'm sending them to you now. Just put the pill in his drink and stir it up to dissolve. It will also dissolve in his body without a trace. It will just seem like he had a heart attack. When he's dead, we'll just cremate his ass. Ashes to ashes, dust to dust. He will finally be gone." Athaliah liked the new plan.

"Why didn't we do this in the first place?" Athaliah asked.

"Just keep an eye on your mailbox," said Vicki.

It was January 7, 2022, the new church I attend, New Chapel, was on a fast. We were fasting on certain foods and drinks to walk closer with God. I cooked dinner that evening. While we sat down, about to eat dinner, I said a prayer.

Athaliah stood up and went into the kitchen. My

daughters and I were talking and enjoying our food. Athaliah came back with a glass of wine for me.

"Honey, go ahead and enjoy some wine with your dinner," she said to me.

"Athaliah, we're on a fast from the church," I said. "I'm not drinking wine."

"No, honey, it's okay," she insisted. "Enjoy the wine."

I rebutted and replied, "No, I don't want it." Athaliah took it back. I said to myself, "That's strange. She never served me wine in our time of marriage. I guess she's trying to repent and be a good wife since all the bad she's done toward me." I had no clue she put poison in the wine. Athaliah was pissed that I didn't drink the wine.

The week after I was out in the backyard barbecuing. I love to barbecue in the backyard; it's my safe place. I had chicken, ribs, corn, and butterfly lobsters on the grill. The week fast was over. So, while I was grilling, I had a glass of wine. While I'm grilling the food, the good smoke was all over the neighborhood. My daughter, Victory, came to the back patio window while I was barbecuing.

"Daddy, someone's at the door," she said.

I went around the front. It was the meat truck bringing me some more meat to grill for a later time. I took my glass of wine in the house and put it on the table. I went to the street where the meat truck was at. I was talking to the gentleman and he was showing me different kinds of steaks I could purchase. While discussing, Athaliah came outside to her car. I was looking at her getting something out. I thought it was weird for her to come out like that with her sweats and shirt and hair looking all messy. She don't like people seeing her like that. It must be something very important in the car she needed. She was so desperate to get something out of that car. What was so important in the car that she had to get looking like she had on a Halloween costume? Athaliah ran back in the house. I purchased the meat. I walked back in the house to put the meat in the freezer. I had to get back to grilling my food.

I went to the table to go get my glass of wine. It wasn't on the table. I turned around. It was by the sink. I said, "I didn't leave my wine here." When I was about to take a sip of it, I heard the Holy Spirit saying, "DON'T DRINK IT! It's poison." I poured it into the sink. I said, "Holy Spirit, how is it poisoned?" I began to think that's why she went into her car. She was in it getting poison to put in my wine. Then she forgot to put the glass back on the table where she got it from. That's why she offered me wine last week. My wife was trying to kill me with poison in the wine. That's why she's watching these crime shows; to kill me. But she was not studying them well. They usually get caught on the shows. I went outside and looked up at the sky and said, "Thank you, Lord, for saving me once again." I felt this power in me. I can't die, I can't be killed. God is with me. I stayed in the backyard to finish my grilling with tears in my eyes thinking there's a God that loves me, that loves us. I didn't run or panic. My wife didn't love me or her daughters. I was in the house with a killer. My daughters and I were not safe.

I finished grilling. We were all at the table eating. Athaliah looked at me thinking why is my husband not dead or on the floor in pain. Athaliah was looking at me like she seen a ghost again. She couldn't really eat her food. I was enjoying the barbecue with my daughters. We got sauce all over our faces going to work on the ribs, chicken, and lobster tails.

The next day, I couldn't work on any music. I needed to get to the police station to let the detective know about her attempt to poison my wine and kill me. Before I left, I checked my emails. I saw something strange. Why was Athaliah's name on my email address as a recipient? I went to my sent emails and I and got up and screamed. She could see the emails I was sending out. She saw the paperwork and information I sent out to the police department and the FBI. Then I put two and two together. That's why she's been crying around the house asking God for mercy. SHE KNOWS THAT I KNOW! She was the one who was trying to have me assassinated. Even last night and the other week she tried to kill me with the poison in my wine. I was running around the house like a chicken with its head cut off. Our marriage reminded me of that movie, *Mr. & Mrs. Smith*, but this was *Mr. & Mrs. Peace.* Thinking about it, it should be more *Mr. & Mrs. War.*

I went back to talk with the detective to see what was going on with my case. I told them about the wine she put poison in.

"Leave the house," said the detective.

"Why do I need to leave?" I asked. "Just come get her."

"We need more proof," said the detective. "Did you talk with the FBI?"

"Yes."

"The FBI have better resources to handle the case."

I called the FBI and told them about my wife trying to poison my wine. "You guys need to come arrest her," I said.

Athaliah called Vicki since she was very upset of

being investigated by the police and the FBI. "I'll kill myself before I go to prison," said Athaliah.

"No, you will not kill yourself," said Vicki. "Get a divorce attorney and have Peace sign the papers to release the daughters over to our dad or one of our family members in New York. And to sign over the house as well."

Athaliah decided to listen to her sister, the devil, again. She went out and got herself a divorce attorney. Later, she asked me to come out to the back patio.

"I want a divorce," she said. "But I need you to sign these papers."

"I'm not signing anything," I said.

I already knew in my mind that she knew she was going to prison. She was trying to make me sign papers to give up my daughters to her family. I might not have gone to college, but I'm not stupid. A week goes by and it felt like they were about to come to the house and arrest Athaliah and all the other killers who tried to kill me. One night, Athaliah was not home yet. I tried calling her to see if she was okay. No answer. "They must have arrested her at her job at the airport," I thought to myself. I felt a peace in my spirit that my daughters and I were safe. Next thing I know the garage opens up and it's Athaliah, but she doesn't drive in. I ran downstairs and ran into the garage and shut it because I was not letting her in the house with me and my daughters. I went outside through the front door and stood between the garage and her car.

"You are not coming in the house," I said.

"Why are you not letting me in?" asked Athaliah.

"I found out you tried to kill yourself," I confronted her. "Why? What's going on with you?"

"Nothing," Athaliah replied. She proceeded to call the police. "Hello? I'm outside my house and my husband has a gun pointed at me and is trying to kill me." Lying ass bitch. I did have my gun, but I was not pointing it at her. The police eventually showed up. They were very calm when they walked up to me.

I put my hands up right away and said, "My gun

is in the flower pot." I wasn't about to be another black man being shot up by the police. I used wisdom right away with my hands up and did not run or act up.

"What's going on, Mr. Peace?" the officer asked me.

"My wife is trying to kill herself because she found out I put a report on her at the police station and with the FBI," I answered.

Athaliah was talking to the other police officers on the street getting her statement. I showed the officers I was talking to the report and an FBI recording of me talking to them. Some Shady hospital paramedics showed up. Athaliah was over there telling the police and the Shady hospital paramedics her story. She was telling them how I was crazy to believe that she was capable to have me assassinated three separate times. The Shady hospital paramedics were just looking at me listening to what I was saying to the police. I was telling the police about how my wife was trying to have me killed and even poisoned my wine. I showed the police the wine that I put in a container. I told them drink some of it, test it, and see if it's poisoned. They obviously refused, while some of them started laughing.

"Take it to the lab and have it tested," I said.

"We can't do that," said the officer.

One of the officers who was reading the report looked at Athaliah and said, "Ma'am, you need to leave and go somewhere else. You don't need to be by Mr. Peace or his daughter. I believe in the report." Athaliah started crying. "Can you go somewhere?"

"Her dad lives here, she can stay with him," I interjected.

Athaliah was crying even louder, but it felt like she was acting. The paramedics called the officer over to them. It was lady and a male paramedic. They were talking with Athaliah earlier. The officer walked back to me.

"You should go with the paramedics to get an evaluation," said the officer. "It's going to make your case look good."

"What you mean look good?" I asked.

"Let the paramedics take you to the hospital," said the officer. "They'll do an evaluation to show that you're okay. Then, when the FBI and detective arrest her, it will show that you were okay."

"I don't want to leave her around my daughters," I said. "She is suicidal."

"We'll go talk with her and make sure she's okay to be around the daughters," said the officer. They came back to me after speaking to Athaliah and said, "She'll be okay with the children."

"I'll do this evaluation for two hours but then I need to get back," I said. I got into the paramedics' truck. "Who's going to bring me back?"

"We have a van that will bring you back in two hours," said the male paramedic. We drove off to the hospital.

Chapter 17

The 13th Floor

I arrived at the hospital with the paramedics twenty-four hours before the new president was sworn into office. I went and sat down with a nurse. She asked me a couple of questions. "What's your name? Your social security number? Where were you born? Who's the next president?" I answered all the questions correctly. The nurse then said, "Okay, Mr. Peace you can go home."

"Okay," I said. "Where's the van at to take me home. I need to get home to make sure my daughters are okay." I saw the paramedics and four doctors talking. I heard the paramedics speaking in a mocking tone with the doctors about my wife trying to kill me, and that the FBI and police were on the case. The four doctors asked me to come in the back room to talk with them.

"No, I have to leave to be with my daughters," I

said.

The lady nurse who did the evaluation on me yelled out, "No, Mr. Peace is okay. Let him go home."

"Yes, I need to go," I said.

One of the four doctors said, "Just come back and discuss your case with us for about five minutes." The four doctors looked at the evaluation nurse with stern faces, silently indicating her to shut up. The nurse put her head down and shook it back and forth.

"Five minutes and I need to go," I said. I went in the back. The door was shut hard after I walked in. I saw two security guards stand by the door. One of the security guards told me to empty my pockets of everything and put a hospital gown on. "No! What's going on? I need to go. Why are you guys doing this to me?" Both the security guards were now standing all up on me, telling me take my clothes off. I rebutted, "No, I got to go."

Then one of the nurses said, "Mr. Peace, this will only take a few minutes. We need to take blood and check your blood pressure."

"I don't need to do all that," I said. But I hurried up and put the hospital gown on. They put my wallet and jewelry in a bag. The nurse came to me and put a long tube in my nose to take a COVID test. She put the tube so deep in my nose that I told her she was hurting me.

"Stop moving," she said. "I'm not hurting you."

"My nose is bleeding!" I said. She then started sticking me with needles, taking IV and blood samples from me as if I was some kind of experiment or animal. They then put me in a small and dirty room despite my protests. They locked the door behind me. It felt like some kind of jail cell hospital room. The bed was hard and the floors where dirty. I was yelling through the door and telling them constantly that I am a businessman and have to get back to work.

Two of the nurses started laughing at me and said, "No, you're not."

"Yes, I am!"

"Stop lying," said one of the nurses. "You're here

now. You belong here." It was starting to feel like a scene from a horror movie. I didn't have my phone on me to call for help. I felt trapped. I noticed the nurses then offered to let another man go home if he took some pills. I told the man not to take those pills. The nurses told me to be quiet. It was 4 a.m. and I was stuck at this hospital with these goons. One of the security guards eventually enters my jail cell of a hospital room and forces me to sit on a wheelchair. He straps me to the chair so I can't get out. I was still trying to stay positive so I asked them if they were taking me home. The nurses just laughed like demonesses.

I was taken to the elevator and the guard took me up to the thirteenth floor. The entire floor was cold and dark and there were several people sleeping quietly on hard beds. They led me to a corner room on the floor, unstrapped me from my wheelchair, and just left, locking me inside. The room was dark and cold with very little light entering in.

In the morning the sun shone into my room through the window. I saw the nurses and the doctors come in. I asked them if I could use the hospital phone. They gave me their phone and I began calling everyone: my neighbors, family, and some of my friends. I told them that I was imprisoned at this hospital. I called one of my best friends, Torey, and told her about my situation. She's a friend who helps direct my music videos. I asked her to call my lawyer, the police, and the FBI.

I was thinking about what Joseph had to go through in the Bible with false imprisonment. I kept telling the nurses to let me go home but they kept refusing. It turns out, the thirteenth floor of the hospital was where they put all the psychiatric patients. They thought to put me there because I was telling them that my wife was trying to get me killed. They wouldn't believe me no matter how much I told them. I told them to give me my phone so I could contact the right numbers and prove to them about the ongoing investigation on my wife. I was imprisoned on the thirteenth floor of the hospital going on so far for three days waiting to get out. Nobody was following any kind of COVID protocol.

There were even patients on my floor walking around naked. It was very filthy. I didn't understand what was going on.

I thought about a scripture from the Bible. "Indeed, all who desire to live a godly life in Christ Jesus will be persecuted." It was 2 Timothy 3:12. All that time I kept thinking that my wife wasn't going through anything, but I was suffering. I guess she wasn't living a godly life. Really, she wasn't; she tried to have me killed, she cheated on me, and she poisoned my wine. I was finally able to convince one of the nurses to let me use my phone so I could at least call my family members and inform them where I was. He led me to an area in the hospital where all my belongings were kept. Thank God my battery wasn't dead. When the nurse wasn't looking, I secretly texted Sergeant Douglas from the airport police. I told Sergeant Douglas that I was being held at the Shady Hospital on the thirteenth floor and that they weren't letting me go. Sergeant Douglas was shocked. He told me to show them his message so they could get me out.

The nurse noticed me texting from my phone and got angry at me. He stopped me from using my phone any further and took me back to my room. I told the doctors about Sergeant Douglas and gave them his number so he could inform them about my case. They went to the other room to give a good scolding to the nurse who let me out of my room so I could get the numbers. I decided to call Torey from the psych ward hospital phone. I gave her all the numbers that I was able to get from my phone and told her to call Sergeant Douglas and inform him of my situation. I told her to also call the FBI and the news reporters so they could investigate the thirteenth floor of the hospital. I was in a desperate situation. Torey was really concerned for me. She was helping me a lot.

They had a talent night in the psych ward one day. I said I was going to rap. But before I could get on stage, I was asked to come to an office room. I went into this room with twelve doctors and nurses. They started asking me questions. They looked very nervous. They wanted to hear the story about my wife trying to have me killed.

"You don't believe me," I said. "You have this black man locked up in the psych ward thinking he's crazy. You have me away from my daughters at home. I gave you the numbers to call the FBI and the police. But they will be calling you guys for you to release me." I was angry with them that I had this one tear come down from my eyes. "When I get out, I'm going to get me an attorney and sue you! You have patients that don't belong here also. You guys are taking regular people who don't need help out of their homes and bringing them here for money. So, the more patients you have the more money you get. That is not cool!"

The love of money is the root of all evil. And this was evil what the doctors and nurses were doing. After finishing what I had to say, I walked out because I wanted to go rap. I went back to the area where the talent contest was being held. It was my turn to perform. I got the mic. They put me on some music and once again I rocked the house; it was a great performance. I had everyone on the thirteenth floor praising God at Shady

Hospital. I was seeing the patients who needed help were healed by the words I was rapping about Jesus. Also, the twelve doctors and nurses were watching me perform with frowns on their faces. I guess they were thinking that no way someone can rap like that can't be sick or needs help. I was really helping the patients on the thirteenth floor. That night the patients came up to me and wanted me to pray for them. I also started getting patients born again giving them the salvation of Jesus. I noticed some patients I could see demons in them, but they wouldn't look me in the eyes. I was seeing a new superman in me. Really, the Jesus in me. The demons knew who I was. It seems like they were bowing down to me. The power of God was working through me in the psych ward. The doctors called Athaliah to ask her questions. "How did your husband get here? Is it true about you trying to have him killed? Is it true an investigation is going on with you with the FBI and police?"

Athaliah yelled, "No! Mr. Peace is bipolar! He is crazy in the brain! Don't listen to him!"

It really wasn't clean up in there. People were getting COVID-19 in the hospital. I wasn't afraid of it or anyone in there. I noticed God was with me. Some patients who had demons tried to act up with me. I just looked them in the eyes and then they would just walk away. The demons in people can't touch me. They saw the Jesus in me. One guy tried to test me. I got into my flesh and ran up to him to pick him up and throw him out the window to bust it open so I could escape. But the doctors and nurses ran up to me and stopped me.

My eyes were really opening up to the spiritual world. I couldn't be harmed by no man. God is with me. There was a little short lady who was a patient who had sex with this tall and strong muscular guy who was a patient. I found out about it. It was a reality show up in here. The next thing I know the strong muscle man was crawling on the floor like a snake. I was like what the hell's wrong with him. Then God revealed to me that the little lady had demons in her, and by them having sex those demons transferred in the big man and had him crawling around like a snake. Excuse the language, religious folks, but I was seeing some weird shit the whole time I was there. Be advised that evening I got the little lady born again and those demons came out. Now on the fifth day in the hospital, I saw the doctors and nurses running around all scared. One of the patients told me the hospital was being investigated by some officers. He said there were important people here. He said, "Mr. Peace, thank you for helping us get out of here. This hospital has us locked up and we don't even have any problems. They get people off the streets and out of their homes. The more people they get on this floor more money the government sends them."

"I noticed that," I said. "This is nothing but a scheme for money."

The patients over there genuinely felt like I was helping them. The doctors and nurses came up to me and wanted to talk again. We sat down and they were looking very nervous.

"We spoke with Sergeant Douglas from airport police," they said. "So, your story is true."

I said, "Okay, get me out."

"We cannot do that right now," they replied. "We need to keep you here a couple more days."

"Why? You know the truth. Get me out so I can be with my daughters."

"Before you leave you need to take some medication."

"For what? I'm not sick. I'm not taking no medication. Let me go home." I have already seen people who take that medication in here. Those pills make you fall on the floor or walk around like zombies, high as a kite. I called Sergeant Douglas from the patient hospital phone. "They're trying to make me take medication."

"Don't take that medication," said Sergeant Douglas. "Why aren't you out yet?"

"They're saying I need to stay for a couple more days so they can evaluate me and make me take medication."

And so it was that Sergeant Douglas reassured me that he would try to get me out as soon as possible and that I had to avoid taking the medication the hospital would force me to take no matter what. And so, I did. I wasn't getting out of this hospital without complying. So, I had to think out the box. I told the doctor that I will take the pills. So, the doctor came in and gave me two pills to take. I took them. But little did they know I had snuck the pills under my tongue and drank water so it appeared like I was taking the medication but I really wasn't. I go to my room and spit the pills into the toilet.

They assessed me after I took the pills. Lucky for me, I had already seen patients drooling and walking around like zombies after taking these pills. So, I decided to use my acting skills and put them to the test. Every time the doctors would want to evaluate me, I put on an amazing show for them. And it worked. I was able to fool these folks. I drooled from my mouth and walked around like a zombie, acting like I was high on the medication pills they gave me. It was really supposed to make you crazier.

The next day was the sixth day of my imprisonment at the hospital. I followed the same old routine of pretending to take the pills. I go back to my acting role by drooling from the mouth and walking like a zombie—yes, I'm ready for my Oscar Award—and then being examined by the doctors. They wanted to make me impressionable by making me take the pills. I know this because this day a doctor came up to me and asked me for assurance that I wouldn't sue them after I got out. I told the doctor exactly what he wanted to hear: "I feel much better now, doctor, and it's all thanks to you guys. I won't sue you because you guys actually helped me."

It was now the seventh day of my imprisonment, but today was finally going to be the day of my release. Now everyone else was being released that morning, but not me. The doctors were trying to keep me as long as possible. They were saying my bloody paperwork was not ready. It was a trick. I stayed back at the hospital till 5pm. I ordered a cheeseburger with fries for my last meal there. But they served me some rice with green sauce on it. It looked like some kind of monster meal. I didn't get mad because I knew what they were up to. If I got angry, they were going to keep me there. So, I kept my peace.

But, once everything was done and dusted, I left. Freedom at long last. An officer escorted me to a van outside the hospital and drove me home. When I got home the first thing I did was hug my daughters. My daughters were so happy to see me and I was so happy to see them.

Chapter 18

Divorce Her Ass

I finally returned home from Shady Hospital.

I had a feeling the FBI would be arresting Athaliah and the people who tried to kill me anytime soon. Athaliah and Shady Hospital had teamed up against me. The first thing she said to me when I returned was, "Shady Hospital wants to make sure you're taking your pills."

"I'm not taking those pills," I said to her. Athaliah was still trying to destroy me. But she was really fighting God. She had no kind of remorse on everything she had done to me. But I couldn't leave the house. I didn't trust my wife around my daughters. I was sleeping downstairs on the couch. I made a fortress around my couch. I put cans on the steps late at night, so that when she would come down the steps the cans would make loud noises to wake me up. I needed to sleep well that night after coming home from Shady Hospital late. The bible says, "Once the enemy is revealed to you, he, she, or them can't harm you." The next morning, I got up and drove to the courthouse and I filed the divorce papers. I had so much evidence from the Holy Spirit of her telling on herself that she doesn't love me. Athaliah was the ringleader of the people who wanted me dead. After I left the courthouse, I went to the police station to speak with the detective. When I arrived at the police station, walking toward the door, two detectives ran up to me and asked me where I was all this time.

"We've been looking for you," they said.

"Man, I been locked up in the psych ward at Shady Hospital," I said.

"What happened?" asked Lieutenant Smith.

"It's a long story," I replied. "I really don't want to talk about it, but you guys need to investigate Shady Hospital on the thirteenth floor."

"We need you to have the FBI call us right

away," said Lieutenant Smith.

"You call them," I said.

"No, you have them call us," said Lieutenant Smith. I really didn't understand. So, I called up the FBI right in front of Lieutenant Smith and the other detective. An FBI receptionist answered the phone.

"My name is Reece Peace," I said. "I'm the one who has a case with Agent Eric Harris." She already knew who I was. "I'm here with Lieutenant Smith and Detective White. They need Agent Eric Harris to give them a call."

The FBI receptionist replied, "What's Lieutenant Smith's phone number?" Lieutenant Smith gave me his card and I read the number to the FBI receptionist. "Thank you. I will give Agent Harris the information."

"What's going on?" I asked Lieutenant Smith and Detective White. "Why do you guys want to get involved now?"

"Your wife came up here saying that the report you put in was false," said Lieutenant Smith. "And that you are bipolar and crazy. While she was talking to us, she said something very strange out of her mouth. She started telling on herself. That's when we knew she was trying to have you assassinated."

"What she say?"

Then Detective White jumped in and said, "Don't worry, Mr. Peace. We got it." Then, we both went our separate ways. My friends and neighbors were hearing about what was going on with Athaliah and I. Our business was getting spread around the atmosphere. I was still at the house, and, yes, I had my gun for protection. I hid all the knives around the house. And when I would drink wine with my dinner, I would buy the individual four pack of red wine, so that I'm just drinking the small bottle and then throw it away. Sleeping downstairs with both eyes open and protecting me and my daughters, I was now just waiting on law enforcement to hurry up and build the case. Athaliah was still trying to make me sign papers and give up my rights of my daughters before she filed the divorce. But Athaliah didn't realize that I already filled the paperwork at the courthouse.

Two weeks had passed, it was late evening around 7:30pm on a Monday night. There was a loud knock on the door. I looked out the window and it was a sheriff patrol car flashing its light. I ran upstairs and said to Athaliah, "There's a sheriff at the door. It might be Shady Hospital coming to take me back to the psych ward on the thirteenth floor. Please don't tell them I'm here. I can't go back to that place. It's worse than hell!" Athaliah goes downstairs while I'm hiding upstairs in the closet.

Once Athaliah opened up the door, she told the sheriff, "Officer, Reece Peace is upstairs. Go get him."

When I heard that I was like, "No, she didn't just do that. She really is the devil!"

The sheriff officer said, "No, I'm here for Athaliah Peace to serve her these divorce papers. Are you Athaliah Peace?

"Yes," she said.

"Sign these please," said the sheriff. Athaliah

signed the papers the sheriff gave her. She closed the door and looked very confused and sad.

"That was wrong what you did," I said. "Telling the sheriff I was upstairs so he could come get me. Athaliah, you really hate me."

"I'm sorry," was all she said.

"Sorry? You should be sorry about many things you did to me, our daughters, our community, and our family.

"I didn't do anything," said Athaliah. "Just take your medication." She still couldn't repent or apologize to me or our daughters. She wasn't really sorry. She was still trying to protect herself from not going to prison.

Weeks passed and there were still no arrests. I headed over to the police station to talk with Lieutenant Smith to see why no arrests had been made yet. Lieutenant Smith advised me that cases take a while to build up all the evidence. "Be patient, Mr. Peace," he said. I walked away not understanding.

Athaliah had her divorce attorney. I didn't even

get an attorney till the last minute. I was thinking she would get arrested already. Thanks to Athaliah's attorney, she called me up one day and told me to get an attorney too. We went through the procedure back and forth with our personal divorce attorneys and the judge. Athaliah's divorce attorney was kinda on my side because she heard about the ongoing investigation with her client. But she still had to work for Athaliah. So, we have joint custody of our children. I got this, and Athaliah got that. I told the judge that Athaliah was being investigated by the police and the FBI, and the girls need to be with me only. "Has she been charged yet?" asked the judge.

"No, but—" I said, but the judge cut me off.

"Since she has not been charged, my hands are tied."

"What!?" I cried. "Your honor, if this was a woman telling you about her husband try to kill her. You would probably have given her everything." The judge winked at me as if telling me to be still. So, I held my peace. I get joint custody of my girls and some other things so I consider that a win. Thank you, Lord. And, remember, this was a virtual court due to the COVID-19 pandemic.

"Will you keep your last name?" the judge asked Athaliah.

"Hell no! She's not keeping my last name!" I interjected.

The judge laughed and said, "She has to answer that."

"Yes, I'm keeping the last name," said Athaliah.

"Judge, she don't deserve that name after all the things she did to me," I said. "She's dishonored the name, my name, Peace, the one God gave me. She's only keeping the name Peace thinking it would help her get away from trying to have me assassinated, her cheating, and the many lies she's told. Baby, it don't work that way. God only named me that, not you. You got that name from me by marriage. That's why God stopped my blessings when I married you. He couldn't give me my blessings because of you. Wow, did I marry the wrong woman again."

"It's her choice," said the judge. I held my peace. Since there was some chaos between Athaliah and I, the judge told her to leave the house for a month and when she would come back then I needed to leave. I was cool with it. I was still thinking that maybe she'd get arrested by then. But all that time, it was God keeping me protected from her. Athaliah moved in with her dad after that court proceeding, but she did visit the girls. I didn't stop her from her visiting the girls. Sometimes she would stay overnight. But, for some reason, I was not afraid. I had already seen God protect me from my killers.

The month was almost over and it was my time to move out. No arrest had been made yet, and I had no family to move in with. I took my things out of the house a day early and put it in a storage unit. My day to move out had come. I had a sore throat and was feeling very weak. So, I decided to stay for a couple of days in the house to get well. While I was laying on the couch to rest, there was a knock on the door. I looked out of the window. It was the police. I also saw Athaliah parked on the side. I opened the door.

"Hello, are you Mr. Peace?" asked the officer.

"Yes," I said.

"We have a court order," said the officer. "You need to move out today."

"I'm not feeling well today," I replied. "So, I've asked to stay a couple of days longer to get well."

"No, you need to get out by 12 noon," said the officer affirmatively.

"This is not fair," I cried. "This is so rude! My wife tried to have me killed five separate times."

"We've heard an investigation is ongoing about this case at the station."

"Okay," I replied. "If you've heard that then why are you kicking me out?"

"It's a court order."

"I let her stay here while she was supposed to be moved out."

"Mr. Peace, just leave and be safe."

God was getting me out, letting me know that it wasn't safe in my home. The same way God allowed Joshua in the Bible to go to prison, to be safe from his brothers because God had a plan for him for a certain time.

I left the house with my clothes packed in the car. I was not feeling well; I was weak and sick. I didn't know if I had the COVID-19 or the common cold because I was stressed out and sick and wasn't able to get myself tested. Also, none of my friends would allow me to stay with them because they heard of my wife trying to have me killed. They were scared themselves. When I moved out at noon, it was pouring rain. I went to a hotel parking lot with tears in my eyes while talking to God. I prayed that my daughters and I would see justice.

So much going on, God it hurts. But like Luke 22:42 says, "Father, if you are willing, remove this cup from me: nevertheless, not my will, but thine be done. So, I rested."

Chapter 19

Long Wait for Justice

No justice, no peace. How can I have peace without justice? Days, weeks, months passed and still no arrest! I was looking toward heaven trying to understand what happened to my beautiful home, my beautiful family. I was talking to God and saying, "You saved me so many times. I escaped death from my mother's womb until now. From you telling my mother not to have an abortion to stopping the witches trying to put a curse on me. First, my ex-wife attempts to kill me. Then my second ex-wife attempts to kill me. Now, today, my wife, or you can say my third ex-wife because the divorce is final, attempts to kill me. She tried five separate times to have me killed." God is not through with me yet. I was still trying to find an attorney for the Shady Hospital case. When I spoke with different attorneys, they all said I have a great case, and they will sign me up to represent me. But later they would send me a letter saying they're not going to represent me in the case. I wasn't stupid. Shady Hospital was paying the attorneys off. I was tired of running to the police station without any answer and the wishy-washy attorneys. It seemed like the enemy won.

Athaliah walked around bad like they were never going to arrest her. She kept saying, "God loves me. I'm the righteous of God." It was the teachings of Reverend Lite Benjamin that she was listening to. He speaks so much about the grace of God, that whatever wrong you've done God's grace and mercy will forgive you. But I know no one is above the law and God's justice. Don't be deceived; God is not mock. Whatever a man or woman sow they shall reap. I told myself to be patient. God works in patterns; He has a track record. I tried to get myself an apartment or a house without luck. I have good credit. I have money in my bank account. I have a business, even a fulltime job on the side. But every time I applied for an apartment or home, it seemed like it was being blocked. So, I had to move into a rent-a-week townhome until I could find a place. It's a place you pay weekly to live almost like a motel, but no one could trace me there.

I saw one of the officers at a hamburger restaurant who knew about my case. "How are you doing?" the officer asked.

"Fine," I said. "Just out here looking for a new apartment or house."

"No!" the officer screamed. "You can't get you an apartment or house or you will put too much information about your whereabouts. You can't have any record about where you're staying until the investigation is finished with your ex-wife. You need to stay with a friend or just move back to California where you're from. Get you some kind of rent-a-week place and pay every week or month till the case is over."

"That's where I'm at now."

"You be safe. No one can trace you there."

I said to myself, "God had already ordered my steps to this rent-a-week."

Athaliah left New Chapter Church to go back to Reverend Lite Benjamin at Planet Dome Church to keep hearing his teachings of grace because that's what she needed now. I was still going to New Chapter Church. I was serving as an usher and working with the youth. My daughters loved the youth services. We would go every week on Sunday evenings and enjoy the youth service. On Thursday there was a youth meeting and I noticed people were looking at me strange. After the meeting, one of the youth leaders wanted to talk to me. We went outside, and he told me I would have to resign from the youth department for the safety of the youth. They knew and found out my wife had put a hit on me. They said I could drop my daughters off, but I couldn't stay. They prayed for justice to be served on my behalf. I was a little hurt, but then I understood about the safety of the children. So, I resigned from New Chapter and went back to Reverend Lite Benjamin's Church. When I went back and joined, I noticed everyone acting very strange when they saw me. I'm not talking about the members. I'm talking about the leadership like Reverend Lite Benjamin to First Lady Benjamin to some head leaders.

They seemed like they were afraid of me. I don't blame them. They knew that my wife, now ex-wife, tried to have me killed. They didn't want no bullets flying in the church house. So, I kept coming to church.

One Wednesday night at bible study, I noticed Reverend Lite Benjamin had his eyes locked down on me. When I got home that night, the Lord spoke to me to leave the church because it wasn't safe there. I said, "Lord, what's really going on?"

I just stopped going to churches. I had to have a relationship with God myself. Well, I am the church. I believe God was building a church in me.

The next day, I go to the barber shop to get my haircut. Everyone in Atlanta knew my life's story and drama, including the barbershops around Atlanta. After my hair was finished the barber was walking outside with me. Then a black car pulled up with black tinted windows. My barber stopped with fear in his eyes and said, "Is that your ex-wife?"

I looked and replied, "I don't think so." The car drove off and we both started laughing. "Man, my little ex-wife can't hurt us. Why is everyone scared of her? She can't kill me or anyone around me. God protected me from her five times." The days were going by and people and the world were getting back to normal. The pandemic was slowing down. The FBI and detectives were finding so much evidence against my ex-wife. They were looking at many people who were involved in the assassination attempts. I was still praying and getting stronger in faith of the Lord. I'm knowing who I am. I felt invincible. I couldn't die. I had a calling from God. There was so much unfinished business. God had too much work to do in me. What was meant to be evil for me turned out to be good.

People were telling me, "Peace, you have a story, a book deal, a movie deal."

The more I thought about it, the more I said, "I really do. I have a movie. My first movie for my film label, Peace Vision Global." I did ask God for a major movie. But, God, I didn't want to be the star in it. Well, God works in mysterious ways. I started getting more calls to be an extra in movies. But I didn't so much care about playing a part. I mostly watched the directors, the film crew, the film help, looking at all angles of the camera shots and production. I worked out, ate better, and always had my hair in shape.

This other time I went to the barbershop, and it was packed. When I walked into the barber's, the clients were already talking about me and my ex-wife's situation. They were in there joking around, laughing about me sleeping with one eye open when I had to live with my wife, the killer. And the fact I had to put couches, loveseats, and chairs as a fortress to surround me while I slept downstairs for protection. I even had to hide all the knives around the house and sleep with a gun like a western cowboy.

The barbers asked me, "Where did you find her at before you married her? In a jungle, in the hood, or a club?"

I said, "No! In the church."

Everyone in the shop said, "The church!?" One of the barbers accidentally nicked off a big piece of his client's hair from the back of his head. Another barbers said, "The devil is in church too."

I replied, "I rather be in church with a few devils then all the devils out the church." So, I decided to joke and play some with the barbershop crew since they wanted to play. There was a lady walking toward the building. I looked at the window from my chair. I said, "There goes my ex-wife coming in here now." Everyone ran to the back. Even the people who were getting their haircut jumped off their chairs to run. I laughed. It was so funny. "I'm just playing," I said. Everyone came back in the shop.

They said, "Stop playing, Reece Peace."

I replied, "I apologize," but I was still laughing.

I was in my apartment safe that no one could trace me. It felt like a small prison cell. Athaliah moved out of the house with the girls. My daughters were still doing virtual learning, but the COVID-19 was disappearing little by little. I didn't know where Athaliah was living at, and she really didn't know where I was living for my safety. There was no way for me to see my daughters. One of my divorce agreements was that we needed to meet at the police station for my safety to get my daughters. But Athaliah didn't like that so she would prevent me from seeing my daughters. She was also trying to make me upset so I could make a threat on her to have me go to jail. God already showed me what she was trying to do. So, I just held my peace.

Athaliah told my daughters lies about me. She told them I was a sick man. Athaliah was trying to make the girls not like me, their own father. You'd think she'd come to her senses and stop her brakes on being so selfish. But that devil was in her deep. I asked God to reveal the hidden secrets to my daughters on what their mother had done to our family. When I had them with me, I didn't talk about what was going on. I just needed to spend time with them as much as I could without the drama. I stopped fighting this battle because I never did anything wrong. I was that good and faithful of a husband. I was that great of father who took care of his daughters and family. I was that man who every night would get my family together before bed and pray and do bible study. Now I was still praying for people and had them repent and live for God. I was like a walking pulpit, a moving preacher you could say.

I was in my small apartment; just a bathroom, a bed, a refrigerator, and a small television. I had to purchase a little portable grill to cook my food in the bathroom. I had to turn on the fans so the smoke detector won't detect the smoke and had the alarm going off. But sometimes it would go off. I'd be fanning the smoke out of my small room before I would get caught. My place was that small you could walk through the front and I'd be out the back in one second. It seemed like a small prison cell, but I could come and go as I pleased. I was thankful. Hey, at least I had a roof over my head. While I was in my place all alone, I got stronger. I'd rather be alone and strong than to have friends and be weak. I felt strong like superman, but superman had a weakness and that was kryptonite. So, I was strong in the Lord, because there's no weakness in Him. I'd do my daily confessions and affirmations. All I could hear in my head was, "Write the book, write the book. Then you have your movie." Maybe this was why God wanted me to be alone, so I could write the book and do God's will. So, I got my computer and started writing. I could remember everything about my life from when I was a baby up to now. While I was writing, I was thinking to myself that I have been through some stuff; too much stuff. Seeing how I came out of this and that problem, I realized it was all God. I was writing everything like a whistleblower; a tell all book. I had nothing to lose. I was not scared. The beast was out.

Athaliah kept asking my daughters to have your daddy tell them where I lived. But I wouldn't tell them or anyone until the investigation was over. Athaliah was trying to call the telephone company or the power company to try to find out where I lived. She would act like she was my wife trying to check on a bill. But they would say that there was no account under that name. I was well hidden from her. God was hiding me. Athaliah would not give up trying to assassinate me. Even though she'd seen that God saved me so many times from the devil working in her. I believe God had hardened her heart. It was like when God hardened Pharaoh's heart to show Moses and Israel the miracle of the red sea. I'm a witness to everything. I remember everything and all the faces. She knew if she got arrested, everyone would be arrested. She got so many people in trouble because of her selfishness. Athaliah was the ringleader. She was still not letting me see my daughters. My daughters were upset as well that she was not letting them see me. The girls were noticing all that their mother was doing. But my daughters were scared to say anything. They feared their mother.

In the room, when my daughters would be alone, they'd be upset. They'd miss their father, and the fun times we've had. They would remember the family they had. Athaliah would lie to my daughters and say that I cheated on her. She would say to them I was lying about her, and that I am sick and bipolar. The only thing I could do was trust in God and pray for my daughters' protection from the enemy. There were many lonely nights without my daughters and no justice. I was crying out to God, "Why have you allowed me to live and to suffer like this?" I lost my home, my daughters, and a wife that tried to have me killed. Lord God, hear my cries. Lord God, see my tears. The earthly authorities and the court system were taking too long. I was crying out for justice to the highest court. And that's heaven above. I needed to be with my daughters. "Why me, Lord?" I heard this soft voice say, "Why not you? You wanted a story. Ever since you were a little boy you will tell stories that was out of this world. Well, here you go! You're in it! You're the star and it's out of this world."

It was my youngest daughter's birthday. Athaliah prevented me from seeing her to bring her gifts. I was very upset. I finally knew this was a spiritual battle. I had to pray in tongues more than I ever did. I needed to pray directly to God. I started to learn something about the devil. The devil can also hear my prayers or anyone. But not when I spoke in tongues. So, I prayed more in tongues than ever. I noticed my prayers were working. Victory's birthday was coming up and I really wanted to spend time with her on her birthday. So, I prayed more in tongues to the Holy Spirit. And, yes, it happened! Victory told her mom that she wanted to spend time with me on her birthday. But I found out Athaliah was coming to the restaurant where I made the reservations. It was a 5-star restaurant. I wasn't afraid of Athaliah or her killers coming to the restaurant. I already knew she couldn't hurt me. I really wanted to see my daughters, and Victory wanted for her father, mother, and sister to celebrate her birthday all together. They showed up. I was there early, already checking out the place, making sure it wasn't a setup. I sat next to Victory and my younger daughter. Athaliah sat across from me wearing dark glasses. "You're in a restaurant. Why do you have glasses on?" I asked.

"I'm free to do want I want to do," Athaliah replied. In my mind, Athaliah hadn't changed one bit. Also, she knew if I looked at her eyes, I could read her thoughts. But really, that couldn't stop me from discerning her thoughts. It was the Holy Spirit that revealed, but I wasn't thinking about all that. I wanted to have fun and celebrate Victory's birthday. But all that time at the dinner table, I was thinking she could redeem herself by repenting to me and my daughters on the actions she did to this family. How could she repent? It would mean condemning herself about trying to have me killed. I could see you saying sorry for stealing someone's bubblegum. Or even kicking someone's cat. But how can you say sorry for trying to have someone killed? Athaliah was not trying to go to prison. I think about the story of the prodigal son in the Bible. When the younger son notices the mistakes he made, he repented to God and came back and repented to his father. Athaliah can't repent to us because she was not trying to go to prison. All the time at the table she was just trying to size me up. Figuring out how to make me fall. God already knows her thoughts.

The dinner party was over. My daughter Victory was happy. She had many gifts from me. I even had gifts for my younger one because I had missed her birthday celebration because Athaliah kept me away from her. The evil that's in her just won't come out. She can't slam the brakes. We all went our separate ways.

During the time I was waiting for justice, I was

still out telling people about Jesus. I know what I was going through, but God was still good. I saw His glory, His love. Athaliah had been telling on herself. Her coworkers and her family members were starting to believe she tried to have her ex-husband, Reece Peace, killed. When someone asked her a question about her ex-husband, Athaliah would reply with an answer like she had something to do with it. Like, Reece Peace should have stepped up and been a man. Peace made me do it. Then she would recognize what she said and shut her mouth. Talk about us was spreading like wildfire. Our story was bigger than some of the Hollywood couples' domestic drama.

The detective and FBI were building the case. They saw this crime triangle going through Atlanta, New York, and Jamaica. They could see the texts, phone calls, and even some video. Athaliah, this sweet Christian woman, wasn't the only one involved. She was using her buddy passes to fly in drug dealers and gangster killers in by their real names. This was a federal investigation by using the airlines to do her dirty crime. The names were already on the FBI database report. There was a paper trail of money being transferred. It was so obvious to everyone involved. So many text messages back and forth served as evidence. From the plots to assassinate me, to the drug lord, Darius Dog, and his cartel. Darius Dog, under his belt, had many bodies. The FBI and the Jamaican authorities had been trying to capture Darius Dog for years. But he would always slip away. Now with him trying to have Reece Peace killed, sleeping with his wife, and transporting drugs, Darius Dog came out the box. The ghost had been revealed, found out. The black oil could be seen all on him. It had been about two years since God revealed to me and when I made the report. It was time for the sweep to capture all the people 's involved that tried to have me killed and Darius Dog's cartel. The Jamaican Defense Force (JDF) and Navy SEALs, with the FBI, were in place in Jamaica to capture Darius Dog and his cartel. The police and FBI were in position to capture Reverend Benjamin and First Lady Benjamin. The FBI and NY police were in position to capture the guys Athaliah flew in from NY. The FBI and detectives were ready and in place to capture Athaliah.

The detective had already called me to be there with them to receive my daughters to take home after the arrest of Athaliah.

The sweep was all in sequence time.

It was five in the morning in Jamaica. The FBI and Navy SEALs joined in with the JDF and went in full force. The snipers took down the watchmen. Then came the tanks and the Blackhawks helicopters. The SEALs came down from ropes from the Blackhawks. The Navy ships came out from the mist of fog. It was a battle with shooting happening back and forth. This was a true warzone, a world war. The law enforcement authorities captured the whole cartel: Heart Attack, Beast Boy, and Darius Dog who tried to run in a cave hole. But he was too drunk and high on cocaine to find it. They made very successful arrests. No one from the good side of the authorities was hurt or killed.

It was four in the morning in New York. The police and FBI captured some of Darius Dog's drug dealer gangsters in NY. They also captured X-Ray, Filter, Skillet, and Maniac who Athaliah flew in from

NY with her buddy passes captured. And, yes, they also arrested Vicki, Athaliah's wicked sister.

It was four in the morning in Atlanta. The FBI and police raided and captured Reverend Lite Benjamin and First Lady Benjamin at their home.

It was six in the morning where I was. Athaliah arrived to work at the airport. She saw FBI units coming up to her. She went into her purse to take a kill pill. Athaliah refused to be arrested; she would rather be dead. The FBI Agent, Eric Harris, slapped the kill pill out of Athaliah's hand before she could take it. Agent Harris told her it was not that easy to escape.

"You shall live and not die and see the results of your sowing and reaping you caused for your family and this community," he said to her. It was a selfish act Athaliah displayed by trying to take herself out and not face the consequences. Many other gang and drug dealers were captured in other cities and states. I got my daughters back and a police unit escorted us to my protection home. God is a just God.

People will say no justice, no peace. But now I received peace because I got Justice.

Chapter 20

I Forgive You

It was a packed courtroom and many news channels were there. The trial to witness the miracle of a man surviving five separated assassination attempts on him was live all over the world. It was a quick two-week trial. Athaliah was found guilty of murder for hire, drug trafficking, and transport of illegal guns. There was too much evidence pointing toward Athaliah, the ringleader, to everyone else who got captured. People were starting to believe that there is a God that sit high and looks low. After hearing my testimony on how I survived being killed, people from all over the world wanted to serve the same God I was serving. The people in the courtroom were talking loudly until the sheriff came out and said, "Order in the court." It was Judge Tom Stickland who walked out.

"Please be seated," he said to everyone.

Everyone sat down, including me with my attorneys and two big sheriff officers and many security personnel next to me for protection. But I didn't really need them because I remembered that my big ten-foot angel was with me. My daughters were seated next to me. Then, a side door opened up and out came Athaliah with handcuffs on her wrist and chains on her ankles that she could barely walk. She had a look on her face like she didn't care. She still had no remorse on her face. There were no tears in her eyes, no concern in her spirit. Everyone one in the courtroom, plus family members, screamed out with disbelief that this sweet church girl was chained up like wild animal. My daughters started to cry. I had tears flow down from my eyes. My daughters heard so much truth and testimony about the first hit on their father when they were in the car, the second hit at the shopping center, and the last hit at the breakfast restaurant. They even heard about the kill pill that was put in my wine, and how those drugs were made by Darius Dog the drug lord. Athaliah walked in front of the judge with her attorney.

"Anything you'd like to say to your children, family, friends, or Mr. Peace before your sentence?" the judge asked Athaliah. Everyone was quiet again.

Athaliah looked at her daughters with tears in her eyes. Then, she looked at me and said, "You didn't have to tell lies. We could've worked it out. The devil is a liar. I'm innocent. I'm the righteous of God. He caused all this to happen." She had absolutely no remorse. She pointed at me with the handcuffs on her and said, "It's your fault, Reece Peace. You should have stepped up and been a man." The judge just shook his head and gave her 25 years in a women's prison. I think the judge was going to give her less time if she would have showed some remorse.

I, Reece Peace, stood up all of sudden and looked at Athaliah and said, "I FORGIVE YOU!"

The sheriffs walked Athaliah out of the courtroom. Darius Dog received life in prison plus 50 years to life without parole for operating an illegal drug enterprise, and conspiracy for hitman for hire that accounted for 200 execution deaths. Vicki received 25 years for conspiracy for hitman for hire and drug charges to distribute cocaine. Everyone Athaliah flew in on her buddy passes all received 25 years for conspiring to kill me drugs charges. First Lady Benjamin received 16 years for conspiracy for hitman for hire. Reverend Lite Benjamin received a lesser charge of 5 years for being an accomplice for the conspiracy for hitman for hire. The Reverend knew about it but never stopped it. And we can't forget about Shady Hospital. There was a big investigation conducted on the thirteenth floor. The doctors were conducting a wrongful operation in that part of the hospital. It was a big lawsuit for the patients who were taken against their will.

The case was one of the biggest stories around the world of how a young man survived all the assassination attempts against him while helping to capture one of the biggest drug lords of all time. Even the FBI, one of the most powerful law enforcement agencies, noticed it was something supreme, like a God that works through people.

I released my book, The Perfect Story, shortly

after the case and it became a bestseller. The Perfect Story sold over one billion copies. I went on book tours signing books and giving autographs all over the world. I went out to speaking engagements, colleges, churches, rallies, and did comedy shows over some of the funny parts in the book.

I went on to write and direct my first movie and did a series based on The Perfect Story. And yes, I played a part in the movie. The movie grossed sales of $2.3 billion and became one of the highest grossing films of all time. I also did a rap soundtrack for the movie. I picked up multiple endorsement deals, television appearances, and music and movie contracts.

Big Green Field put his big mansion up for sale and, yes, I purchased it from him so that my daughters and I could move in it. It was the same big mansion that he saw when he first moved to Atlanta. I also started my own business, Peace Vision Global, signing music artists and producing and directing more movies.

Look how the story changed. Athaliah, who went to college and received a bachelor's degree in management was now in prison. While I, Reece Peace, who didn't go to college and have been in jail multiple times owned a billion-dollar company and living in a big mansion. All I remember is what God had told me and also what the three white angels once told me in the restaurant back in California. God spoke through those three angels.

God is real. God is not a man who tells lies. After all I had been through, the rough times since I was born until now, I have trust in God. I had to turn my lemons into lemonade, apples into apple pie. And since I'm at it, I might as well turn my sausages, shrimps, potatoes, corn, chicken, and crab legs into a seafood gumbo, my test into a testimony, my mess into a message. I was walking like a barefooted priest. Since I helped capture one of the biggest drug lords in the world, the FBI asked me sarcastically if I wanted to work for them. Of course, I said no! I work for God. I'm all about my Father's business.

Peace Out!

The Black Widow, *Latrodectus Mactans*, the

female of which is black with red markings, highly venomous, and commonly eats its mate.

The Butterfly protects itself through camouflage. By folding up their wings, they reveal the undersides and blend in with their surroundings. Through this strategy, known as crypsis, they become nearly invisible to predators. Bright colors and distinctive wing patterns can, however, be advantageous.

The toxins that most poisonous butterflies have aren't potent enough to kill a large predator, but they are potent enough to make the butterfly taste so bad that a predator learns to avoid other members of the species in the future. Interestingly, most butterflies are not poisonous, but many imitate and hang out with butterflies that are. The very distasteful monarch butterfly, for example, is mimicked by the viceroy, who also doesn't taste good. Many butterflies start storing the poison in their bodies when they're caterpillars.

Were Reece Peace's steps ordered by God all this time? Did Reece Peace marry the wrong woman again or was this God's plan all this time? God has so many ways to bless His people. It may not come the way you want it. It may look crazy; no kind of red-carpet treatment. You will have to walk by faith and not by sight. But God will bless His people, His chosen, His way. God allows things to happen or God sends things to happen for His will. So that He, the Lord, may get the glory. Athaliah's purpose from the devil was already set to kill her first husband. Did God allow or send her to meet Peace? Because Reece Peace couldn't be killed, God had too much work and purpose in him to write the book and film the movie. God has many ways to bless us. But all God needs is one. God already knew the path He was going to bless Peace with, or even you. The battle wasn't with Athaliah, Vicki, Darius Dog, the witches, or the killers sent by Athaliah. The battle was with the devil, who comes to kill, steal, or destroy. But none of it worked or prosper against Reece Peace. Think about what the front of the book scripture says. I had to go through Babylon to get to this point.

Jeremiah 29:11. Really this scripture is the part of going through the fire without the smell of smoke. But the same way the evil is real, God is real, His love is real, His Grace is real, The Holy Spirit is real, and, oh yeah, angels are real. IT'S A BATTLE! A true spiritual battle out here. But the devil can't stop you. We stop ourselves. The devil works through the mind. So have the mind of Christ.

"For I know the plans I have for you," declares the Lord, "plans to prosper you and not to harm you, plans to give you hope and a future."

Who really was the true hero in The Perfect Story. God, Jesus, The Holy Spirit, the Host of Angels. All of them.

2 King 6:16. Fear not: for they that be with us are more than they that be with them.

This wasn't Reece Peace's story. This was God's story, The Perfect Story.

SHALOM!